NOLO® Products & Services

➯ Books & Software

Get in-depth information. Nolo publishes hundreds of great books and software programs for consumers and business owners. Order a copy—or download an ebook version instantly—at Nolo.com.

➯ Legal Encyclopedia

Free at Nolo.com. Here are more than 1,400 free articles and answers to common questions about everyday legal issues including wills, bankruptcy, small business formation, divorce, patents, employment and much more.

➯ Plain-English Legal Dictionary

Free at Nolo.com. Stumped by jargon? Look it up in America's most up-to-date source for definitions of legal terms.

➯ Online Legal Documents

Create documents at your computer. Go to Nolo.com to make a will or living trust, form an LLC or corporation or obtain a trademark or provisional patent. For simpler matters, download one of our hundreds of high-quality legal forms, including bills of sale, promissory notes, nondisclosure agreements and many more.

➯ Lawyer Directory

Find an attorney at Nolo.com. Nolo's consumer-friendly lawyer directory provides in-depth profiles of lawyers all over America. From fees and experience to legal philosophy, education and special expertise, you'll find all the information you need to pick the right lawyer. Every lawyer listed has pledged to work diligently and respectfully with clients.

➯ Free Legal Updates

Keep up to date. Check for free updates at Nolo.com. Under "Products," find this book and click "Legal Updates." You can also sign up for our free e-newsletters at Nolo.com/newsletters/index.html.

NOLO® **The Trusted Name**
(but don't take our word for it)

"In Nolo you can trust."
THE NEW YORK TIMES

"Nolo is always there in a jam as the nation's premier publisher of do-it-yourself legal books."
NEWSWEEK

"Nolo publications... guide people simply through the how, when, where and why of the law."
THE WASHINGTON POST

"[Nolo's]... material is developed by experienced attorneys who have a knack for making complicated material accessible."
LIBRARY JOURNAL

"When it comes to self-help legal stuff, nobody does a better job than Nolo..."
USA TODAY

"The most prominent U.S. publisher of self-help legal aids."
TIME MAGAZINE

"Nolo is a pioneer in both consumer and business self-help books and software."
LOS ANGELES TIMES

1st edition

The Craft Artist's Legal Guide

Protect Your Work, Save on Taxes, Maximize Profits

Attorney Richard Stim

FIRST EDITION   MAY 2010

Editor   BETSY SIMMONS

Cover Design   SUSAN PUTNEY

Book Design   TERRI HEARSH

Proofreading   ROBERT WELLS

Index   MEDEA MINNICH

Printing   DELTA PRINTING SOLUTIONS, INC.

Stim, Richard.
  The craft artist's legal guide : protect your work, save on taxes, maximize profits / by Richard Stim. -- 1st ed.
    p. cm.
  ISBN-13: 978-1-4133-1212-6 (pbk.)
  ISBN-10: 1-4133-1212-8 (pbk.)
  1. Artisans--United States--Handbooks, manuals, etc. 2. Handicraft industries--Law and legislation--United States--Popular works. 3. Handicraft--Law and legislation--United States--Popular works. I. Title.
  KF390.A69S748 2010
  343.73'0787455--dc22
                    2009046168

Please note

We believe accurate, plain-English legal information should help you solve many of your own legal problems. But this text is not a substitute for personalized advice from a knowledgeable lawyer. If you want the help of a trained professional—and we'll always point out situations in which we think that's a good idea—consult an attorney licensed to practice in your state.

Acknowledgments

Although I have no crafts skills, I'm fortunate to have had several family members (my wife Andrea, sister Barbi Jo, and niece, Sasha) who are skillful crafts artists and who provided advice. I've also been lucky to have many wonderful crafts artists as clients. They provided helpful information and comments. Thanks also to my editor, Betsy Simmons (and her trusted companion, Nikki Bean), as well as the Nolo production staff.

About the Author

Richard Stim specializes in small business, copyright, patent, and trademark issues at Nolo. He practices law in the Bay Area and has represented photographers, software developers, crafts people, publishers, musicians, and toy designers. He is the author of many books, including *Wow! I'm in Business, Music Law,* and *Profit From Your Idea.*

Table of Contents

7 Protecting Appearances With Design Patents and Trade Dress 221

8 Names and Trademarks 255

Forms on CD-ROM

Invoice

Consignment Agreement

Commission Agreement

Collection Letter #1

Collection Letter #2

Collection Letter #3

Work-Made-for-Hire Agreement

Nondisclosure Agreement

Sales Representative Agreement

Partnership Agreement

Basic Copyright Assignment

Artwork Assignment Agreement

Unlimited Personal Release Agreement

Limited Personal Release Agreement

Merchandise License Agreement

Merchandise License Worksheet

Your Legal Companion

There's a wonderful feeling the first time that you spot a woman wearing your jewelry, or you see a baby decked in your colorful crocheted hat, or you watch an older gentleman walking with one of your hand-carved canes. It's the realization that someone appreciates what you are doing. Wouldn't it be ideal if your crafts effort consisted solely of the satisfaction of making your great artworks and seeing other people use them?

Unfortunately, a lot happens between your creation of goods and someone else's purchase. There's the business of obtaining supplies, hiring help, renting a studio, insuring your business, protecting your artwork, naming your products, doing your taxes, and dealing with contracts.

This book is my attempt to help with all that "other stuff" and to offer tips for steering your business on a "no problems" course. I've tried to incorporate the experiences of various crafts artists as well as my own experience working with crafts clients. So if you have a few hours, put down that sander, soldering gun, crochet needle, or safety glasses and this book will guide you through:

- **Selling your work.** I analyze pricing, consignment, retail, wholesale, and commissioned sales, and I provide model sales agreements.
- **Determining the form of your crafts business.** I discuss the advantages and disadvantages of basic business forms such as sole proprietorships, partnerships, LLCs, and corporations. I also explain how to create these business forms.
- **Securing your workspace.** I provide information on the legalities of a home studio and explain how to secure and lease a studio.
- **Going online.** I offer some business and legal tips for taking your business online.
- **Working with employees and contractors.** I help you sort through your legal obligations and rights with employees, independent contractors, and sales reps.

- **Protecting trademarks and business names.** I explain how to register and protect your trademarks.
- **Protecting your work with copyrights, design patents, and trade dress.** I offer information about registering a design patent and copyright.
- **Licensing your crafts.** I provide information about how to license a crafts work and how to analyze a license agreement.
- **Avoiding liability and legal problems.** I advise you how to find a lawyer, examine your insurance options, and avoid expensive contract disputes and rip-offs.
- **Paying taxes.** I help demystify the world of income taxes for the self-employed.

Pricing and Selling

A few blocks from the Pacific Ocean in San Francisco's foggy Sunset District, you'll find *The Last Straw,* a small shop with an eclectic mix of jewelry, fabrics, and crafts. Marge Heard has operated the shop for over 30 years, buying and reselling crafts from locals. Heard defies many of the rules of retail crafts success—in some cases contradicting the advice provided in this chapter! For example:

- She doesn't require ID from customers writing checks: "If a check bounces I call the person, and they usually come right over. In the history of the shop, I don't think I've lost more than $100 total."

- She doesn't accept credit cards: "People say that they would buy a lot more if I would accept credit cards, but I don't want to. I feel people will spend more than they can afford."

- She allows people to take items home and pay for them in installments: "It works well for the more expensive stuff. I tell them, pay when you can, and please don't die in the meantime!"

- She operates in a working class neighborhood with very little foot traffic. "Most of my business is word of mouth, although some customers don't tell others because they want it for themselves."

As The Last Straw proves, running a problem-free crafts shop can be accomplished using common sense, developing business radar, and doing business with artists and customers that you trust. "The thing is," says Heard, "customers and artists who come into the shop become my friends. I don't know if they feel like my friends, but that's the way I feel—that we're attracted to the same kind of things."

The Pricing Dilemma: How Much Do You Charge?

Your price should reflect your costs and a reasonable profit. But how do you calculate costs and how do you measure a reasonable profit? Author Christopher Morley once said that when you sell someone a book "you don't sell just twelve ounces of paper and ink and glue." In other words, creative products have many costs that aren't visible. For example, there's your time, your overhead, and your training—all of which go into the costs of your crafts product. How do you sort through all those calculations and come up with the right price for your merchandise? And after you do this number crunching, will the customer consider your price to be fair, or say, "No thanks, it's not worth it"? In this section, I'll walk you through a few calculations that will help you determine your prices.

Overhead

Let's start with overhead. Overhead refers to your fixed costs—that's usually your rent, insurance, and other regular, set expenses. Here's an example of overhead costs, broken down into monthly and daily expenses:

Overhead

	Monthly	Daily
Rent	$ 300	$ 10.00
Insurance	100	3.33
Electricity and Gas	100	3.33
Water	30	1.00
Transportation	30	1.00
Cable/Internet/Phone	60	2.00
Total Overhead	$ 620	$ 20.66

Direct Costs (Material Costs)

Next consider the direct costs (sometimes referred to as "material costs") for crafts goods that you make and sell. Direct costs refer to your cost of materials—the expenses that are directly attributable to the particular item you are selling. If you work with crochet, it would be your yarn, buttons, or fabrics incorporated in your work. Pick one item and focus on that. For example let's say you make leather pouches with decorative leather buttons. your direct costs might look like this:

Direct Costs (Material Costs)

Item: Leather Pouch	Cost	Unit Cost
Leather	$20 per yard (4 pouches per yard)	$ 5
Leather ties	$60 for 30	2
Decorative Metal button	$50 for 10	5
Total Direct Costs Per Unit		$ 12

Labor Costs

What's your time worth and how long does it take to produce one of your crafts items? Many crafts artists underestimate the value of their time. If you're not sure what your time is worth, why not start by using the minimum wage (currently $7.25) and multiply that times the number of hours it takes to produce one item. If you have an employee or independent contractor making this item for you, calculate the time spent by that worker.

Labor Costs

Item	Time required	Labor Costs (Time Spent x $7.25)
Leather pouch	1 hour per pouch	$7.25

Your labor costs also provide you with another piece of information—the number of those particular crafts items you can make in a day. In the case of the leather pouch, you can say conservatively—considering interruptions, meals, and other business—that you can make six pouches per day.

Putting Your Cost Together

Once you know your overhead, direct costs, and labor costs, you figure out your wholesale price. This the total cost to make the item—that is the price needed to reimburse you for all your costs.

Cost Per Pouch

Item: Leather Pouch	Cost
Overhead per pouch = Daily Overhead ($20.66) ÷ the number of pouches per day (6)	$ 3.44
Direct Costs per pouch	12.00
Labor Costs	7.25
Total (Cost Per Pouch)	$22.69

Markup and Profit

Markup is the difference between the cost and the price. Sometimes it is expressed as a percentage. For example doubling costs (a 100% markup) is common for many crafts items. Profit is the difference between your revenue and your costs. So, markup and profits are closely related.

Putting Your Price Together

If you are selling the item yourself—for example at a crafts show—the typical markup is double the wholesale price. So if your costs for your pouch were $22.69, you would be selling your pouches for $45.00. Things get more complex when you place your crafts on consignment. Galleries and shops usually mark up your price further, so your $45 pouch may sell for $90. If it sells for $90 in shops, should you raise your direct price when selling to customers? Or should you lower your profit margin so that consignment prices will be more appealing? Here are a few things to consider:

- **Is your pricing based on your own wallet or the consumer's?** As Barbara Brabec, author of *Handmade for Profit,* writes, "Beginners look at their product and say 'I wouldn't spend more than $10 for this ....' Which is a very big mistake because most crafters aren't very rich. What they have to do is research the marketplace and see what others who are making similar products are charging for their wares."

- **What do people pay for similar crafts?** You can get a bead on this question by checking the Internet, walking through a typical crafts show, or by checking local consignment shops and galleries for similar items.
- **How strong a motive is money?** You may have sufficient savings or income so that you don't need to live off your crafts. You may not need a generous profit as long as you don't lose money. If that's the case, lower your markup to reflect a price that is appealing to consumers. Keep in mind that you don't want to also disrespect yourself by setting your price so low that it reflects poorly on your work (see below).
- **Is price considered a measure of artistic value?** This is a double-edged question. Some crafts artists believe that the only way to get customers to take their crafts seriously is to charge a high price. Others may believe that their work is so inspiring that it deserves to be recognized and priced like fine art. This is a decision you'll have to make on your own, but regardless whether either theory applies to your work, consult competitor's pricing to be sure you're not over- or under-pricing your work.
- **Consider using formulas.** Many crafts artists adopt formulas for pricing. For example, if consignment shops are selling your work at a final markup of 200%, perhaps you can sell your crafts at fairs at a 150% markup (raising it from 100%). For some crafts artists, formulas don't work. "I have no formula for pricing," says jeweler Susan Brooks. "I may do a little bit of market research, but I rely more on intuition. Through trial and error, I hit a price that's comfortable for galleries."

How to Increase Your Profit

Besides raising prices, here are two simple and time-tested methods for increasing your profit.

- **Become more efficient.** For crafts artists, one of the largest expenses is labor. Can the time you spend creating crafts be streamlined? Step back and look at your production process.

Consider the sequence of events for each piece. Can you do the work in a piecemeal fashion, concentrating on batches? Can you organize your work space better so that there is less moving things or looking for things? What can you do to be able to make just one or two more items a day?

- **Cut costs and inventory.** You may think you have already cut costs to the bone but maybe you just need to take a fresh look at your operation. Is there any way you can spend less on materials by buying in bulk with a group of artists? Can you cut overhead costs by subletting your space? Can you cut labor costs by using contractors instead of employees? The same approach should be taken with unsold inventory. Items that are not selling are actually adding to your costs because they take up space that might be better used for new hotter selling work. If that's the case, lower prices on slow selling inventory (and increase your cash flow, as described in "Cash Flow Management," below).

Your Break-Even Forecast

Another way to look at pricing is to consider how much you'll need to earn each month to break even. For example, how many $45 pouches do you have to sell each month to break even? To calculate your "break-even," you'll need to determine your gross profit percentage. This is a percentage based on what's left after you deduct the direct costs for each sale. In the case of your pouches, you would calculate it as follows:

Calculating Gross Profit Percentage

Price of Pouch	$ 45.00
Minus Direct Costs and Labor Costs	19.25
Gross Profit	$ 25.75
Gross Profit Percentage (Profit ÷ Selling Price)	57%

To calculate your break-even amount, divide your monthly overhead expenses by your profit percentage (as a decimal). For example, if your crafts business has fixed monthly costs of $620 and your profit percentage is 57%, then you will need total sales revenue of $1,087 a month to break even

So, as a practical matter, if you were selling pouches at $45 apiece, you would need to sell approximately 24 pouches a month to break even—that is, to avoid losing money. (24 pouches @ $45 a pouch = $1,080.)

Calculating Monthly Breakeven

Fixed Monthly Costs	$ 620
Profit Percentage for Leather Pouches	÷ 57%
Monthly Breakeven	$ 1,087
Monthly Breakeven	$ 1,087
Retail Price Per Pouch	÷ $ 45
Number of pouches needed to sell to break even each month.	24

If this amount is below your anticipated sales revenue, then you're facing a loss—and you'll need to lower expenses, increase prices, or increase sales (or some combination) to break even.

Cash Flow Management

You've probably heard people complain about cash flow and maybe wondered what exactly that means. Simply put, the money that comes in and goes out of your crafts business is your cash flow. Business cash flow is really no different from personal cash flow. For example, when you're in a furniture store trying to decide whether to spend money on a new futon, that's a cash flow decision. If you use the money on the futon, you may not have enough to pay for your new laptop.

Proper cash flow management is the key to profitability for your crafts business (and for its survivability). Think of cash flow as your business's lifeblood. If it is interrupted—and this is true even for highly profitable ventures—it can lead to your crafts business's demise. The four most common reasons that crafts businesses have cash flow problems are:

Accounts receivables are late. When people are not paying you in a timely manner, you'll always be short of cash. Are you reluctant to approach your customers? I discuss how to deal with collections later in this chapter.

Inventory is turning slowly. Inventory—the crafts work you sell—is cash transformed into products. So when you're holding unsold inventory, you're really preventing access to cash. In addition, inventory costs create a financial burden. That's why it's sometimes wise to sell inventory at break-even prices rather than have it take up space without generating revenue.

Expenses are not controlled. It may be axiomatic, but your failure to control costs can be a major factor in cash flow problems. Always look for ways to lower expenses. Throughout this book I provide tips on lowering fixed and variable expenses. You'll be surprised: Even the leanest business can shed a few pounds.

Bills are paid before they're due. When possible, I recommend paying your bills early. Often, however, there are benefits to waiting—say, 30 days—and then paying the bill. In fact, in terms of holding on to your cash, it's even better to get longer terms for paying back your suppliers.

Selling Wholesale

Okay, now that you have an idea how to price your work, you're ready to sell. Let's start with wholesale transactions—where you sell quantities of your work to a dealer or a retailer, usually at a discount. In other words, you charge your costs plus a markup that generates a profit (although usually not as large a markup as when you sell the item directly to consumers). That dealer or reseller resells your work to the general public.

Don't expect to get a check as soon as the wholesale deal is made. Payments for wholesale sales are traditionally made 30, 60, or 90 days after the goods have been transferred. In effect, your crafts business is extending credit to the retail outlet. You may not feel like you're extending credit—after all, you're just waiting for payment—but from a legal perspective, you're making an unsecured loan to the store or gallery. (The intricacies of unsecured loans are explained below.) Your "creditor" status can have a significant impact on your business, particularly if you extend a lot of credit to a store that has financial problems. (I talk about collections later in this chapter.)

Can You Trust the Retailer?

When People's Pottery, the 47-store chain specializing in American-made crafts, filed for bankruptcy in December 2001, it claimed $20 million in debts. That sum included $3 million that remained owing to approximately 250-300 crafts vendors. An attorney working on the case told one of the crafts artists that it would be a victory if the crafts businesses got 1% of the amount owed them.

What happened to the $8 to $10 million in assets that the company still had when it declared bankruptcy? It was used to pay secured creditors—lenders who had demanded that their loans be secured with property. If the debt wasn't paid, the secured creditors could demand that the bankruptcy court sell the assets and turn the proceeds over to the creditors. Crafts artists who had used Net 30 or Net 60 terms were considered unsecured creditors and would only be paid if money remained after paying the secured creditors. In other words, the crafts artists were left holding an empty bag!

It would be difficult, perhaps impossible, for a small crafts vendor to avoid the results of the People's Pottery debacle. Unless a crafts business has somehow secured its loan, that is, required in writing some collateral as a condition of a wholesale purchase, the purchaser's bankruptcy will effectively wipe away the debt.

Since there's not much you can do once a store goes into bankruptcy, you'll need to minimize your risks beforehand. Below are some suggestions:

- **Avoid putting all your eggs in one basket.** In the case of People's Pottery, crafts artists who had a range of retail accounts suffered less than those who had relied exclusively on People's Pottery. On the same note, don't ditch your smaller retailers because of large orders from one retailer. Loyal smaller accounts give a business a constant, reliable source of income.

- **Don't wait to pursue those who owe you money.** Some vendors managed to successfully pursue People's Pottery before it went under. Manufacturers Credit Cooperative (MCC) began taking claims against People's in the summer of 2001. "We had 16 clients," said Jim Dempster, CEO of Manufacturers Credit Cooperative (www.mcccredit.com), "and all of them obtained some payments. Four collected in full. The earlier they came in, the greater percentage they received."

- **When in doubt, don't extend credit.** Some larger retailers will promise you anything to get your merchandise into the store under a Net 30 or 60 arrangement. That's because the store may have an "asset-based" loan with its bank. Under this arrangement, the more merchandise in the store, the more money the store can borrow. Don't play into a failing store's problems. There's no sense extending credit when you have doubts. In these cases, obtain prepayment or payment upon receipt of the goods.

The Wholesale Order Form (Invoices)

When selling wholesale, you don't need a custom-made wholesale order form. Perfectly suitable order forms can be purchased at an office supply store. You can personalize these forms, if you wish, with a rubber stamp with the name of your business. Alternatively, many business software accounting suites include customizable forms and invoices.

 FORM ON CD-ROM
In the event you want to create your own custom invoice, you can find an Invoice template on the CD-ROM at the back of this book.

At a minimum, your order form should include:
- information about your company (name, address, phone, and so on).

- date of the order
- information about the buyer, including customer account number, "ship to" address, sales tax number, and "bill to" person
- order number
- ship date and method of shipping, and
- order information including quantity, item number, description, price each, and total cost.

It's normal to include a statement in the invoice that the order cannot be canceled. After all, a deal is a deal, and most stores understand that. If you want, you can seek compensation in the event of cancellation. For example, in the sample invoice, check the box, "Buyer agrees that in the event the order is cancelled, there is a cancellation fee of ___% of balance due." Although some crafts businesses use such language, always keep in mind that if a store fails to pay it, you must go to court to enforce the agreement. The same is true for the optional statements regarding interest payments and collection fees. When preparing your own invoices, you can decide whether to use this language in (or delete it from) your invoice.

> **RELATED TOPIC**
>
> **Using PayPal to create invoices.** In Chapter 3, I discuss how to use PayPal (an online payment system) for creating invoices that are emailed to customers.

Selling Retail

Retail sales are when you sell directly to the public, whether at a crafts fair, an open studio, or as the result of a special custom order. Such sales are the bread and butter of the crafts industry and the source of more than half of the money made by crafts artists. The good news is that you probably won't need much legal advice for retail sales. All you need is a trusty receipt book and a system for accounting for your income. This section provides advice on the few areas of retail sales that sometimes

Invoice

Bill to: _____   Ship to: _____

_____   _____

_____   _____

_____   _____

_____   _____

Date	Your Order #	Our Order #	Sales Rep.	Ship Via	Terms

Item Number	Description	Quantity Ordered	Quantity Shipped	Retail Price	Discount	Unit Price	Total

Subtotal	
Tax	
Shipping	
Miscellaneous	
Balance Due	

☐ If payment is late, interest shall accrue from the date the payment was originally due, and the interest rate shall be 1.5% of the unpaid balance.

☐ If this account is delinquent, it shall be referred for collection, and Buyer shall pay all collection fees and costs including reasonable attorney fees.

[*Choose one*]

☐ This order may not be canceled.

☐ In the event the order is canceled, there is a cancellation fee of _____% of balance due.

raise legal red flags—sales tax, handling checks and credit cards, and returns.

Sales Tax

Did you ever dream of working as a tax collector? If your state has a sales tax law and you sell directly to customers, then your dream has come true. Sales tax is added to your selling price, usually after you ring the item up. You will need a permit from the state authorizing you to make sales and collect sales tax from customers within the state. Sometimes, the permit lets you buy items from wholesalers (for resale to customers) without paying sales tax. Some states call this a seller's permit; others call it a resale permit or something similar. (Note: You might need a permit even if your state doesn't have a sales tax. Even in the handful of states that don't impose a sales tax—Alaska, Delaware, Montana, New Hampshire, and Oregon—local governments sometimes impose sales taxes, which you may be required to collect and pass on.) If you're caught doing business without a permit, you could be subject to a number of penalties—such as having to pay the sales tax you should have collected from your customers, along with a fine. Also note that you may be subject to sales tax if you live on the border between two states or regularly sell in a neighboring state—some states have arrangements with neighboring states for combined tax certificates.

Finding the Forms

You can find information on seller's permit requirements at the website of your state's tax agency. For a list of links to these agencies, go to the IRS website at www.irs.gov, choose "Business," then "Small Business/Self-Employed," then "State Links." You can also find state tax rates online at the Tax and Accounting Sites Directory (www.taxsites.com/state.html) or the Federation of Tax Administrators' website (www.taxadmin.org).

Accepting Checks

Considering that over 200 million checks bounce each year, it's best to follow some commonsense procedures for minimizing your risks. For example, check your state's law regarding what ID you can demand. Some states, such as California, have established limits on the types and number of identification that can be requested from a customer. For information, check with your state attorney general's office. Other tips:

- Avoid taking checks that lack the person's name or address.
- Require ID, preferably a driver's license—and really look at it, for example, by comparing the address on the ID with the address on the check.
- Never accept a postdated check.
- Never accept two-party checks (checks written by someone other than your prospective buyer).
- Never accept the following as identification: membership cards, library cards, any card or ID that appears to be altered, Social Security cards, or temporary driver's licenses.
- Record the buyer's license number and phone number on the check.

Accepting Credit Cards

Though some retailers such as Marge Heard don't like to use them, many small crafts businesses find that accepting credit cards is a business necessity. More and more customer's wallets contain only plastic, and the ATM machine may be nowhere in sight at your local crafts fair.

Handling credit cards is fairly straightforward when the customer is physically present (not online). You'll need to establish a merchant account, set up through a bank associated with a credit card processing company. The latter handles the actual credit card orders. You must pay application fees, which can range from $200 to $600.

The percentage you have to pay Visa or MasterCard (usually 2% to 3% of sales)—depends on your expected sales revenue and the bank. Although the percentage takes a cut from your revenue, there's an upside to it—payments by credit cards don't require collections or a credit check. Because banks may reject your merchant application if it seems suspicious (you're estimating way-high sales revenue), it's wise to estimate conservatively. Expect bank approval to take one to two months.

Credit card fees can eat into your profits, so you need to check them thoroughly before you sign up to be a credit card merchant. You can do comparison shopping on the Internet (type "merchant credit card compare" into your search engine).

Going Online With Credit Cards

If you're taking credit card orders online, you'll need an e-commerce provider who manages your shopping cart and credit card acceptance. The credit card processing is handled by the provider's credit card transaction clearinghouse, a company that collects money from a customer and then pays the credit card companies their percentage of the sales. The balance is then deposited into your bank account within three days. There's a simpler solution (see the discussion of PayPal and Google Checkout, in Chapter 3) but for more information on e-commerce providers, type "shopping cart services" into a search engine.

Credit Card Fraud

In the offline (real) world, where a person must show you the credit card, it's sometimes easier to avoid fraud. You have an opportunity to judge the customer's demeanor and (in most states) to verify with identification that the customer and card owner are one and the same. If in doubt, you can call the issuing bank and check that the credit card is in good standing.

Although fraud is harder to prevent online, the good news is that credit card transaction clearinghouses use fraud prevention systems that can flag risky transactions—for example, they may use Card Identification Codes, the three- or four-digit numbers that are printed on the back of the credit card in addition to the 16-digit embossed number. Ask your e-commerce provider or credit card transaction clearinghouse about its antifraud protection.

Nevertheless, when accepting credit cards in person, here are some precautions:

- If at all suspicious, require proof of identity, check a "Hot Sheet" (a list of bad cards), or telephone the issuing bank for authorization.
- Avoid any transaction where a card has been altered, has expired, is not yet valid, or shows a signature that doesn't look like the one the customer writes on the sales slip.
- Always be careful processing an order from a new customer—especially if the customer places a large order or wants overnight delivery.
- Consider rejecting purchases when a bank in a foreign country has issued the credit card. This may seem harsh, but foreign credit cards are reported to have a higher fraud rate than those issued by U.S. banks.
- When you ship merchandise, choose a shipment method that requires the card owner to sign upon receipt. This approach adds some expense to the transaction, but you'll know whether or not the shipment arrived—thereby preventing claims by the customer that it didn't.

As for online purchases, "gateway software" or a transaction clearing-house can also provide additional fraud protection services. Some popular software add-ons include:

- **Fraud protection.** This system lets you rate the chances that a particular transaction will be fraudulent based on criteria that you select. If a transaction is flagged as especially risky, you can seek further information from the customer or reject the transaction entirely.
- **AVS.** This system (short for Address Verification Service) takes the first five numbers of the street address and the ZIP code information from the customer's stated billing address and compares that data to the billing address the card issuer has. You're told if there's a good match. If not, you can decide to reject the sale.

- **CIC.** Every credit card has a Card Identification Code, a three- or four-digit number that's printed on the credit card in addition to the 16-digit embossed number. You can minimize fraud by including a feature that checks this number, since only someone who actually has the card in hand will know the number. Some companies call the number a CVV2, CVC2, or CID.

Credit Card Chargebacks

Look out for excessive chargeback fees—the money a bank takes out of your business account when a customer disputes a credit card transaction. Disputes about online transactions can pop up in several ways. For example, a customer may order merchandise, get it and keep it—but dispute that it was ever received. Or a customer may have some other complaint about the transaction. Unfair as it may seem, a bank typically can take a chargeback in any situation in which the customer is dissatisfied. In a retail store, chargebacks are rare, accounting for a mere 0.14% of credit transactions; but at an online store it's 1.25% of transactions. In other words, chargebacks are nine times more frequent in online transactions than in traditional store transactions. So compare chargeback rates at merchant banks before signing with a merchant bank.

Getting Paid via PayPal

Some crafts artists use PayPal (www.paypal.com), an automated online payment system that enables anyone with an email address to make payments from across the country or around the world. Because the system works so well, it is the clearly preferred way to pay for many online purchases. Sending money via PayPal is free, but receiving money may be subject to a fee depending on the type of PayPal account you have.

Although developed and owned by eBay, PayPal is not just for use in eBay transactions. You can also use your account to accept payments via your website regardless of whether you have an eBay account. As part of its Merchant Services program, PayPal offers a free PayPal Shopping Cart system.

FTC Rules for Jewelry Ads

The Federal Trade Commission has established rules for advertisements and catalog sales of jewelry containing diamonds, gemstones, and pearls. For more information, call the FTC toll-free at 877-FTC-HELP (382-4357), or read the guidelines online at www.ftc.gov.

Selling at Crafts Shows

Although this book, like many crafts artists, uses the terms crafts fairs and trade shows interchangeably, the term "crafts fair" often refers to a retail show where the artist sells directly to the consumer. "Trade show" commonly refers to wholesale shows where the artist takes wholesale orders to be completed and delivered at some future date. By the way, for practical advice about entering and exhibiting at crafts fairs, check out the *CraftMaster News Guide* (www.craftmasternews.com).

Crafts shows are like small communities that spring up overnight and disappear a few days later. And as in a small community, a wide range of problems can develop as artists try to sell their wares. For example, while attending one outdoor crafts show, I watched the customers quickly disappear as a Bible-toting evangelist confronted them about sin and damnation. For two hours he continued while the ten booths in the vicinity saw little or no sales. The crafts show promoters explained that they could do nothing, since the law guaranteed the man the right of free speech in a public place. At another outdoor crafts show, I watched sales dissipate when the smoke from a nearby barbecue stand poured through a line of booths. Another time, participants at a crafts fair spent many hours in the dark after the electricity blew in the convention center.

It's difficult, if not impossible, to resolve disputes like these during the two to three intense days of a crafts show. An artist who has paid hundreds of dollars in booth fees and traveled quite a distance wants to generate revenue, not get embroiled in battles with a promoter. And once the show is over, most artists can't afford and don't want to waste time traveling to an out-of-state courtroom or endanger their relationship with the promoter. The tendency is to chalk it up to a bad show, express an opinion on a crafts message board, and factor the experience into the decision whether to attend next year. Not only that, many crafts show agreements contain provisions that relieve the promoter from damages in situations like those I've described. For example, one promoter's agreement states:

> I agree not to hold [*Promoter*] responsible for personal injuries or property damage and I agree not to be party to any legal action against [*Promoter*]. All exhibit personnel, merchandise fixtures, etc., on the premises are my sole responsibility and I agree to indemnify and hold harmless [*Promoter*] from all liability stemming from their presence or their acts.

(Note: The statement "and I agree not to be party to any legal action against [*Promoter*]" may not be enforceable in some states. In such cases, the provision would probably be severed from the agreement.)

Other crafts show promoters' agreements shield the promoter from lawsuits through what is known as a Force Majeure (or "Acts of God") contract provision. For example, one promoter's agreement says:

> [*Promoter*] will not be liable for refunds, loss of profits and out of pocket expenses, or any other liabilities whatsoever for the failure to fulfill this contract due to any of the following reasons:
>
> ☐ The facility in which the exhibition to be produced is destroyed by fire or other calamity.
>
> ☐ By an act of God, public enemy or strikes, the requirements of statutes, ordinances, or any legal authority, or any cause beyond the control of [*Promoter*].
>
> ☐ The bankruptcy or insolvency of the facility.

Just in case such broadly written clauses aren't enough, many contracts itemize the ways in which the promoter holds all the cards, such as:

- **Prohibition on refund of booth fees.** Most crafts show agreements contain a provision stating that there will be no refund of exhibit space fees.
- **Penalties for unqualified exhibitors.** Crafts show agreements often contain language allowing the promoter to remove the exhibit if it is not "up to show standards." In reality, most promoters will not act on infractions during the show; they will wait until after the show to decide how to investigate and resolve the matter. And in general, enforcement of show rules by promoters is inconsistent.
- **No recourse for lack of promotion.** If a show is not properly promoted, there's not much that a crafts artist can do. Crafts show agreements sometimes contain statements indicating that the promoter makes no promises as to sales or attendance.

Selling on Consignment

Consignments to galleries are the third-largest method of craft sales in the United States. Consignments account for over $3 billion in annual U.S. crafts sales. But consignment obviously comes with risks and obligations. What if the store doesn't pay? How do you retrieve unsold merchandise? Who's responsible when crafts are damaged? And—dread of dreads—what do you do when a gallery goes belly up?

Consider the crafts people left holding the bag when a Minneapolis gallery filed for bankruptcy while owing artists a total of $97,000. Said one crafts artist at the time, "We're the canaries down the coal mine. When the gas comes we're the first to die."

Consignment occurs when an artist (the "consignor") provides work to a gallery (the "consignee"), who agrees to pay the artist the proceeds from a sale minus the consignee's commission (usually 40% to 50% of the sale price). If the work doesn't sell, the consignee can return the work to the crafts artist. Under this arrangement, the consignee takes very little risk since it does not have to purchase the goods. The advantage of consignment is that it gives crafts artists access to sales outlets that might not otherwise be open to them.

Below I discuss three types of legal protection for consignors: the Uniform Commercial Code, state consignment laws, and written consignment agreements. You may find some of these legal principles difficult to comprehend, inconsistent, and expensive to enforce. Of the options provided below, I would recommend the use of written agreements as the best option.

By the way, regardless of these options, never forget to do some research and trust your common sense. Ask other crafts persons about their experiences with specific stores and galleries. Avoid large orders until you have built a level of trust with an unknown shop. And if you have doubts about a consignment, ask the store for references from other crafts people. If you've got a funny feeling about a shop, trust your intuition and don't hand your work over to it.

The Uniform Commercial Code

Some version of the Uniform Commercial Code (UCC)—a set of model laws—has been adopted by every state. Under the UCC, if damage to your consigned crafts results from the store's negligence, the store must pay for the loss. If the damage is not the fault of the store—for example, there's a flood or fire—the store may or may not be liable, depending on how the courts in that state interpret the UCC.

Normally, under the UCC, if a store files for bankruptcy, the store's creditors can seize your consigned goods as payment for debts. In other words, anyone owed money by the store can take your crafts as payment. You must stand in line behind the other creditors and hope that the judge awards you some compensation. However, the UCC gives crafts artists ways to prevent the creditor of a gallery from claiming your work as payment in the event of the gallery's insolvency or bankruptcy. You can avoid this unhappy outcome by fulfilling one of three requirements:

- file a UCC form (known as UCC Form 1 or UCC-1) at the time of the consignment, in the county where the store is located

- have the store owner post a sign telling the public that the goods are consigned (not applicable in all states), or
- prove that the creditors were aware that the gallery sold consigned goods.

These efforts are referred to as "perfecting a security interest." Having a security interest gets you certain rights over other creditors—for example, you can seize the property if the gallery doesn't pay you. Although crafts people rarely use these cumbersome UCC requirements, you may find it worthwhile, in the case of high-ticket one-of-a-kind crafts items, to file the UCC form. The filing creates a lien (a legal claim over property) elevating you to the level of a "secured creditor" and putting you at the head of the line in bankruptcy court. If you do file the form and obtain the lien, you must remove the lien at the time of any sale.

Having the store or gallery post a sign—the second UCC requirement—is a troublesome request. In general, galleries prefer not to post such notices. However, some galleries are complying with such requests, and I have included an optional provision in the sample consignment agreement for this purpose. It requires that the gallery post a notice such as "Crafts at this gallery are sold under the terms of a consignment agreement." As noted, this may not be effective in all states.

Most crafts workers will find the third requirement difficult to accomplish. It requires some legwork when it comes to obtaining proof that creditors of the store were aware of the consignment. Some consignors have accomplished this by sending creditors a copy of the consignment agreement. As you can imagine, the average crafts worker—who does not know who the store's creditors are and who may not have a written consignment agreement—would find this impractical.

Keep in mind that in the event of a store bankruptcy you must prove to a bankruptcy court that you have met one of these three conditions—which usually means hiring an attorney.

State Consignment Laws

Because the UCC has proven to be a frightening trapdoor for crafts people, many states have passed special consignment laws to protect artists from gallery abuses and bankruptcy. So far, 31 states have passed art consignment laws—Alaska, Arizona, Arkansas, California, Colorado, Connecticut, Florida, Georgia, Hawaii, Idaho, Illinois, Iowa, Kentucky, Maryland, Massachusetts, Michigan, Minnesota, Missouri, Montana, New Hampshire, New Jersey, New Mexico, New York, North Carolina, Ohio, Oregon, Pennsylvania, Tennessee, Texas, Washington, and Wisconsin.

Each of these laws is unique, but all of them operate under one basic presumption: Whenever art is handed over to a gallery, store, or dealer, it's presumed to be a consignment unless the artist is paid by the time of delivery. Most of these laws provide two benefits:

- any art held under a consignment arrangement or any money from a consignment sale is held in trust by the gallery for the artist (that is, the artist always owns the work and the proceeds), and

- the artist is shielded from bankruptcy, because creditors are prohibited from seizing consigned goods. (In reality, enforcing these laws usually requires hiring a lawyer and filing claims in bankruptcy court.) Half of the state laws require a written consignment agreement as a condition for enforcing the law.

The problem for crafts artists in these states is proving that their work qualifies as "art" under state laws. The determination can be confusing. Some state consignment laws apply only to "fine art." Fine art is traditionally defined as a painting, sculpture, drawing, graphic art, or print, but not multiples. Many states—for example, Arizona and Ohio—specifically include crafts in the definition of "artwork" (defining them as any work made from clay, textile, fiber, wood, metal, plastic, or glass). Some statutes are vague, and it's not clear whether crafts are covered.

Landing Consignment Accounts and Avoiding Consignment Problems

"Consignments can be an ideal situation for my riskier work," says jeweler Alison Antelman (www.antelman.com), who has built her business with a combination of wholesale and consignment sales. "By taking it on consignment, the gallery takes less risk, and these works are available in outlets that might not buy wholesale. I also like consignments because I can pull back items or switch my line if I choose." But, Antelman adds, "It's a shared responsibility. The gallery has to make payments on time and has to keep track of the inventory, too."

Antelman locates consignment accounts the old fashioned way, by visiting shops and investigating their inventory. "I check out galleries to see if my work fits with their taste and what they are trying to promote.

"Never assume they can see you when you drop in. I always ask if I can make an appointment. If they're willing to see me then, that's fine, too. I bring samples of my work and slides and literature such as an artist statement, bio, contact information, and tear sheets from magazine articles. The important thing is to always maintain a professional approach."

And what about rejection or rudeness? "I always, always, act friendly and calm, leave, and thank them for the time. You can't be insulted personally. You have to be thick-skinned. After all, my work is not suitable for all galleries."

Here are some tips for assessing a gallery before committing to a consignment:

- If you can't visit a gallery, ask someone you know in the area to check out the customer traffic and report back to you.
- Get names of other artists exhibiting at the gallery, preferably on your own rather than through the gallery owner. Then contact the artists and ask about the gallery's practices.
- Be wary of a gallery that won't give you financial or credit information.
- Check online about a gallery at crafts chat rooms (for example, www.craftsreport.com).
- After placing your work in the gallery, stay in contact. Regular communication may alert you to any financial problems and will also prepare you for success. You may need to get to work and build up stock to ship out because of ongoing sales.

In those rare cases when you have a problem, either because of late payments or suspicions that the gallery is having financial problems, follow Antelman's simple strategy: "Take your work out. Put all of your energy and talent in another place."

Written Consignment Agreements

Traditionally, consignments are made by written agreements, often furnished by the gallery, or through oral agreements. I recommend, when possible, using a written consignment agreement. It can provide benefits for you, obligations for the gallery, and, most important, it is required under many state consignment laws. A consignment agreement should cover:

- the inventory being consigned
- the retail prices for the goods
- the store or gallery's responsibility for damage to the goods
- the gallery's fees for consigned goods
- who pays for shipping
- whether discounting is permitted
- promotional responsibilities, if any, and
- the gallery or store's obligation to post a sign regarding consignment (a condition that may protect you in the event of consignee bankruptcy).

I also recommend including an attorney fee provision (requiring that the loser pays the winner's attorney fees) and an arbitration provision (requiring settlement by a private arbitrator, not a judge). These provisions create incentives for rapid settlement of all nonbankruptcy-related disputes. (A discussion of these provisions is provided in Chapter 11.)

Many galleries furnish their own consignment agreements. If you are furnished one of these agreements, compare it to the sample agreement below. It is possible that a gallery may refuse to modify its consignment agreement. If the agreement compares unfavorably to model consignments, you will have to decide whether there is any risk in proceeding. Usually, however, galleries are flexible about negotiating some terms and conditions.

How do you convince a gallery to use your consignment agreement? The best approach is to bring up the subject in your introductory conversation. Ask the gallery if they have a contract. If they do, ask them to send or fax it, and then compare it to the professional guidelines. If it's unacceptable, or if the gallery doesn't have a contract, tell the gallery you have a contract and ask if they're comfortable reviewing your agreement.

> **CAUTION**
> **Don't use the sample agreement for vanity galleries or auctions.** The agreement below is not intended for vanity galleries or auctions. Under a vanity gallery arrangement, the artist pays a fee for the right to exhibit works and may pay to rent the space, install his work, and use the gallery's mailing list. The consignment agreement is also not intended for use at auctions. Auctions often involve more specialized financial arrangements covering advances or loans to an artist, catalog costs, reserves, and estimates of minimum payments. For more information on your legal rights in auctions, read *Legal Guide to Buying and Selling Art and Collectibles*, by attorney Armen R. Vartian.

Discounts: What are they? Discounts are used by galleries to provide special customers with an incentive to make regular purchases. For example, a gallery might give a favorite collector a 10% discount. When the practice started, discounts were usually only offered to collectors of higher priced crafts works, for example works valued at $10,000 or more. That's changed, and galleries now may attempt to inflate prices to cover the discounts.

If the consignment price is not inflated to absorb the "discount," who absorbs this loss? Many artists believe that the gallery, not the artist, should take the hit because the discount reflects the relationship between the gallery and the collector. They reason that the artist and the collector usually don't have an ongoing business or personal relationship. Obviously this is a matter of negotiation between the artist and gallery. The sample consignment agreement in this chapter provides three choices for the artist, ranging from no discounts to splitting the loss.

Sample Crafts Consignment Agreement

FORMS ON CD-ROM

You'll find a sample Consignment Agreement on the CD-ROM at the back of this book.

Here are explanations for certain important provisions of the consignment agreement:

Introductory paragraph. Insert your name as artist and insert the name and street address of the gallery.

Appointment of Gallery. This provision establishes whether your relationship with the gallery is exclusive or nonexclusive, and establishes the geographic area within which the gallery will represent your works. Exclusive means that while the agreement is in force, only the gallery (not you or another gallery) can represent the sale of the artwork within the territory you define. If the agency relationship is nonexclusive, then others (including you) could solicit potential sales within the territory. If it's exclusive, insert a statement in the territory section to reflect the regions in which you have granted rights, for example, "New York State."

Fees and Payments. Under this provision, the gallery agrees to accurately account to you for your commission (a percentage of the sales income). There are two optional provisions: one provides for your right to audit the gallery's books; the other provides that the gallery will provide contact information for purchasers.

Discounts. The sample agreement provides two choices: subjecting all discounts to your prior approval, or having the artist and gallery split the difference. Check the choice that's applicable.

Shipping. Three choices are provided for shipping costs: an open choice in which you can describe your arrangement; the traditional approach of "whoever ships, pays"; and a negotiated approach that is established by using Attachment B. Check the choice that's applicable.

Insurance. This is standard language, requiring that the gallery's insurance cover and protect your works.

Termination. After the initial period of sale (within a reasonable time period that you establish), this agreement is drafted to permit your immediate termination of the consignment agreement.

Ownership; Loss or Damage. This provision establishes the gallery's legal liability for any damage that occurs to your work while it is consigned to the gallery. The reference to "secured parties" and the Uniform Commercial Code is to prevent the gallery's creditors from seizing your work to pay the gallery's debts.

Miscellaneous provisions. The assorted provisions at the end of the agreement—"Entire Agreement," "No Joint Venturer," and so on—are explained in Chapter 9.

Attachment A: Inventory Listing. Complete the inventory listing. It's important to provide a detailed description of the artworks and to establish the price at which each item will be sold. You may need to determine the price with the assistance of the gallery, since the gallery is likely to better know the market and prices within the territory. But keep in mind that the final decision as to the price is up to you, not the gallery. If you are submitting this sheet when modifying consignments—for example, supplying new work—it's wise to have the gallery sign and send back the new Attachment A (you don't need to sign it). I have included an optional signature section on this Attachment.

Attachment B: Expenses. This optional section establishes how any applicable expenses will be paid (or split, as the case may be). It's more likely you will use this attachment if you are dealing with a lot of high-ticket crafts or if the gallery is providing a special exhibition, not merely offering your work for sale. You and the gallery should agree on estimates for each expense and insert that sum in the attachment. If certain estimates are inapplicable, insert "N/A." You can also request approval of any expenses over a certain amount (for example, over $500).

Send two signed copies of the agreement to the gallery. One copy is for the gallery's records, and the other is to be returned to you with the gallery's signature.

Consignment Agreement

_____ ("Artist") is the owner of the original works and accompanying rights in the works listed in Attachment A (referred to as the "Works"). Artist desires to have _____ (the "Gallery") located at _____ _____ _____ represent Artist with regard to the exhibition and sale of the Works. From time to time, the parties may revise the list of Works specified in the inventory listing and such revisions, if executed by both parties, shall be incorporated in this agreement.

Appointment of Gallery; Agency Relationship. Artist appoints Gallery as its: [_Choose one_]

☐ exclusive agent for the sale and exhibition of the Works in _____ _____ (the "Territory").

☐ nonexclusive agent.

Gallery shall use its best efforts to promote and sell the Works and to provide attribution of the Works to Artist.

Fees and Payments. Gallery shall sell the Works at the retail prices established by Artist in this agreement. All income paid as a result of the sale of any Works by the Gallery shall be paid directly to Gallery, and Gallery shall issue payment to Artist within _____ days of Gallery's receipt of such income along with any accountings, including identifying inventory numbers.

For sales of Works, Gallery shall receive a commission of _____ % of any sales income.

[_Optional_]

☐ Gallery shall keep accurate books covering all transactions relating to the Works, and Artist or Artist's authorized representatives shall have the right, upon five days' prior written notice and during normal business hours, to inspect and audit Gallery's records relating to the Works.

☐ Gallery shall provide Artist with the name and contact information for purchasers of the Works.

Discounts

[*Choose one*]

☐ Gallery will obtain Artist's approval before changing retail prices or offering the Works at discount.

☐ Gallery may offer discounts to selected customers up to _____% and Gallery and Artist will split the discount equally, provided that Artist does not receive less than _____% of the sale price.

Custom Order Commissions

[*Choose one*]

☐ In the event of custom orders resulting from exhibition at Gallery, Gallery shall receive a commission of _____% of any sales income.

☐ Gallery shall not be entitled to any commission on custom orders resulting from exhibition.

Shipping

[*Choose one*]

☐ Costs for shipping shall be as follows: _____ .

☐ Costs for shipping: (a) from Artist to Gallery shall be paid by Artist; (b) from Gallery to Artist shall be paid by Gallery; and (c) from Gallery to anywhere other than Artist (for example, to customers) shall be paid by Gallery.

☐ Costs for shipping shall be as set forth in Attachment B.

Insurance. Gallery shall maintain adequate insurance for the wholesale value of the Works (the retail price minus potential commission) and shall pay all deductibles.

Termination. This Agreement may be terminated at any time on or after _____ at the discretion of either Artist or Gallery. This Agreement shall automatically terminate if Artist dies or if Gallery becomes insolvent, declares bankruptcy, or moves from the Territory. In the event of termination, all Works in Gallery's possession shall be promptly returned to Artist at Gallery's expense.

Ownership; Loss or Damage; Security Interest. Gallery agrees and acknowledges that the delivery of the Works to Gallery is a consignment and not a sale of the Works to Gallery. As Artist's agent, Gallery shall have a duty to protect the Works and shall be strictly liable for any damage to the Works once in Gallery's possession and until returned to Artist. If Works are destroyed while within Gallery's possession, Gallery shall pay Artist the full value as established by the retail price. Artist shall retain full title to all Works consigned to Gallery and shall in no event be subject to claims by creditors of Gallery. Title of the Works shall pass directly from Artist to purchaser, and, in the event of default or breach by Gallery, Artist shall have all rights of a secured party under the Uniform Commercial Code and Gallery agrees to execute all forms necessary to perfect such interest.

[*Optional*]

☐ **Posting Consignment Notice.** Gallery agrees to prominently post the following notice in its gallery: "Crafts at this gallery are sold under the terms of a consignment agreement."

General Provisions

Entire Agreement. This is the entire agreement between the parties. It replaces and supersedes any and all oral agreements between the parties, as well as any prior writings. Modifications and amendments to this agreement, including any exhibit or appendix hereto, shall be enforceable only if they are in writing and are signed by authorized representatives of both parties.

Successors and Assignees. This agreement binds and benefits the heirs, successors, and assignees of the parties.

Notices. Any notice or communication required or permitted to be given under this agreement shall be sufficiently given when received by certified mail, or sent by facsimile transmission or overnight courier.

Governing Law. This agreement will be governed by the laws of the State of _____ _____ .

Waiver. If one party waives any term or provision of this agreement at any time, that waiver will only be effective for the specific instance and specific purpose for which the waiver was given. If either party fails to exercise or delays exercising any of its rights or remedies under this agreement, that party retains the right to enforce that term or provision at a later time.

Severability. If a court finds any provision of this agreement invalid or unenforceable, the remainder of this agreement will be interpreted so as best to carry out the parties' intent.

Attachments and Exhibits. The parties agree and acknowledge that all attachments, exhibits, and schedules referred to in this agreement are incorporated in this agreement by reference.

No Agency. Nothing contained herein will be construed as creating any agency, partnership, joint venture, or other form of joint enterprise between the parties.

[*Optional*]

☐ **Attorney Fees and Expenses.** The prevailing party shall have the right to collect from the other party its reasonable costs and necessary disbursements and attorney fees incurred in enforcing this agreement.

☐ **Jurisdiction.** The parties consent to the exclusive jurisdiction and venue of the federal and state courts located in _____ [*county*], _____ [*state*], in any action arising out of or relating to this agreement. The parties waive any other venue to which either party might be entitled by domicile or otherwise.

☐ **Arbitration.** Any controversy or claim arising out of or relating to this Agreement shall be settled by arbitration in _____ in accordance with the rules of the American Arbitration Association, and judgment upon the award rendered by the arbitrator(s) may be entered in any court having jurisdiction. The prevailing party shall have the right to collect from the other party its reasonable costs and attorney's fees incurred in enforcing this agreement.

Signatures

Each party represents and warrants that on this date they are duly authorized to bind their respective principals by their signatures below.

GALLERY:

_____
Signature

_____
Typed or Printed Name

_____
Title

_____
Date

ARTIST:

_____
Signature

_____
Typed or Printed Name

_____
Title

_____
Date

Attachment A

Title of Work	Inventory No./Description	Retail Price
_____	_____	$ _____
_____	_____	$ _____
_____	_____	$ _____
_____	_____	$ _____
_____	_____	$ _____
_____	_____	$ _____
_____	_____	$ _____
_____	_____	$ _____
_____	_____	$ _____
_____	_____	$ _____
_____	_____	$ _____
_____	_____	$ _____
_____	_____	$ _____
_____	_____	$ _____
_____	_____	$ _____
_____	_____	$ _____
_____	_____	$ _____
_____	_____	$ _____
_____	_____	$ _____
_____	_____	$ _____
_____	_____	$ _____
_____	_____	$ _____
_____	_____	$ _____
_____	_____	$ _____
_____	_____	$ _____

_____

Date

_____

Consignee

Attachment B (Optional)

Expenses. Gallery shall pay expenses as listed in this Attachment B. In the event that an expense shall be shared between Artist and Gallery, the relative percentage of Gallery's payment shall be set forth below, and Artist shall be responsible for the remainder. For any shared expenses, Gallery shall provide an estimate of the expense and, in the event the actual amount of the expense exceeds the estimate, Gallery shall pay the difference.

Expense	Percentage Paid by Gallery	Estimate	Deductible by Gallery
Promotional mailing	_____	_____	☐ Yes ☐ No
Advertising	_____	_____	☐ Yes ☐ No
Party/event (opening)	_____	_____	☐ Yes ☐ No
Frames	_____	_____	☐ Yes ☐ No
Installations	_____	_____	☐ Yes ☐ No
Catalog*	_____	_____	☐ Yes ☐ No
Photographic reproductions	_____	_____	☐ Yes ☐ No
Shipping to purchasers	_____	_____	☐ Yes ☐ No
Shipping to artist	_____	_____	☐ Yes ☐ No
Other _____	_____	_____	☐ Yes ☐ No
Other _____	_____	_____	☐ Yes ☐ No
Other _____	_____	_____	☐ Yes ☐ No
Other _____	_____	_____	☐ Yes ☐ No
Other _____	_____	_____	☐ Yes ☐ No
Other _____	_____	_____	☐ Yes ☐ No
Other _____	_____	_____	☐ Yes ☐ No
Other _____	_____	_____	☐ Yes ☐ No

*Gallery shall furnish Artist with ten copies of catalog.

Custom Orders

"I love your work," a customer tells you at a crafts fair, "but could you make it in mauve with chartreuse green trim?" Assuming you're willing to prepare the work according to the customer's specs, the best method of following up on the sale is with a commission agreement (also known as special or custom order).

Prior to pulling out any paperwork, you'll need to agree on the basic terms, that is, get an agreed-upon estimate, schedule, and payment plan. Sometimes a custom order will cost more than the pieces you're currently selling, for example, if it involves a limited production method or more expensive raw materials. Crafts artists often must explain how a work is made in order for a buyer to understand custom order prices. Once you've agreed on that, you should sign an agreement.

 FORM ON CD-ROM
You'll find a sample Commission Agreement on the CD-ROM at the back of this book.

Sample Commission Agreement

The sample Commission Agreement I've provided in this book is drafted in terms that are fair for both the buyer and the artist. Below I help you understand the provisions of the Commission Agreement and give you some tips on filling it out.

Basic information. Include the names of the parties (you and the buyer), the relevant job information (delivery dates and fee), and a description of the job.

Payment. Choose the method of payment that you have agreed upon with the buyer. Sometimes, in the case of larger, more expensive commissions, a buyer may spread the payment over several installments and also insist upon the right to approve the progress of the work at each stage.

Additional Expenses [optional]. If you are to be paid for additional expenses that you incur in filling this custom order, insert the supplies and services for which you seek compensation. If the buyer is to pay for shipping, include that information here. Also included is a reference to repayment of sales tax.

Credit [optional]. If the work will be shown and you wish to be credited, insert the appropriate statement. Although it is not mandatory to include any notice, the use of a copyright notice may provide some benefits in the event you are involved in an infringement lawsuit.

Termination; Cancellation Fee [optional]. If you wish to give the buyer the opportunity to terminate after making the order, insert an amount that is equitable, usually one-fourth or more of the amount for the total job.

Liability. This "legalese" section limits the amounts that buyer and artist would have to pay if a dispute arises under the agreement. With this provision, the only amounts due in the event of a breach would be the sum that would correct the problem, usually the fee paid for the artwork.

Reservation of Rights; Ownership of Original. This provision makes it clear that you own the copyright in the work. If the buyer wants to own the copyright, that is a fundamental change to the agreement that can only be accomplished by adding an assignment provision (an example is provided in Chapter 6) or, if the work qualifies, making it a work made for hire (see Chapter 4).

No Destruction or Alteration [optional]. In the case of certain high-ticket, one-of-a-kind crafts works, the artist may choose this optional provision that establishes that the works cannot be destroyed or modified. For some crafts works, this right may also be acquired without the contract under some federal or state laws.

Miscellaneous Provisions. The remaining provisions are explained in Chapter 9.

Commission Agreement

Number: _____ Job Number: _____

To: _____ ("Buyer")

From: _____ ("Artist")

Delivery Date(s): _____ Fee: _____

Job Description ("Work").

_____

_____

Payment. Buyer shall pay Artist as follows:

[*Choose one*]

☐ An initial nonrefundable payment of $_____ upon signing this agreement and the remainder upon receipt of the Work.

☐ Payment in full within _____ (_____) days of signing this agreement.

[*Optional*]

☐ **Additional Expenses.** Artist shall be remunerated for the following expenses:

_____

_____

_____

Buyer shall also pay all applicable sales taxes due on this assignment.

[*Optional*]

☐ **Credit.** All publications or displays of the Work by Buyer shall contain the following statement: _____

☐ **Termination; Cancellation.** In the event this agreement is canceled by Buyer for any reason other than Artist's breach of this agreement or inability to complete the work as agreed upon, Buyer shall pay to Artist the cancellation fee of $_____ along with expenses incurred. In the event of termination by Buyer, Artist shall retain all works in progress and any payments already made.

Liability. Neither party shall be liable for incidental or consequential damages, nor for any claims in tort (or for punitive damages) which may arise from any breach of this agreement or any obligation under this agreement.

Reservation of Rights; Ownership of Original. Artist retains copyright and all other intellectual property rights in all artwork furnished under this agreement.

[*Optional*]

☐ **No Destruction or Alteration.** Buyer agrees not to intentionally destroy or modify the Work.

General Provisions

Entire Agreement. This is the entire agreement between the parties. It replaces and supersedes any and all oral agreements between the parties, as well as any prior writings. Modifications and amendments to this agreement, including any exhibit or appendix hereto, shall be enforceable only if they are in writing and are signed by authorized representatives of both parties.

Successors and Assignees. This agreement binds and benefits the heirs, successors, and assignees of the parties.

Notices. Any notice or communication required or permitted to be given under this agreement shall be sufficiently given when received by certified mail, or sent by facsimile transmission or overnight courier.

Governing Law. This agreement will be governed by the laws of the State of _____ _____ .

Waiver. If one party waives any term or provision of this agreement at any time, that waiver will only be effective for the specific instance and specific purpose for which the waiver was given. If either party fails to exercise or delays exercising any of its rights or remedies under this agreement, that party retains the right to enforce that term or provision at a later time.

Severability. If a court finds any provision of this agreement invalid or unenforceable, the remainder of this agreement will be interpreted so as best to carry out the parties' intent.

Attachments and Exhibits. The parties agree and acknowledge that all attachments, exhibits, and schedules referred to in this agreement are incorporated in this agreement by reference.

No Agency. Nothing contained herein will be construed as creating any agency, partnership, joint venture, or other form of joint enterprise between the parties.

[*Optional*]

☐ **Attorney Fees and Expenses.** The prevailing party shall have the right to collect from the other party its reasonable costs and necessary disbursements and attorney fees incurred in enforcing this Agreement.

☐ **Jurisdiction.** The parties consent to the exclusive jurisdiction and venue of the federal and state courts located in _____ _____ [*county*], _____ [*state*], in any action arising out of or relating to this agreement. The parties waive any other venue to which either party might be entitled by domicile or otherwise.

☐ **Arbitration.** Any controversy or claim arising out of or relating to this agreement shall be settled by arbitration in _____ [*county*], _____ [*state*], in accordance with the rules of the American Arbitration Association, and judgment upon the award rendered by the arbitrator(s) may be entered in any court having jurisdiction. The prevailing party shall have the right to collect from the other party its reasonable costs and attorney's fees incurred in enforcing this agreement.

Signatures

Each party represents and warrants that on this date they are duly authorized to bind their respective principals by their signatures below.

GALLERY:

_____
Signature

_____
Typed or Printed Name

_____
Title

_____
Date

ARTIST:

_____
Signature

_____
Typed or Printed Name

_____
Title

_____
Date

Shipping and Delays

The Federal Trade Commission's Mail or Telephone Order Merchandise Rule, also known as the "30-Day Rule," imposes basic shipping and refund rules on businesses. When you advertise merchandise online— for example at eBay—and don't say anything about when you plan to ship, you're expected to ship within 30 days from when you receive the payment and all the information needed to fill the order. If your listing does state when you'll ship the merchandise—for example, within two days of payment—you must have a reasonable basis for believing you can meet this shipping deadline.

If there's a delay, that is, it will take longer than 30 days for you to ship (or longer than you promised), you have two choices:

- You can ask for the customer's consent. If you can't get consent to the delay, you must, without being asked, refund the money the customer paid you for the unshipped merchandise.
- You can simply cancel the order, notify the customer, and refund the payment.

Keep a record of how you notified the customer about the delay, whether by email, phone, fax, or regular mail, when you gave it, and how the customer responded.

Returns and Refunds

The legal rules for returns and refunds are straightforward: Once a sale is complete, you don't have to give a refund. The only exceptions are if:

- you broke the sales contract—for example, your goods were defective, or
- you have a policy that allows a refund for returns.

If you want to provide refunds and impose conditions on when merchandise can be returned, post your return and refund policy prominently at your shop, booth, with your listing in your catalog, or mailing, or at your online store or website. A typical policy might require the customer to return the merchandise within 30 days for a refund.

State rules on refunds. A few states have laws regarding refunds. It's not always clear whether these laws apply to online retailers doing business with residents of these states. California's law seems to apply to Internet transactions because it applies to "other sellers of goods at retail, and mail order sellers which sell goods at retail in California ...." New York's law is silent on the issue. So far, there have been no cases enforcing this issue, but if you prefer to err on the conservative side, then sellers dealing with residents of these states should consider abiding by the retail rules as follows:

California. You must post your refund policy unless you offer a full cash refund or credit refund within seven days of purchase. If you don't post your policy as required, the customer is entitled to return the goods for a full refund within 30 days of purchase.

Florida. If you don't offer refunds, that fact must be posted. If the statement isn't posted, the customer can return unopened, unused goods within seven days of purchase.

New York. If you offer cash refunds, that policy must be posted, and you must give the refund within 20 days of purchase.

Virginia. If you don't offer a full cash refund or credit within 20 days of purchase, you must post your policy.

For more information about the FTC rules, call the Federal Trade Commission at 877-FTC-HELP or visit their website (www.ftc.gov). You also may get helpful information from the Direct Marketing Association (www.the-dma.org).

Ten Tips for Collecting Past-Due Accounts

One of the most frustrating aspects of running a crafts business is dealing with customers who are slow in paying. Should you pursue the debt aggressively, or write it off as a waste of time?

In a sense, getting paid is actually an element of your marketing. If you can work with people having financial problems, you may end up with devoted customers for life. Late-paying customers usually fall into three categories:

- customers who want to pay but, because of real financial problems, can't do it on time
- customers who prefer to delay or juggle payments, and
- customers who will do whatever possible to avoid payment.

For the first two categories, there is hope. You may be able to manage these debts and to convince the debtors to make partial or full payment. This is especially true if you have encouraged customer loyalty and your customers sincerely want to support you. As for the last category, you need to recognize this type as quickly as possible and take serious action—perhaps turning the account over to a collections agency. Here are ten tips.

Get busy and stay at it. According to a survey by the Commercial Collection Agency Association (www.ccascollect.com), after only three months, the probability of collecting a delinquent account drops to 73%. After six months, it's down to 57%. After one year, the chance of ever collecting on a past due account is a dismal 29%. Send bills promptly and rebill monthly. There's no need to wait for the end of the month. Send past-due notices promptly once an account is overdue.

Read about collections. Debt collectors can offer helpful tips, and you can learn many of them by reading either *Collections Made Easy*, by Carol Frischer (Career Press), or *Paid in Full*, by Timothy R. Paulsen (Advantage). Although these editions are both over ten years old, most of the information remains accurate, and helpful.

Don't harass debtors. It's rarely a successful strategy and it's sometimes illegal. If a customer asks that you stop calling, then stop calling. If a customer asks you to call at another time, find out the right time to call, and call then. Don't leave more than one phone message a day for a debtor, and never leave messages that threaten the debtor or contain statements that put the debtor in a bad light.

Be direct and listen. Keep your calls short and be specific. Listen to what the debtor says and keep a log of all of your collections phone calls.

Look for creative solutions. If the customer has genuine financial problems, ask what amount they can realistically afford. Consider extending the time for payment if the customer agrees in writing to a new payment schedule. Consider entering into a simple promissory note with the debtor that details the new payment schedule. Call the day before the next scheduled payment is due to be sure the customer plans to respect the agreement.

Write demand letters. Along with phone calls, send a series of letters that escalate in intensity. You can find sample collection letters (sometimes referred to as "demand letters") on the CD-ROM that comes with this book and at various online resources. You may find it useful to develop a set of past-due notices to use when customers fall behind in their payments. Your first letter may suggest that perhaps the bill was overlooked, and that payment should be sent now so that the customer can maintain a good credit rating. Your second and third letters should be polite but increasingly firm. Vary the format of your letters; each one should look a little different. Samples are shown below. Save copies of all correspondence with the customer and keep notes of all telephone conversations (in case you hand the matter over to collections or take the customer to court). You can also pay a collection agency a fixed fee to write a series of letters on your behalf. (This is different than turning over the debt to an agency.)

FORM ON CD-ROM

You'll find sample collection letters on the CD-ROM at the back of this book.

Deal with excuses. How can you tell if the customer is simply delinquent with a payment or whether the delinquency is a precursor of bigger financial problems? That is, how can you sift through the excuses given by a debtor without a lie detector? Carol Frischer considers excuses like a puzzle. You must solve each one and then stay a few steps ahead of the next one. If you're given an excuse—the person writing checks is sick this week—then you must determine whether it is true or not. If it turns out not to be true—that is, another excuse arrives the following week—then you should become less tolerant and more aggressive. Always maintain your sense of urgency. For example, if the company is "expecting a big check next week," insist on a partial payment this week and the remainder when the big check arrives.

Offer a one-time deep discount. If an account is fairly large and remains unpaid for an extended period (say six months) and you're doubtful about ever collecting, consider offering in writing a time-limited, deep discount to resolve the matter. This way, the customer has the incentive to borrow money to take advantage of your one-time, never-again offer to settle. You can finalize this with a mutual release and settlement, a legal document that terminates the debt. You can find such forms at Nolo's website (www.nolo.com).

Turn the account over to a collection agency. Turning a debt over to collections is your last resort. A collection agency will usually pay you 50% (or less) of what it recovers. Of course, in some cases, half is better than nothing. You're likely to want the help of collection agency when the customer lies to you about the transaction or becomes a serial promise-breaker, assuring you on various occasions that payment is on the way, when it isn't. The Commercial Collection Agency Association (www.ccascollect.com) provides more information on collection agencies.

Consider a lawsuit. You can also take the debtor to court. Small claims court is inexpensive, though it can take a good chunk of your time. Furthermore, any judgment that you receive may be worthless if the debtor lacks a job or bank account. For an excellent guide to using small claims court and collecting after you win, see *Everybody's Guide to Small Claims Court*, by Ralph Warner (Nolo). You can hire a lawyer for larger debts (say, over $5,000). But beware of filing a lawsuit to chase a debt; your legal fees may exceed the amount owed.

TIP

If a customer goes bankrupt, pursuing a creditor into bankruptcy is rarely worth the effort. The worse your customer's financial condition, the harder it is to recover any money. When a customer declares bankruptcy, you've got a big problem. A bankruptcy will effectively wipe out your debt unless you're a secured creditor (the customer promised some property to secure your debt).

Seven Reasons to Send an Account to Collections

The Commercial Collection Agency Association (www.ccascollect.com) provides seven reasons to send an account to collections. We reprint them below, with permission from the CCAA. They include:

Two or more broken promises of payment. Payments were promised, but no checks have been received, and customer will not send immediate payment by overnight delivery.

Customer's telephone is disconnected. If no new listing can be obtained, place the account in collections immediately.

The customer repeatedly requests documentation, even though they have been supplied the documentation previously. This common practice is used to delay payment of the account.

Your customer indicates that they do not adhere to your terms of sale. For example, they may indicate that they pay bills in 60 or 90 days and not according to the agreed-upon terms of sale. If you did not have an agreement with the customer before shipment for extended terms, this is just a delaying tactic. Explain to your customer your terms of sale and request immediate payment. If they refuse or fail to send a check as promised, place the account with a certified collection agency.

Your customer indicates an inability to pay and refuses to provide a specific date for payment or to initiate a realistic payment schedule. This is a sure indication of a serious cash flow problem, and immediate steps should be taken to protect your interests.

Your customer states they will "take care of the account," but refuses to make a realistic commitment for payment or to work out a payment schedule. This is another indication of a serious cash flow problem.

Your customer suddenly indicates, in response to your requests for payment, a dispute regarding the merchandise shipped or your terms of sale. Such a dispute was not raised previously. If your investigation shows the dispute groundless and the customer will not take steps to make payment or resolve the matter, the account should be placed with a certified collection agency.

Collection Letter #1

Account No. _____

Dear _____ :

Our records show that you have an outstanding balance with our company of

$_____ . This is for _____

_____

_____ (*describe the goods or services*).

Is there a problem with this bill? If so, please call me so that we can resolve the matter. Otherwise, please send your payment at this time to bring your account current. I'm enclosing a business reply envelope for you to use.

Until you bring your account current, it's our policy to put further purchases on a cash basis.

Sincerely,

_____

P.S. Paying your bill at this time will help you to maintain your good credit rating.

Collection Letter #2

Re: Overdue Bill ($_____)

Account No. _____

Dear _____ :

Your bill for $_____ is seriously overdue. This is for the _____
_____ (describe the goods or services furnished)
we supplied to you last _____ (state the month). More than
60 days have gone by since we sent you our invoice. You did not respond to the letter I
sent you last month.

We value your patronage but must insist that you bring your account up to date.
Doing so will help you protect your reputation for prompt payment.

Please send your check today for the full balance. If this is not feasible, please call me to
discuss a possible payment plan. I need to hear from you as soon as possible.

Sincerely,

_____

Collection Letter #3

Re: Collection Action on Overdue Bill ($_____)

Account No. _____

Dear _____ :

We show an unpaid balance of $_____ on your account that is over 90 days old. This is for the _____ that we supplied you over _____ days ago.

I have repeatedly tried to contact you, but my calls and letters have gone unheeded.

You must send full payment by _____ or contact me by that date to discuss your intentions. If I do not hear from you, I plan to turn over the account for collection.

Sincerely,

_____

Selling and Buying Outside the U.S.

Selling Across the Border

If you're selling outside the U.S., here are two tips: Get the payment up front, and get the payment up front. You don't have the ability to chase down rubles, drachmas, or pesos in a faraway land. These payments can be made by credit card, bank transfers, or bank letters of credit. To avoid confusion about currency conversion, keep your dealings in U.S. dollars. For more information on exporting goods, check out the U.S. Trade Information Center (www.export.gov).

Importing Crafts for Sale in the U.S.

Have you ever traveled to another country and thought, "This is an inspiring place to create handcrafted works!"? That's what happened to designer Andrea Serrahn when she traveled to India in 1990. "When I got there, I felt like I had arrived." Inspired by the vivid colors and fabrics, she worked with Indian tailors to create her unique clothing. There was only one catch—bringing her radiant designs back to the U.S. to sell.

"I think the average traveler would be daunted by what you have to go through to bring work from India to the U.S.—the red tape and bureaucracy. There's a lot of protocol, and you can't just walk into the post office and ship it back with the same expediency as one would in the States. On both sides—U.S. and India—you have to hire people to move it in and out. Textiles need proper visas, and the U.S. government is a stickler. There's also a quota for fabrics. One way to do it is to find an exporter, or another way is to use a courier. Sometimes I've actually dragged it back (over 100 kilograms) on the plane with me.

"Be prepared for surprises when you ship," warns Serrahn. "I've had packages broken into. Nothing is missing, but everything is rearranged. And customs agents slice not only the boxes with their cutters! People want to look through it for antiques or drugs."

Andrea was able to fund part of her work when she qualified for a Fulbright Foundation grant for artists that gave her "cachet and clout, which goes a long way for a woman trying to do business in India."

After ten years of shuttling back and forth, Serrahn decided to open a shop in Oakland, California. At her shop, called Serrahna (www. serrahna.com), she offers her passionate, colorful clothing designs for men and women.

"You've got to have a couple of screws loose to try something like this," says Serrahn. "It really takes a true dedication to bring your work in from a foreign country. I think you could benefit from taking a course on import/export, but I did it through the school of hard knocks."

For more information on importing and exporting, check out: the U.S. Small Business advisor website (www.business.gov), and U.S. Customs (www.customs.gov).

Your Studio

Jeweler and fine artist Susan Brooks (www.susanbrooks.com) knows something about crafts studios. She grew up in one, among a family of artisans. As an adult, she operated her first studio in her home, then later leased workspaces in the Bay Area. She has firsthand knowledge of other artist's studios as well, having directed the Berkeley Artisans Holiday Open Studios program (www.berkeleyartisans.com) since 1991. And like many crafts artists, she's familiar with commercial lease agreements—and has "heard every [lease] horror story in the book."

Brooks's number one suggestion for a crafts artist leasing a workspace is to find a studio that's in a building with other crafts artists. "You'll find that quite often you need the cooperation or assistance of other artists. That's very important. For example, if you want to do an open house or participate in an open studio event, the more artists in the building, the more success you are likely to have.

"And," adds Brooks, "remember that leasing space in an 'artist' building doesn't necessarily mean you will be working amongst other crafts artists. The 'Use' provision of the building lease may say 'Artists Only,' but that can also mean graphic artists, Web designers, and, in some cases, architects or even engineers. These people may make good neighbors, but for purposes of selling your work or sharing ideas, you'll be better off working amongst other artisans. So check out the tenants before committing to an artist building."

Should you take a short-term or long-term lease? Brooks suggests trusting your intuition. "Do what you think is right. I've always wanted long-term leases, but in one instance I was glad I had a short-term lease because I was able to leave."

Brooks also suggests checking out the landlord. "You don't need for them to be your friend. You're in a business relationship. You just want to make sure you can do honest business with the landlord or the management company. Find out what people are saying about the landlord and their experience in the building. Is the landlord concerned about safety, etc.? Talk to tenants in the building. In some cities, you can go to the Planning Commission and learn about problems with landlords."

What about operating a home studio? "I did it for many years," says Brooks. "The only problem was that I didn't know when to stop working. And, of course, you have to be careful that your home studio creates a professional atmosphere. It shouldn't smell like dinner."

No doubt about it, establishing your studio is often one of the most difficult activities of establishing a crafts business. Home studios may run afoul of neighbors and zoning restrictions. Leases may require enormous financial commitments and produce anxiety over keeping up on the rent. In this chapter I discuss workspace issues, including establishing a studio in your home, finding a studio to lease, evaluating the essentials of a lease agreement, and maintaining a safe workplace.

Working From Home

There are many tempting reasons to operate your crafts business out of your home. It's convenient and economical, there's no studio rent, and best of all, no commuting. And did I mention the potential tax deduction? Under IRS rules, you may be able to deduct part of your rent from your income taxes. If you own your home, you may be able to take a depreciation deduction. You may also be eligible to deduct a portion of your total utility, home repair and maintenance, property tax, and house insurance costs, based on the percentage of your residence you use for business purposes. For information on claiming the home office deduction for your home studio, see Chapter 10, on taxes.

As long as your business is small, quiet, and doesn't create traffic or parking problems or violate local zoning rules, operating in your home is usually legal. But before setting up a home studio, review the laws that restrict a person's right to operate a business from home.

Zoning Laws

In most areas, zoning and building officials don't actively search for violations. Hundreds of thousands of home-based businesses exist in violation of zoning laws but go undetected by local officials. The majority of home-based businesses that run into trouble do so when a neighbor complains—often because of noise or parking problems, or even because of an unfounded fear that the business is doing something illegal—for example, a neighbor smells chemical solvents or soldering and thinks illegal drugs are being manufactured. Your best approach is to explain your business activities to your neighbors and make sure that your activities are not worrying or inconveniencing them.

RESOURCE

Read your local ordinance. If you'd like to determine the zoning rules that apply to your home, get a copy of your local ordinance from your city or county clerk's office, the city attorney's office, or your public library. Zoning ordinances are worded in different ways to limit business activities in residential areas. Some are extremely vague, allowing "customary home-based occupations." Others allow homeowners to use their houses for a broad—but, unfortunately, not very specific—list of business purposes (for example, "professions and domestic occupations, crafts or services"). Still others contain a detailed list of approved occupations, such as "law, dentistry, medicine, music lessons, photography, cabinetmaking." If you read your ordinance and still aren't sure whether your business is okay, you may be inclined to ask zoning or planning officials for the last word. But until you figure out what the rules and politics of your locality are, it may be best to do this without identifying and calling attention to yourself.

Many ordinances, especially those that are fairly vague as to the type of business you can run from your home, also restrict how you can carry out your business. The most frequent rules limit your use of on-street parking, prohibit outside signs, limit car and truck traffic, and restrict the number of employees who can work at your house on a regular basis (some prohibit employees altogether). In addition, some zoning ordinances limit the percentage of your home's floor space that can be devoted to the business. Again, you'll need to study your local ordinance carefully to see how these rules will affect you.

RESOURCE

Do you want to fight? In many cities and counties, if a planning or zoning board rejects your business, you can appeal—usually to the city council or county board of supervisors. This can be an uphill battle, but it is likely to be less so if you have the support of all affected neighbors. In some communities, people are working to amend ordinances that have home-based business prohibitions to permit those that are unobtrusive. For more information on home-based businesses and zoning, consult Entrepreneur.co. (Go to www. entrepreneur.com and click "Home Based Biz" on the home page.)

Leases, CC&Rs, and Other Contractual Limitations

If you live in a subdivision, condo, or planned unit development that required you to agree to special rules when you moved in—typically called Covenants, Conditions, and Restrictions (CC&Rs)—these will govern aspects of property use. CC&Rs pertaining to home-based businesses are often significantly stricter than those found in city ordinances.

Your legal right to set up a home studio may also be affected by your property and lease agreements. If you rent your home or apartment, your written lease (if you have one) may prohibit you from using the premises for business purposes. Your only means of resolving this is for you and your landlord to amend the lease.

Noise Restrictions

Frequent use of your band saw will likely result in zoning investigations and may violate local municipal noise ordinances. Before operating noisy machinery, check your local noise ordinance at your local library. For information on noise ordinance violations throughout the nation, check out the Noise Pollution Clearinghouse (www.nonoise.org).

Insuring Your Home Studio

Don't rely on your homeowner's or renter's insurance policy to cover your home-based crafts business. These policies often exclude or strictly limit coverage for business equipment and injuries to business visitors. For example, if your inventory is stolen, your home studio is destroyed in a fire, or a client trips and falls on your steps, you may not be covered.

> **TIP**
>
> **Avoid surprises.** Sit down with your insurance agent and disclose your planned business operation. You'll find that it's relatively inexpensive to add business coverage to your homeowner's policy, and it's a tax-deductible expense. Some insurance companies provide special cost-effective policies designed to protect your home and home-based business.

It Gets Lonely ...

According to a survey of the Craft Organization Development Association (CODA—www.codacraft.org), 64% of crafts artists work alone in a studio, 18% work with a partner or family member, and 16% work with paid employees.

Finding the Right Space at the Right Price

If your crafts sales won't rely on foot traffic—for example, you don't wish to operate a retail space—your best bet is to search out convenient, low-cost, utilitarian surroundings, preferably among other crafts artists. Even if people do visit your location, a low-cost, offbeat location may make more sense than a high-cost, trendy one. The major issues to consider when leasing are the obvious ones. Figure out the maximum rent your business can afford to pay per month, determine what type of security deposit you can pay, and consider how much money you can afford to spend to alter the space to fit your studio needs.

> CAUTION
>
> **Don't assume your landlord will tell you about zoning rules.**
> As with a home office, you'll need to be sure that there are no zoning laws that would prohibit you from using your leased space for your studio or retail use—usually, a simple matter of getting appropriate documentation from your landlord. Never sign a lease without being absolutely sure you will be permitted to operate your business at that location.

Rent

Calculating the monthly rent for a leased studio is more complicated than what you're used to when paying monthly rent for an apartment or house. That's because many landlords charge you not only for square footage, but also for other regular expenses such as real estate taxes, utilities, and insurance. If you rent in a multitenant building, you're likely to be asked to pay your share of common area maintenance, too. If you rent the entire building, you may be asked to foot the entire bill for these costs. How to determine the cost of a rental space is explained later in this section.

Deposits

Many commercial landlords require tenants to pay one or two months' rent up front as a security deposit. The landlord will dip into this deposit if the tenant fails to pay the rent or other sums required by the lease (such as insurance or maintenance costs). The amount of the deposit for commercial rentals is not regulated by law, but is instead a matter of negotiation. Landlords tend to demand high deposits from new or otherwise unproven businesses—which are often the least able to produce a large chunk of cash.

Improvements and Expenses

Unless you are fortunate enough to find space that was previously owned by a crafts person in the same field as yourself, you'll need to modify the space to fit your needs and tastes. These modifications are known as "improvements." There are several ways that landlords and tenants can allocate the cost of improvements. You might find a landlord willing to foot the entire bill. But for now, don't count on it. The tenant usually pays for this work. You'll need to determine what it would cost to make your space usable.

Length of the Lease

The "term" of your lease means its chronological life. Your lease could be as short as 30 days (in a "month to month" agreement), or run for one, five, or ten years. As long as you satisfy the important conditions of the lease (such as paying rent and other costs), you have the right to remain in the space until the lease is terminated or expires. And unless the other terms of the lease provide otherwise, they, too, are guaranteed for the life of the lease. For example, your landlord's promises to provide on-site parking and janitorial services can't be ignored.

　　Reasons to opt for a short-term lease. A short term lease may be attractive if you:

- are just starting just want to test the waters
- are feeling uncertain about your business's prospects for success, or
- would like the freedom to leave on short notice.

There are two ways to establish a short-term lease. You can:

- **Enter into a month-to-month tenancy**—a system in which the rental is automatically renewed each month unless you or your landlord gives the other the proper amount of written notice to terminate the agreement. Under a month-to-month agreement, the landlord can raise the rent or change other terms with proper written notice. You can negotiate how much notice is required. If you don't address the issue in your rental agreement, the law in your state will dictate the amount of notice required. In most states, this is 30 days.

- **Set up a short-term tenancy.** Sign a lease for a short but fixed period of time—say, 90 days or six months. This type of lease terminates at the end of the time period you've established. Unlike a month-to-month tenancy, it's not automatically renewed. You and the landlord can, however, negotiate lease language specifying what happens at the end of the fixed period covered by the lease. You could provide, for example, that if you stay in the space beyond the stated period, your tenancy becomes a month-to-month tenancy. A fixed-term lease, even for a short term, gives you the assurance that the landlord can't boot you out on short notice. It also means, of course, that you're obligated to pay rent throughout the lease term, unless you can negotiate an escape clause that gives you the right to end the lease earlier.

Reasons to opt for a long-term lease. A long-term lease may be attractive if you want to:

- Minimize transaction costs. (It takes a lot of time (and money) to find and secure good rental space.)
- Minimize improvement costs and get the most in the way of improvements. Chances are that you'll have to pay to alter your space to fit your studio needs. You may not want to do it again soon. Also, with a longer lease, the landlord is much more likely to pay for substantial improvements, or at least pick up a good chunk of the tab.
- Lock in a good deal. If the space is desirable, you may want to make sure that you'll have it for some years to come.
- Get the most in the way of improvements.

Elements of a Lease

Typically, you'll be working with a lease that's been written by the landlord or the landlord's lawyer—and you can bet that neither one of them will be looking out for your best legal or economic interests.

So treat the landlord's proposed lease as the starting point from which you'll negotiate changes.

Don't fall for the line that "this is a standard lease." There's no such thing. Even if the landlord starts with a lease that's widely used in your community, printed and distributed by a big real estate management firm, or accepted by other tenants who lease from this landlord, it can always be modified.

When you identify your business as the tenant in a lease—both at the beginning of the lease and at the end where you sign—make sure that you correctly name the business. You must also designate its legal form (partnership or corporation, for instance). For an explanation of how to identify your business, see Chapter 5 about business forms. The legal nature of your business entity, for example, sole proprietorship, partnership, corporation or LLC, determines whether or not you'll be personally responsible for paying rent and meeting the other obligations stated in the lease. (If you're not personally responsible, creditors can reach the assets of your business but no more.)

Changing the common areas. Landlords often write clauses that give them the right to change the common areas at will. For example, in order to create a larger space for another tenant, the landlord might someday want to narrow the entryway to your studio. Changes in the common areas can make your own space less convenient, or usable. If you see language in a premises clause that gives the landlord the right to adjust the common areas as he sees fit, try to eliminate it or at least build in a bit of protection—for example, by having the landlord agree in writing not to reduce the access to your space or make your space less visible from the street.

The use clause. A use clause can be either a restriction on how you do business—telling you what you can't do—or a prescription, telling you what you must do. In general, you'll want to avoid strict restrictions on your use of the rented space. And if you want to offer a retail space as well as a studio, that should be clear, as well.

The landlord's remedies if you fail to pay rent or breach the lease. Since most landlords understand that a tenant breach may be inadvertent, they agree in the lease to notify you of the problem (called "notice") and give you a specified amount of time to rectify (or "cure") the problem before they take sterner measures. And even when it comes to deliberate breaches—such as failing to pay the rent because you can't—landlords typically extend the same second chance. They'd rather get their money late than have to start over with a new tenant. Typically, the notice and cure period will be rather short for monetary misdeeds (such as failure to pay the rent), but longer for problems that take more time to fix.

If you fail to live up to a lease obligation during the notice and cure period, the landlord may decide to "fix" your error. Known as a landlord's right of "self-help," it means that the landlord can correct your breach of the lease, then sue you for his expenses (or deduct them from your security deposit, which you will then have to top off). For example, if you're late with the rent, the landlord will take it from the security deposit (and then demand that you bring the deposit back up to its original sum). Or, a tenant who doesn't maintain the property as required in the lease, or who parks in others' spaces, may find the maintenance done or his car towed—and a bill from the landlord for the work or the services of the tow truck.

Consider arbitration and attorney fees provisions. Your lease may include ways you can iron out problems using mediation and arbitration and a provision explaining who pays for attorney fees and court costs if the dispute boils over into litigation. These provisions, common to many agreements, are discussed in Chapter 11.

Terminating the Lease

The next weapon in the landlord's arsenal is his right to terminate the lease. If the landlord terminates, you'll have to move out. If you don't, the landlord may file an eviction lawsuit against you. Clearly, neither would be a welcome event. Although your lease clause probably won't address it, be sure you understand what happens after the landlord terminates the lease. Contrary to what you might expect, you won't normally just walk away without financial consequences. In fact, depending on market conditions, you might end up paying a considerable amount of money in damages. Here's why.

When you and the landlord signed the lease, you promised to pay a certain amount of rent for a specified number of years. The landlord is legally entitled to that money, regardless of the fact that your misbehavior caused him to terminate the lease. In most states, however, the landlord cannot sit back and sue you for unpaid rent as it becomes due. Usually, the landlord must take reasonable steps to rerent the space. Once the space is rerented, the landlord credits the new rent money against your debt. If the new rent doesn't cover what you owe, you pay the difference. In legal jargon, the landlord's duty to rerent and credit your debt is called "mitigation of damages."

You can see that your continued responsibility for rent will depend on market conditions. If you were paying below-market rates, or if the new tenant was simply unable to negotiate as low a rent as you did, you may end up with no rent liability, since the new tenant's rent will cover (or exceed) what the landlord had been charging you. But if the value of the location has gone down or the income from the new tenant doesn't match yours, you'll pay the difference.

Agreeing on the Rent

Your biggest concern with your lease is probably the rent. Determining the monthly payment can be fairly complicated. Here are the factors used to determine the rent.

- **Square footage.** If your rent is tied to the square footage—for example, $10 per square foot—you should find out how the square footage is measured. Some landlords measure square footage from the outside of the walls—so that you end up paying for the thickness of the walls—while others measure from the inside.

- **Net lease or gross lease.** Do you have a "gross" lease or a "net" lease? A gross lease is one in which you have a fixed monthly rate with periodic increases. The increases may be based on a flat percentage—for example, 3% a year—or ten cents per square foot per year. Or, the increase may be variable and tied to increases in a national indicator, commonly the Consumer

Price Index. In this case, if you're paying $5,000 a month and the CPI jumps 5% in one year, your payments will jump to $5,250. Under a net lease, you pay a base rent—say, $10 per square foot—as well as additional periodic expenses such as taxes, insurance, and maintenance. (You may also have to pay periodic increases, such as CPI tied to the base rent.) Some of the issues you face with a net lease are highlighted below.

- **Allocation of taxes.** Many net leases state that if property taxes increase during the lease, the tenant must pay some percentage of that increase. Usually, your tax payment is tied to the percentage of space you are leasing—for example, if you rent one-fifth of the total space in the building, you may be obligated to pay one-fifth of any increase. Try to negotiate your tax obligation based on your pro rata share of the taxable value of the property. Also, try to limit the amount of tax increase you must pay. This type of cap may protect you if the property tax jumps drastically or the building is reassessed and sold.

- **Insurance.** Insurance policies protect the landlord from property damage from fires or other disasters and from claims made by third parties who are injured at the building. Most net leases require that the tenant contribute to the insurance for the building (in addition to purchasing separate insurance policies that the tenant needs to cover its own business). Like tax obligations, you want to make sure you are only paying a contribution to the landlord that is based on how much space you take up—for example, if you're occupying one-fifth of the building, you should only have to pay one-fifth of the insurance.

- **Common area maintenance.** Most net lease tenants must pay for common area maintenance (CAM). If you lease a whole building, you'll get stuck with all of the maintenance costs for the common areas. If you lease a portion of a building, you often must pay a percentage of the costs to maintain the lobbies, hallways, garages, and elevators. Sometimes you must pay for maintenance of the heating and ventilation system.

Other Important Lease Elements

In addition to the business terms, you'll need to evaluate elements of the property that are important to you personally and in the operation of your studio.

Fresh air/open windows. Many landlords feel that windows—ones that open and close—will compromise the efficiency of the building's heating, ventilating, and air-conditioning system, known in the trade as HVAC. (And if the heater is blasting while the windows are wide open, you, too, will bear some of the cost, since tenants typically pay for a portion of the HVAC costs.) So if you highly value fresh air on demand, make this a priority when studio searching.

Soundproofing. Good sound insulation between rooms within your space and in the walls separating your space from that of adjacent tenants may be very important—especially if you're the one who will be making noise with machinery or tools.

Control of heating and cooling. In some buildings, you have to take whatever the HVAC system happens to be pumping out. In others, you may have one or more thermostats within the space you lease. Individual control of your work climate will be a high priority if you or employees work on weekends or nights, when building-wide ventilation and heating controls are typically turned off.

Storage space. Some buildings have extra storage space for tenants in a basement or other out-of-the-way area. If you need space for items that you use only occasionally, access to a separate storage area may be a priority. This can reduce clutter and free up your rental space for important uses.

Private restrooms. Many buildings offer restrooms that are shared by several tenants. However, if you're willing to pay a higher rent, it may be important to you to have restrooms within your leased space for the exclusive use of employees and customers.

Other tenants and services in and near the building. As discussed at the opening of this chapter, there are many advantages to being in a building with other crafts tenants.

Parking. If parking is a necessity for you, your landlord may impose an additional charge for on-site parking. You won't be guaranteed a specific number of spaces or spaces at a designated location unless the lease says so.

Security. If you're concerned about security, check on the neighborhood. Your local police department is a good source of information on the safety of various areas in your town. Also check on the internal building security—flimsy locks on doors or windows are invitations to opportunists. Reasonable security steps may include adequate outside and inside lighting, strong locks, limited entry, alarm systems, and even security guards.

Ability to expand space. Some craftspeople forget to plan for success. After the first year or two, you may need more space. Depending on your expectations for growth, you may feel that the ability to take over additional space in the building is a high-priority factor. You'll want to nail down your right to occupy additional parts of the building in a lease clause giving you the right of first refusal when space opens up.

Studio Safety

More than 200 years ago, a doctor wrote, "Many an artisan has looked at his craft as a means to support life and raise a family, but all he has got from it is some deadly disease, with the result that he has departed this life cursing the craft to which he has applied himself."

Things have improved, right? Actually, it was only 30 years ago that jewelers used asbestos fibers, cadmium solder (now banned), and carcinogenic solvents including trichloroethylene, benzene, and carbon tetrachloride—often without suitable ventilation. Fortunately, in recent decades, there's been progress in crafts safety standards, much of it led by crafts artists themselves.

It goes without saying that it is absolutely essential for your studio to maintain adequate safety standards. Not only can it affect your short- and long-term health, but ignoring these standards may violate the law and lead to lawsuits by employees and neighbors.

In 1998, engineer Milt Fischbein wrote four basic principles for maintaining studio safety:

- understand the hazards associated with each chemical, tool, and machine in your studio
- design your studio to minimize hazards
- use safe procedures for each of your work processes, and
- make absolutely sure that each safety procedure is followed and that no shortcuts are taken.

Chances are good that you are already aware of the recognized risks within your field—risks that come with the territory when working with and around polishing machines, rolling mills, infrared radiation, dermatitis-causing dust, propane tanks, and so on. Determining what is right for your crafts business requires research. Before you snap on your safety goggles (with side shields), review the material below to best identify dangers and prevent injuries:

Material Safety Data Sheets. One key to maintaining a safe studio is to familiarize yourself with product labels, and if possible with the Material Safety Data Sheets (MSDS) that are issued by the chemical makers or product manufacturers. This information can be found on the Web at any of these sites:

- Vermont Safety Information Resources site (http://hazard.com/msds)
- MSDS Search (www.msdssearch.com), and
- MSDS Solutions (www.msds.com).

It is also usually available at the source of your supply, or you can write to the manufacturer or check their website. The MSDS lists hazardous ingredients, short- and long-term effects of exposure, flammability, precautions, and recommended protective gear.

Ventilation and PPMs. Safety-conscious crafts artists can lower the exposure limits created by toxic fumes by choosing the right chemicals and properly ventilating the workspace. Keep in mind that exposure varies depending on the individual—for example, children and pregnant women may be more susceptible to toxics. You can find exposure limits for most common crafts supplies via the MSDS (above). Exposure standards are expressed in parts per million (PPMs). Higher PPM limits are usually better—for example, you are better off using odorless paint thinner (300 ppm) than mineral spirits (100 ppm). Ventilation is key to a healthier environment because ventilated air dilutes the toxicity in an evaporated chemical.

Volatility and flashpoints. It may seem obvious but I'll say it anyway: to avoid fire dangers, keep solvents, welding gases, and oxidizing chemicals sealed when not in use. These substances are considered volatile. They mix easily with the air to create an explosive combo of air and vapors. And they have a low flashpoint (the temperature at which the substance ignites—the lower the flashpoint, the more danger). Ideally you should use low volatility, high flashpoint substances.

Foundries and kilns. It's best to wear eye protection and keep your distance, when possible, from devices and processes that generate high heat. For example, kilns and glass-blowing processes generate infrared radiation. Devices such as carbon-arc lighting generate ultraviolet radiation. Prolonged exposure to both can lead to a variety of ailments.

Noise injuries. If you have a noisy workspace, don't wait: start using sonic reducing headphones immediately and if possible, isolate noise-producing devices within your studio. Excessive noise can cause a range of hearing problems the worst of which—tinnitus—is permanent.

Physical injuries. Repetitive stress injuries—doing the same motion over and over—can lead to many physical ailments. Poor posture—for example, stooping to use a spinning wheel—can result in back and other muscular-skeletal ailments.

Much of the factual material I've mentioned above is derived from a helpful online guide, *Safety Guide for Art Studios,* by Thomas Ouiment. Search for it on the Web where it's posted as PDF. Two other well-respected resources are by Michael McCann. They are:

- *Health Hazards Manual for Artists*
- *Artist Beware, Updated and Revised: The Hazards in Working with All Art and Craft Materials and the Precautions Every Artist and Craftsperson Should Take.*

Going Online

Holly Yashi Jewelry, founded in 1981, produces stylish jewelry with luminous colors and innovative materials. The company has had considerable success in the marketplace and when the Internet exploded in the late 1990s, Holly Yashi considered its options and decided on a slow, steady approach to entering the online business world.

The company's site (www.hollyyashi.com) debuted in 2000. At first, it basically reproduced Holly Yashi's print catalog. "We shot with a digital camera," says cofounder Paul Lubitz, "so that made it easier to transfer our images to the Web." The company later added some handy features including tips on jewelry care, Holly's Picks (gift ideas), and a search feature called Find A Retailer. The search feature allows the customer to locate nearby stores selling Holly Yashi's Jewelry products. Although the search feature wasn't cheap—it cost approximately $1,000—it served a secondary purpose: allowing Holly Yashi to avoid publishing a list of all its retailers, which would have been easy for competitors to copy.

"In 1998 and 1999, I didn't get the Internet," said Lubitz. "Now, I think it's incredible! I see it as another cost of doing business, just like your electric bill."

No doubt about it, if you're looking for an efficient, relatively inexpensive way to reach customers, clients, and fans, establishing a presence in cyberspace fits the bill in many respects. Your site can provide images of your work instantly and globally. If you want to invest a little more time and effort, your site can be used for direct sales—an efficient way to increase your profits and reduce your need for agents, galleries, and distributors.

Creating and hosting a website can now be accomplished by even the most tech-challenged crafts worker. If you've got other priorities, you can hire a website developer to custom design the site for you. In this chapter, I'll discuss the legal and practical issues involved in going online.

For experienced Internet users, this chapter may seem too elemental; for those without any experience, it may seem too technical. I extend apologies to both. I'm trying to provide a middle ground, basic enough not to scare away newbies, and detailed enough to be informative.

> ### TIP
> **No, you don't have to have a website.** Don't let me (or any other nerds) talk you into a website if you don't really want one. If you're happy with the way you do business or you already have more orders than you can handle, you probably don't need to bother establishing a presence in cyberspace.

Where Do You Start?

The Web provides the opportunity for a crafts business owner (at home in her pajamas) to present a product line that appears as competitive and inviting as its big-business cousins. At the same time, the Internet allows your crafts business to communicate with existing customers—perhaps providing access to a calendar of sales events—and to send out information that sells your work to potential customers.

Whether your crafts business operates primarily on the Internet or just has some Web-based component—for example, you sell at fairs and also sell at eBay—you'll find that you'll need and benefit from some knowledge about going online. In this chapter you'll learn how to:

- Get lots of cool stuff for free.
- Invoice customers and get paid using online payment systems.
- Sell stuff via Etsy or eBay.
- Earn money using Google Adsense and affiliate accounts.
- Learn the (very) basics of driving traffic to a site.
- Set up a website in 24 hours.
- Understand the basic legal rules for operating online.

If you're staying away from the Internet for any of the following reasons: fear (you're afraid of computers and don't know how to use Google); confusion (you know a little bit but the whole thing seems overwhelming); or costs (you're pretty sure you can't afford it, whatever it is), then you'll be surprised at how much you can manage on your own. And remember, having a high I.Q. is not a requirement for cyberspace, as you'll quickly become aware.

Free Stuff

Many crafts artists are unaware of the great free business stuff that's available on the Web. There are many business and personal services available gratis and the number of such services seems to be increasing as online entrepreneurs realize that giving some things away for free is a great way to sell other stuff. Consider this scenario: you set up a free blog to describe jewelry-making tips and your custom jewelry business. You include—at no charge to you—Google Adsense, which peppers your blog with ads for jewelry supplies. Users are attracted to your tips, they click on the ads, and each time they do so, pennies drop into your Google account. Talk about low start-up costs! (Of course, it's not always so easy, as I'll describe below.) Here's an idea of some of the free stuff that can help your crafts business.

Free Email

Every crafts artist can benefit from an email account, and for the less than 2% of crafts artists who don't have an email account, here's some good news. You don't need to own a computer to get an email account and you don't even need an Internet connection. If you have access to a public computer at a library or Internet café, you can create a free email account in minutes. If you don't know how, ask someone to show you how to get on the Internet (it usually involves two or three clicks), go to any of the free email websites—Gmail, Yahoo, Hotmail—and set up an account. (If you've never used a computer mouse, you may need an explanation.) For the small fraction of readers who are unaware, you can also track your email on your cell phone, smart phone, and a variety of other handheld devices (although you may pay extra for that).

RESOURCE

Hotmail (www.hotmail.com), Gmail (www.gmail.com), and Yahoo (www.yahoo.com) are three popular free mail sources.

Free Blogs

A blog—short for Web log—is the fastest way to acquire Internet real estate. Initially, blogs were used as journals. Nowadays, they've come to mean any frequently and easily updated Web page. Blogs provide a way for people to learn about your business or they may be a marketing adjunct for your business by providing information on a related topic—for example the history of knitting. Check out setting up a blog; it really is very simple. You can list contact information, provide a bio, and post regular updated information about your business.

For example, check out The Jewelry Blog (http://jewelrytrends. blogspot.com), where daily postings discuss jewelry trends, design tips, and related information. The advantage of a blog is that you can establish one in less than an hour. The disadvantage is that in order to maintain interest, you'll need to regularly refresh it with new information. And if you're really serious about making money from your blog and driving traffic to that blog, you may eventually have to liberate it from the free blogging site and set up your own site (more on that, later).

RESOURCE

Three free resources for setting up a blog are Blogger (www.blogger. com), Typepad (www.typepad.com), or WordPress (www.wordpress.com).

Free Online Calendars, Spreadsheets, Photo Storage, and Documents

Welcome to the "cloud." In tech parlance, cloud computing is when your services are provided and stored online. Instead of searching for that document, photo, or calendar on your work computer or your home computer, it's stored in the cloud—that is, cyberspace. To see how it works, sign up for a Gmail account, sign in, and click one of the links in the upper left-hand corner—calendar, documents, or photos.

These links provide you with free word processing software and storage of documents, free spreadsheet software and storage, free photo galleries, and a free calendar. All of these tools may help you in managing your crafts business and they may have an extra benefit in that you can provide limited public access to them to your customers or clients. So, for example, if you'd like sales reps to schedule appointments, you can have them access your free calendar to see what's available. Want customers to see examples of the sweaters you knit? Post them free at your free photo gallery.

RESOURCE

See Gmail (www.gmail.com), Zoho (which has free and paid platforms) (www.zoho.com), and ThinkFree (which offers some free and some paid services) (www.thinkfree.com). Also, although it doesn't offer online services, OpenOffice.org offers a free suite of downloadable office software similar to Microsoft Office (www.openoffice.org).

Free Surveys

If you're looking for customer feedback or you're doing some market research, sites such as Survey Monkey allow you to do it for free.

RESOURCE

See Survey Monkey (www.surveymonkey.com).

Free To-Do Lists

Keeping track of your to-do list is tricky when you've got multiple lists living on your work computer, home computer, smartphone, and iPod. Sites such as Doris and Toodledo manage your lists for you by keeping the main list online and syncing them to smaller applications widgets that live on your personal devices.

RESOURCE
See Doris (www.dorisapp.com) and Toodledo (www.toodledo.com).

Free Faxes

Say goodbye to that clunky fax machine with free online fax services. You upload documents and provide the fax number and these sites deliver, usually with a paid ad on your cover sheet. If you want the ad-free version there's usually a fee of one or two dollars per fax.

RESOURCE
See Faxzero (www.faxzero.com) and Freefax (www.freefax.com).

Free Websites

Let's say you just want to provide a site that provides some basic information, a biography, a synopsis of your work, and perhaps some useful material for customers—like tips on maintenance of your pottery and your most popular bowls. You can use one of the many free offerings—for example, Google Sites—which make it easy to create a professional-looking website. The disadvantage is that your site may look slightly generic (since you'll choose from a limited number of templates) and your domain name (your address on the Web) will be more complicated than most. At Google Sites, for example your address would be http://sites.google.com/site/mobilehairsalon (instead of www. mobilehairsalon.com if you created a paid site as described below).

RESOURCE
See Google Sites (www.sites.google.com), Yola (www.yola.com), Webs (www.webs.com), Wetpaint (www.wetpaint.com), and Weebly (www.weebly.com).

Invoice Customers and Get Paid Online

PayPal (www.paypal.com) is an automated online payment system that enables anyone with an email address to make payments from across the country or around the world. Because the system works so well, and because it also enables the use of credit cards (as part of its Merchant Services), PayPal has become a premier payment system for small business owners. Sending money via PayPal is free, but receiving money may be subject to a fee depending on the type of PayPal account you have. In other words, if you're selling stuff online, PayPal offers a simple way to accept payments without establishing a credit card merchant account (and dealing with the associated fees and expenses).

But wait, there's more! The system also allows anyone to create invoices that enable your customers (even those who know nothing about PayPal) to use the system. You can create invoices in several ways:

- **Email.** Create an email invoice by filling out PayPal's online invoice form.
- **Request Money.** Use PayPal's "Request Money" page to send a customer an invoice directly from PayPal.
- **QuickBooks.** Use the Payment Request Wizard for QuickBooks, which enables you to create an invoice from within your QuickBooks program.
- **Outlook.** Use the Payment Request Wizard for Outlook, which enables you to create an invoice from within your Microsoft Outlook email program.

Some alternatives to PayPal include:

- **Google Checkout.** Another alternative to establishing an online credit card merchant account is to create a Google Checkout Merchant Account. Google Checkout is primarily for the sale of tangible and digital (downloadable) goods, although it can also be used to process transactions for services and subscriptions. Like PayPal, Google Checkout accepts major credit and debit cards, including VISA, MasterCard, American Express, and Discover. Buyers enter their credit or debit card information when they first sign up for Google Checkout and can select their preferred payment type during checkout.

- **Checkout by Amazon.** Amazon bills this as a "complete e-commerce checkout solution." Using the Amazon checkout system, customers at your website get the same checkout experience as they would at Amazon, including Amazon's 1-Click tools.

RESOURCE

See PayPal (www.paypal.com), Google Checkout (www.checkout. google.com), and Checkout by Amazon (www.payments.amazon.com).

Battle of the Community Stores: Etsy vs. eBay

Community stores offer a complete turnkey solution—that is, they'll help you quickly set up your crafts store online and make it possible for you to accept credit card payments. All you'll need to do is pay the fees and provide photos and copy for your products.

eBay is the pioneer of community stores. If you set up an eBay store, you are provided with a series of Web pages that showcase your inventory and cross-promote your eBay auctions. The logic behind an eBay store (instead of a straight eBay auction) is that consolidating your eBay crafts products in a store supposedly increases the likelihood of sales and gives customers an overall view of your business. Additionally, the About the Seller function of an eBay store enables you to describe your business in detail and to link to other websites.

For crafts artists there had always been drawbacks to working at eBay. The sheer size of the site—the company posts six to seven million listings a day—combined with the amazing variety of items for sale, made it difficult for crafts artists to break out of the garage sale atmosphere. Not only that, items at eBay stores did not show up in searches of eBay auctions. In addition, eBay sellers thrived on the automation of their listings ... and one-of-a-kind crafts items did not lend themselves to this model. (eBay has several formats for listing items for sale, but the vast majority of transactions are completed by means of a Standard Auction listing.) Some other drawbacks were that eBay auctions are open for short fixed time periods—typically five to seven days.

Along came Etsy (www.etsy.com) in 2005, founded as a retail site where artists could sell one-of-a-kind handmade merchandise. The primary rule for sellers at Etsy is that you have to hand-make the items you sell—or put another way, you can't sell goods created by someone else, even if they are handmade. Despite some internal shuffling—two of the founders departed in 2008 along with a number of employees—Etsy has become (and remains) the most popular site for buying and selling handmade crafts (you can also sell vintage clothing—as long as it's over 20 years old—and crafts supplies).

At Etsy, a seller sets up a community store (or "shop"), gets a unique Etsy domain—for example, hookwooky.etsy.com—and ships the item when a sale is made. The rest is up to Etsy, including collecting payments and customer service. A group of crafts artists can even set up a collective Etsy store. Etsy supports the crafts community with forums, profiles, blogs, handy features—for example, a "Custom" feature that permits buyers to request commissioned works. You can sign up to sell your work for free. To start, you'll need to register for an Etsy account and you'll need a credit card for verification purposes. It costs 20 cents to list each item for four months. Etsy also charges a 3.5% transaction fee for each item sold. For the most part, these fees are the same or lower than at eBay, where an auction listing fee can range from 15 cents to $4, and eBay's cut of the auction sale price starts at 8.75% and climbs higher based on the sales price, or—in the case of buy-it-now items (fixed price)—eBay's percentage starts at 8%. To start selling on eBay, you need to register. It's free (you must be over 18 and have a valid email address) and you must obtain a seller's account (you'll need a credit card).

💡 **TIP**

By the way, although not as popular with crafts artists, you can also set up an Amazon WebStore. The setup procedure is quite simple (slightly easier and more user-friendly than at eBay stores), and it also includes some bells and whistles that you might not expect—for example, your WebStore will be hosted on your own public domain (www.yourstorename.com), a factor that may increase your search engine rankings and increase traffic. You can also easily incorporate Amazon affiliate listings and promotions. Although pricier than the standard eBay store (Amazon WebStores are $59.95 per month), the ease of use, the Amazon placement and security, and the feature-rich services make it worth the extra price for some sellers. Amazon often offers a free 30-day trial so you can test it out.

Earn Money With Google Adsense

Google Adsense ads appear on the side of your Web pages and you earn revenue—usually a few cents—each time someone clicks on one of the Google ads (and is transported to the advertiser's website). Adsense business is booming and Google pays out over $1 billion per quarter to its Adsense partners. Still, income is highly speculative and is directly tied to your ability to generate website traffic and click-throughs. Once you sign up to host ads, you'll be given a choice as to categories, and you can filter ads from competitors, as well.

RESOURCE
Learn more about Google Adsense (www.google.com/adsense).

The (Very) Basics of Driving Traffic to Your Crafts Site

As anyone who has launched a website business knows, success on the Internet requires hypervigilance, patience, a lot of hard work, and luck. The key is driving traffic to your website. So many people make their living by instructing others on how to increase traffic it's no wonder cynics say the only ones earning money from the Internet gold rush are the people selling the pans.

So, how do you get people to come to your website or blog? If your blog is simply a calling card on the Web, then there's no pressure to drive traffic. But if you're trying to generate online sales, you'll need to attract eyeballs. Here are explanations for some common approaches. If you're serious about pursuing traffic, check out some of the resources, below.

Great content and links. The most effective and low-cost method of driving traffic to your site is to create great content that encourages other sites to link to you. For example, Nolo, the publisher of this book, provides extensive free legal information at its website (www.nolo.com), making it one of the most linked-to legal sites on the Web. (By the way, if you're interested in seeing who is linked to your website, type "link:" followed by the address of your website into the Google search engine; for example, type "link:www.nolo.com.")

Search engines and keywords. Say hello to SEO (or search engine optimization), the science of making your website appear high in search engine rankings. Most people find their Web destinations via search engines, which have two types of listings: relevant and sponsored. Relevant listings are the primary search results that appear on the search page. Relevance (the order in which they are listed) is determined by the search engine algorithm, a mathematical formula that uses factors such as the content in a site, its domain name, material in its header (the headline that appears in the bar on top of your browser), information buried in the website code, and the number of sites that are linked to it. (There are numerous ways to increase your relevance at a website and you can pursue those through the resources listed below. Or type "increase traffic website" into a search engine and view the avalanche of results.)

Sponsored links usually appear at the top and in the right margin of the page. You can become a sponsored link by purchasing (or bidding on) keywords at a search company. For example, at Google.com, you can click on the "Advertising Programs" link and buy keywords (Google calls them "Adwords") for a setup fee of approximately $5. Keywords are the terms that people type into the search engine. For example, if you had purchased the words "crochet" and "baby," then your ad would pop up when a user searched for crocheted baby hats.

In reality, keyword buying is a lot more complex. Your choice of keywords is crucial, because if you use terms that are not specific or appropriate, you'll have wasted your money. Often, you must bid for keywords against competitors, and if you have the top bid, you will pay that amount every time someone clicks on your link when it appears in the search engine results.

There's strong sentiment for and against keyword buying. Some marketing people believe that it's useless trying to outbid competitors all the time and that the only one who profits is the search engine company. In addition, keyword prices have escalated in the past few years, making them a more expensive form of marketing.

Others, in crowded fields, believe that keyword buying is an effective way to rise to the top of the heap. In any case, everyone agrees that if you do buy keywords, you must closely monitor their effectiveness. If you are not getting results from the purchase of certain keywords, ditch those terms—fast. And, of course, if keywords in general are not generating sufficient returns, stop paying for them. For more information, type "Buy keywords" into your search engine. Finally, some search engines, such as Overture, merge relevance and sponsorship. The more you bid, the more relevant your search results.

Banner ads. Banner ads are short advertising messages that appear on websites. Like billboards, you can buy this advertising space and place your ads strategically across the Web. Like any form of advertising, you have a challenge: to get the viewer's attention and to motivate the viewer to click though to your site. It's a big challenge for a small ad and I don't recommend them.

Affiliate programs. You can offer commissions or other rewards to other sites that drive customers to click through and buy those products. For example, someone who specializes in leather golf club covers may wish to establish an affiliate system with golf websites.

Building a community. If your customers have something in common, you have an opportunity to unite them in a community at your site. For example, if your business specializes in knit hats for people undergoing chemotherapy, or if you provide mobiles for newborns, you may want to set aside a portion of your site for community exchange. The key is to unite your customers in a community atmosphere.

> **RESOURCE**
> *Search Engine Optimization: Your Visual Blueprint for Effective Internet Marketing,* by Kristopher B. Jones (Visual), *A Practical Guide to Affiliate Marketing: Quick Reference for Affiliate Managers & Merchants,* by Evgenii Prussakov (AM Navigator LL), *Ultimate Guide to Google AdWords: How to Access 100 Million People in 10 Minutes,* by Perry Marshall and Bryan Todd (Entrepreneur Press), and *Adwords for Dummies,* by Howie Jacobson (For Dummies).

How to Build a Website in 24 Hours

If free prefab free sites, described above, are not for you, you can build a site from scratch. You'll need three elements:

- **A domain name.** You can buy one at a domain name registrar (assuming your choice is available) or through a hosting company. Expect to pay between $10 and $15 a year.
- **A hosting company.** A hosting company, referred to as an Internet Service Provider or ISP, rents you space on its equipment. You give the host your domain name information (or they'll get the domain name for you) and they broadcast your website for the world to see. Expect to pay $5 to $50 a month for Web hosting, depending on the bells and whistles.
- **Website development software.** This is what you use to create your website. If website construction is not your thing, you can hire a website developer or use an ISP such as GoDaddy.com that provides templates.

Building a store from scratch. An online store is like a jukebox; it has to look good on the outside but also house some complex inner mechanics. Buyers need to examine images of your crafts items, fill shopping carts, pay with credit cards, and process orders. If you're building a store from scratch, you'll have to go through the same basic steps as for typical sites described above—get a domain name, design your site, and locate an ISP—with one twist: You need to incorporate a shopping cart and credit card payment system. There's a simple solution (see the discussion of PayPal and Google Checkout, above), but if you want buyers to pay you directly through your own credit card merchant account, you've got some programming tasks ahead of you. For more information on shopping cart providers, type "shopping cart services" into a search engine. These companies will handle all of your back-end details and deposit payments into your account.

RESOURCE

If you're creating a site from scratch and want your own domain name, consider GoDaddy (www.godaddy.com), one of the least expensive ISPs. See also *Creating Web Sites: The Missing Manual,* by Matthew MacDonald (Pogue Press).

Dealing With Developers

If you can't or don't want to deal with website creation then get a developer to do it for you. Expect to pay between $500 to $2,000 for a basic site (five to ten website pages). Developers may also assist you on a regular basis by offering Web hosting and regular maintenance. Keep in mind that websites are not static; they need to change as your business changes. So unless you set up a system to update the site yourself, you'll have to keep returning to a developer for every fix. The best solution: Have the developer set up the site and then teach you how to update it. There's an added benefit of using developers: They are often savvy in methods of popularizing sites and you may benefit from their online marketing and traffic-driving knowledge.

Basic Legal Rules When Going Online

Many sites post "terms and conditions" somewhere on the site. Do you need them, too? Maybe. If your site sells goods, you may need notices regarding credit card use, refunds, and returns (known as "transaction conditions"). For example, you might want to announce that your business will accept returns up to 30 days after purchase. You may also want to include disclaimers—statements that inform customers that you won't be liable for certain kinds of losses they might incur. For example, you may disclaim responsibility for losses that result if pottery breaks when a customer ships it back for return.

Rules for Refunds

I discussed the Federal Trade Commission's Mail or Telephone Order Merchandise Rule, also known as the "30-Day Rule," in Chapter 1. Basically, when you advertise merchandise on eBay and don't say anything about when you plan to ship, you're expected to ship within 30 days from when you receive the payment and all the information needed to fill the order. Not every business needs an unlimited return policy, but I do recommend that you establish a customer-friendly policy of some sort and that you communicate it to your customers. Review Chapter 1 for more details.

Other Terms and Conditions

Here are some other items you may want to include at your website or online store.

Disclaimers. You may want to include disclaimers—statements that inform customers that you won't be liable for certain kinds of losses they might incur. For example, you may disclaim responsibility for losses that result if pottery breaks when a customer ships it back for return.

Privacy. If you're gathering information from your customers, including credit card information, you should post a privacy policy detailing how this information will be used or not used. Yahoo!'s privacy policy is a good example of a broad, easy-to-understand policy. Whatever policy you adopt, be consistent, and if you're going to change it, make an effort to notify your customers by email of the change.

Chats and postings. If your website provides space for chats or postings from the Web-surfing public, you'll want to limit your liability from offensive or libelous postings or similar chat room comments. There are three things you can do. First, regularly monitor all postings and promptly take down those you think are offensive or libelous. Second, if a third party asks you to remove a posting, remove it while you investigate. If you determine—after speaking with an attorney—that you're entitled to keep the post, then you can put it back up. Third, include a disclaimer on your site that explains you don't endorse and aren't responsible for the accuracy or reliability of statements made by third parties. This won't shield you from claims, but it may minimize your financial damages if you're involved in a lawsuit over the posting.

Copyrights and trademarks. Include notices regarding copyright and trademark—for example, "Copyright © 2010 RichandAndrea.com" or "DEAR RICH is a trademark of Richard Stim."

Kids. If you're catering to an audience under 13 years old, special rules apply. You should learn more about dealing with children at the Federal Trade Commission website, www.ftc.gov.

Hiring Workers and Sales Reps

I n 1984, a dispute arose as to who owned the rights to Hummel figurines, one of the world's most collectible crafts products. At issue was whether the copyright in these cherubic creations was owned by the estate of the creator, Sister Berta Hummel, or by the German convent in which Sister Hummel toiled.

Under copyright law, the creator of the work—with one major exception—is the owner. The exception is that when someone is hired to create a work, the hiring party may, in some circumstances, be the owner. This is known as the "work-made-for-hire" (or "work for hire") principle. A manufacturer, trying to preserve its license to manufacture the Hummel figurines in the United States, argued that Sister Hummel was employed by the convent and that the drawings were works made for hire. The manufacturer pointed out that Sister Hummel had taken a vow of poverty and intended that all the fruits of her labors pass to the convent.

The U.S. federal court disagreed with the manufacturer. It was true that Sister Hummel performed artistic work for the convent—designing ecclesiastical vestments and artifacts—but the convent did not ask her to create the secular and spiritual drawings that were to become the basis of the figurines. Even if Sister Hummel was an employee of the convent, spending time on the spiritually inspired figurines was not part of her job description. Sister Hummel had created and controlled the drawings and supervised the creation of the ceramic figures. She, not her "employer" (the convent), owned the rights, and her rights passed to her mother, her only surviving relative. (*Schmid Brothers, Inc. v. Goebel*, 589 F.Supp. 497 (E.D. N.Y. 1984).)

It may seem odd that, 40 years after her death, lawyers are arguing about whether Sister Hummel was an employee when she created her art work. But the dispute demonstrates the crucial importance of correctly classifying an employee's status. Workers—those people you hire for your crafts business—provide important services and can increase your profit margins. The Craft Organization Directors Association (CODA), reports that craftspeople that have paid employees have three times the household income and ten times the sales/revenue of those who work alone. But employees and contractors can also be the source of disputes over a wide range of issues, including employment tax reporting responsibilities, hiring and firing, ownership of designs created by the worker, and misuse of confidential information. In this chapter, I discuss issues that arise when you hire workers and sales reps.

Employee vs. Independent Contractor— What's the Difference?

An independent contractor (IC) is a person who generally provides specialized services on a per-project basis for a number of businesses. Some common examples of ICs include website developers, bookkeepers, and electricians. An IC is hired to provide a service, usually one that requires a certain level of skill, experience, and on an ongoing basis.

An employee, on the other hand, is not running his or her own business. An employee follows the rules and standards required by the employer. An employer exercises a lot more control over an employee (than over an IC), from setting work hours to imposing a dress code to dictating exactly how the employee does every aspect of the job. Although employees can be hired for a short-term project (such as helping you with a seasonal mailing crunch or gift-wrapping items during a holiday rush), it's more common to hire employees on an open-ended basis, until the work runs out or the employee quits or doesn't meet your expectations.

If your crafts business misclassifies a worker, you may run into problems with the state unemployment insurance agency, the state workers' compensation board, and the IRS. (The IRS, in particular, imposes hefty penalties for misclassification.) The IRS test considers workers employees if the company they work for has the right to direct and control the way they work—including the details of when, where, and how the job is accomplished. In contrast, the IRS considers workers independent contractors if the company they work for does not manage how they work, except to accept or reject their final results.

The important thing to remember here is not to treat workers as ICs if they are really employees. If you're attempting to avoid taxes and legal requirements, there are a number of government agencies that might call your bluff (no government agency is ever going to tell you that you should have classified an employee as an independent contractor). If you're curious about how the IRS makes its consideration, here are some factors that they use.

Factors the IRS Considers	
Factors That Make a Worker Look Like an IC	**Factors That Make a Worker Look Like an Employee**
Worker can earn a profit or suffer a loss from the activity.	Worker is paid for his or her time, regardless of how well or poorly the hiring company is doing.
Worker furnishes the tools and materials needed to do the work.	Worker receives tools and materials from the hiring business.
Worker is paid by the job.	Worker is paid by the hour.
Worker decides how to do the work.	Worker receives instructions and training on how to do the work.
Worker decides when and where to work.	Worker has set hours, usually at the hiring company's place of business.
Worker hires and pays any assistants.	Worker's assistants (if any) are provided and paid for by the hiring company.
Worker pays for business and travel expenses.	Worker's job-related expenses are paid by the hiring company.
Worker works for more than one business at a time.	Worker provides services to only one business.
Worker does not receive employee benefits from hiring company.	Worker receives employee benefits from hiring company.
Worker can be terminated only for reasons specified in contract.	Worker can quit or be fired at any time.
Worker provides services that fall outside of the hiring company's usual operations.	Worker provides services that are an integral part of the hiring company's regular operations.

Five Reasons Why Hiring an IC Is Usually a Better Choice for Your Crafts Business

If you're considering hiring someone for your crafts business, you're usually going to prefer hiring an IC, (assuming that the worker qualifies as an IC). Here's why:

ICs require less training. Unlike an employee, whom you may have to train, an IC will be ready to go on day one—and will have the skill and background to do the job right. ICs also have a stronger incentive to finish the work quickly.

ICs are always a better choice for short-term tasks. If you have a specific project or task you need done (for example, a one-time electrical job or help designing your packaging), you'll probably want to go with an IC.

Costs are lower with ICs. Your total cash outlay will probably be lower for ICs than employees. Although an IC is likely to charge you more to do a project than you'd have to actually pay an employee, employees are more expensive overall after you add on taxes, insurance costs, the price of equipment, materials, and workspace, and other cash outlays.

ICs are better for your cash flow. State and federal laws set strict guidelines for paying employees. You have to pay at least the minimum hourly wage, and you have to pay them according to a schedule set by state law (anywhere from once a week to once a month). If you don't follow these rules, you could face fines and penalties. For an IC, you and the IC will set the pay schedule yourselves. If your clients pay you by the project, you can pay the IC when you get paid. If you won't be able to pay for a while, you can work out an installment arrangement with the IC.

ICs require fewer rules and red tape. Unless you're ready to learn your legal obligations as an employer and set up a payroll system to withhold taxes and pay them over to the IRS, don't hire employees. You can run into trouble quickly if you don't handle employee matters by the book; for an IC, on the other hand, the paperwork is minimal. Keep in mind, however, that government agencies will take a close look at ICs to make sure they shouldn't have been classified as employees. This means you may be a more likely target for an audit if you hire ICs.

Independent Contractors

Don't hire an IC to do anything other than a very minor project without signing an agreement. An IC agreement helps you and the IC clarify the terms of your deal, creates a written record of exactly what you agreed upon, and can help convince the IRS and other agencies that you and the IC did not intend to create an employer-employee relationship. A written agreement is especially important if you are hiring someone to do creative work for you—designing crafts items, for example. An IC will own the creative rights to the work unless you make a written agreement signing the rights over to you. A sample IC agreement transferring rights is included in this chapter.

There are only a couple of legal rules you have to follow when hiring an IC—and they kick in only when the hiring party pays the IC $600 or more in one year.

Complete and file IRS Form 1099-MISC, *Miscellaneous Income.* This form is very straightforward—you simply enter identifying information about your business and the IC, then enter the amount you paid the IC in the box marked "Nonemployee compensation." You must provide copies of the form to the IC no later than January 31 of the year after you made the payment. You also have to file copies of the form with the IRS and your state taxing authority (you have to file with the IRS by February 28 of the year after you made the payment; check with your state tax agency to find out its filing deadline). When you file the 1099 with the IRS, you must send along IRS Form 1096, *Annual Summary and Transmission of U.S. Information Returns.* Form 1096 is essentially a cover letter on which you add up all payments you reported on 1099 forms for the year.

CAUTION

You can't file a downloaded 1099 or 1096. Although you can download both Form 1099 and Form 1096 from the IRS website, www.irs.gov, you cannot file these copies. Instead, you must file an original of each, which you can get by contacting your local IRS office (you can find a list of offices at the IRS website) or calling 800-TAX-FORM.

Get the IC's taxpayer identification number. The IRS knows that many ICs work under the table—they're paid in cash, which they don't report (or they underreport) to the IRS. To put a stop to this, the IRS requires those who hire ICs to get a copy of their taxpayer ID—their employer identification number or Social Security number that they use on their tax returns. If an IC won't give you an ID number or the IRS informs you that the number the IC gave you is incorrect, you have to withhold taxes from the IC's pay and remit that money to the IRS. (The IRS calls this "backup withholding.") Obviously, you want to avoid this extra chore—and you can, by requiring the IC to fill out IRS Form W-9, *Request for Taxpayer Identification Number.* If the IC doesn't have an ID number yet, you don't have to start withholding until 60 days after he or she applies for one.

Employees

There are more forms to fill in—and rules to follow—when you hire an employee than when you hire an IC. Fortunately, most of the paperwork is fairly simple, and you can find the forms online. When you hire an employee, you must do all of the following:

IRS Form W-4. Have the employee complete IRS Form W-4, *Employee's Withholding Allowance Certificate.* On this form, the employee provides basic identifying information and tells you how much money to withhold from each paycheck. You must have this form in your files, but you don't have to send it to the IRS.

> **RESOURCE**
> **You can download W-4 forms from the IRS website,** www.irs.gov, or get them by contacting your local IRS office (you can find a list of offices at the IRS website) or calling 800-TAX-FORM.

USCIS Form I-9. Complete USCIS Form I-9, *Employment Eligibility Verification.* This form confirms that the employee is eligible to work in the United States. The employee must complete a portion of the form and then give you documentation of his or her eligibility. The form tells you what kinds of documents are acceptable; a U.S. passport or a driver's license and birth certificate or Social Security card are the typical showing for U.S. citizens. You don't have to file this form, but you must keep it on hand for three years after you hire the employee or one year after the employee quits or is fired, whichever is later.

RESOURCE

You can download I-9 forms from the website of the United States Citizenship and Immigration Services (USCIS, formerly the INS), at www.uscis. gov. You can fill in the form on your computer or print out a blank copy and fill it in by hand. I-9s can now be completed and stored entirely electronically, signatures and all; check the USCIS website for more information on this.

State reporting agency. Report the employee to your state's new hire reporting agency. Employers must submit basic information on new employees to the state, which uses that information to track down parents who owe child support. You will have to submit your employee's name, address, and Social Security number; some states require additional information, such as the employee's date of birth or first day of work.

RESOURCE

To get the information and forms you need, start at the website of the Administration for Children and Families (www.acf.hhs.gov), a subdivision of the federal Department of Health and Human Services. Click the tab for "Working with ACF," then scroll down to the heading "Employer Info." This will lead you to several publications about the new-hire reporting program as well as a list of state requirements and links to the agency in each state that administers the program. Go to your state agency's website to download the required form and find out what information you have to provide.

Register with your state's labor department. Once you hire an employee, you will have to pay state unemployment taxes. These payments go to your state's unemployment compensation fund, which provides short-term relief to workers who lose their jobs. Typically, you must complete some initial registration paperwork, then pay money into the fund periodically. Unemployment compensation is a form of insurance, so the amount you pay in will depend, in part, on how many of your former employees file for unemployment (just as your insurance premiums depend, in part, on how many claims you file against the policy).

RESOURCE

Start at the federal Department of Labor, which administers federal/state unemployment programs. Go to http://workforcesecurity.doleta. gov/map.asp, which provides a link to each state's unemployment agency. Once you get to your state agency's website, look for a tab or link on unemployment, or find the material for employers or businesses. Many states provide downloadable forms and online information on your responsibilities.

Don't forget workers' compensation insurance. Many states require all employers to have workers' comp coverage, either by paying into a state fund or buying a separate policy. (Workers' comp is not needed for ICs, but general business liability insurance is recommended. I talk about this in Chapter 5.) Some states exempt employers with no more than two or three employees from this rule, but it might make sense to purchase coverage anyway. Beyond the legal requirements, having workers' comp coverage can save you a bundle if one of your employees is hurt on the job.

Hang up required posters. Even the smallest businesses are legally required to post certain notices to let employees know their rights under a variety of workplace laws. The federal government wants you to put up a handful of notices; many states have additional posting requirements.

RESOURCE

The Department of Labor's website, www.dol.gov, lists workplace posters. (Search for "posters" in the A-Z index to find what you need.) Your state's labor department probably also has any required posters on its website.

If you're having trouble figuring out which requirements apply to you (or you don't want to post a dozen different notices), you can get an all-in-one poster that combines all required state and federal notices from your local chamber of commerce for about $20.

Ten Tips When Hiring Family Members

There's something to be gained by bringing the family into the business —for example, loyalty, respect, and a sense of mission. Besides that, family businesses have a better chance of survival over the first five years than nonfamily businesses. But working with family members can also trigger emotional, legal, and business issues. Here are ten things you should know about making your crafts business a family business:

Family members are easy to hire and hard to fire. How do you know whether to bring a family member into your business? First consider whether they share your vision or interest in the business. Next, consider whether they're competent. Neil Koenig, author of *You Can't Fire Me, I'm Your Father* (Hillsboro Press), suggests a simple standard. Just ask: "Is this person hirable at our competitors?" If not, don't consider the relative for a job. If you're unsure about qualifications, business counselor James Hutcheson suggests asking family members to come in for a short specified period of time to avoid painful terminations if things don't pan out.

Family businesses affect the family's bottom line. Don't bring in a spouse (or other relative) until you project the short- and long-term impact on your family balance sheet, especially if the spouse must curtail other money-making (or money-saving) activities.

Be clear with directions and compensation. You should be able to explain to your spouse or child how long and how often their help will be needed—for example, weekly, monthly, or seasonally. Accurately describe the work and spell out the type and variety of tasks. Compensation must be reasonable. If not, you'll likely trigger resentment or disputes that will soon spill over to the dinner table.

Establish boundaries for family members. For most people, the boundary between work and family is clear, but that's not always the case when a family member joins the business. "If you can't turn it off at home," says business counselor Dr. Rachna Jain, "your whole relationship rises and falls with the business." One approach is to establish no-biztalk-zones or ban crafts business discussions during certain times (such as dinner).

Take advantage of tax benefits when hiring kids. If you hire your children, you can deduct salaries you pay them. Your children, particularly those under age 18, probably pay taxes on this income at a lower tax rate (starting at 10% for amounts under $8,025) than you pay on your business income. Not only that, a minor child who performs services for the family business does not have to pay any taxes on the first $5,700 in wages earned in a year (as of 2009). If your child is under 18, you don't even need to pay payroll taxes—that is, payments such as FICA (Social Security and Medicare) and FUTA (federal unemployment) that are required for all other employees. Even more tax can be saved if the child establishes an IRA, the contributions for which are tax deductible up to $5,000 per year. In that case, your working offspring won't have to pay taxes on the first $10,700 of earned income. For more information on employing your child, see IRS Publication 929, *Tax Rules for Children and Dependents*. Keep in mind that these rules don't apply for hiring anyone's kids—only your own. If the IRS questions you, the primary concern will be whether the child does real work and is paid reasonable wages. In general, as long as you are paying for a task you would pay someone else to do—for example, sweeping up the studio, putting stamps on promotional postcards, running errands, doing clerical tasks, entering data into a computer, or answering the phones—and as long as the payment is commensurate with what you might pay an outsider, the IRS will likely accept the categorization.

Hire your parents. If you hire your retired parents, you can deduct the expense, lowering your taxable income. Your parents will probably be taxed at a lower tax rate than what you pay. But before Mom and Dad punch the time clock, check what effect the extra income will have on their Social Security. In some cases—for example, for parents under 65, income from your business could reduce their Social Security income.

Understand spousal co-ownership rules. If spouses own the business in a community property state (Arizona, California, Idaho, Nevada, New Mexico, Texas, Washington, or Wisconsin), they can report their business income on a Schedule C (as a sole proprietorship) as part of the joint return. This doesn't save money but it does save the time and hassle of filing a K-1 partnership return, which is required of spouses who co-own a business in a non-community property state. If one spouse owns the business and the other works for it, however, it's a sole proprietorship, and income is reported on the individual family member's tax return.

Tread carefully with Family Limited Partnerships. Family Limited Partnerships (FLPs) are a business form popularized in the 1990s that shields a business from many liabilities and provides tax benefits, especially when you're transferring assets of the business to another generation. In the typical FLP, the parents act as the general partners. The children are the passive limited partners, who cannot run the business and are prevented from transferring their interest to others outside of the family. If the parents are sued, the business assets of the limited partners can't be touched by creditors. Using FLPs, savvy accountants and lawyers have helped family businesses achieve nearly tax-free transfers of millions of dollars of money and business property to their heirs. Chances are that you won't need to think about FLPs for your family business because the tax benefits usually won't kick in unless your family has millions in assets. In any case, the IRS is suspicious of FLPs. In 2004, a federal tax court knocked out a Texas FLP, obligating heirs to pay over $2 million in taxes. In another 2004 case, however, a court of appeal upheld an FLP, though it stated that a transaction between family members will be scrutinized more thoroughly to assure that the arrangement is not a sham transaction or a disguised gift. (*Kimbell v. U.S.,* 371 F.3d 257 (5th Cir. 2004).) In short, tread carefully and with the sound advice of an attorney or accountant before forming an FLP.

Beware of divorce business-style. Even if only one spouse operated the crafts business, the ownership will likely be split between both after divorce. Unless there is an agreement to the contrary—for example, a prenuptial or buyout agreement—divorce laws generally require that the value of the business ownership be split by the separating spouses. In community property states (Arizona, California, Idaho, Louisiana, Nevada, New Mexico, Texas, Washington, and Wisconsin), each spouse is entitled to an equal share unless the business was acquired with one spouse's separate property. In other states, a similar rule makes each spouse entitled to an equitable (fair) share of the business. Most ownership issues can be anticipated with a buyout agreement (also known as a buy-sell agreement). Buyout agreements are like a prenuptial agreement for your business. They can require that a person sell an ownership interest back to the company or to other co-owners, according to a valuation method provided in the agreement. Preparing the valuation can be tricky, which is why a buyout agreement can be helpful. It establishes a way to put a value on the business and usually requires that the value of the business be calculated on two dates: marriage and divorce. An attorney can assist in preparing a buyout agreement or you can prepare one yourself by reading *Business Buyout Agreements: A Step-by-Step Guide for Co-Owners,* by Bethany Laurence and Anthony Mancuso (Nolo).

Incorporating the family business may save money at tax time. Incorporation has extra benefits when family members work in the crafts business. If you incorporate a family business, you can shift income from higher tax brackets to lower ones (known as "income splitting") by giving stock to family members in lower tax brackets—for example, giving stock to kids under age 14.

Statutory Employees

Special rules apply for workers who make or sew buttons, quilts, gloves, bedspreads, clothing, needlecraft products, or similar products. Under these rules, your workers will be considered statutory employees (that is, the government says they are employees by law) if the following requirements are satisfied:

- your crafts business produces quilts, gloves, bedspreads, clothing, needlecraft products, or similar products
- the worker performs services away from your place of business— usually in his or her home or workshop, or in another person's home
- the worker performs this work only on goods or materials that you furnish
- the work is performed according to your specifications; generally, such specifications are simple and consist of patterns or samples, and
- the worker is required to return the processed material to you or a person designated by you.

If the work meets all these requirements, you must pay half the employer's share of FICA and withhold FICA taxes from the worker's pay and send it to the IRS, just as for any other employee. However, no FICA tax is imposed if you pay the worker less than $100 during a calendar year.

> **EXAMPLE:** Rosa sews quilts at home. She works for various quilt makers, including Upscale Quilts, Inc. Upscale provides Rosa with all the fabric and supplies she must sew. The only equipment Rosa provides is a needle. Upscale gives Rosa a sample of each quilt and a pattern. When Rosa finishes each batch of quilts, she returns it to Upscale. Rosa is a statutory employee.

You also must complete a Form W-2, *Wage and Tax Statement,* for each of your statutory employees. (If you were allowed to treat them as independent contractors, you would instead complete Form 1099-MISC, the form used to report independent contractors' income to the IRS.) The W-2 will show how much Social Security and Medicare tax was withheld from the worker's pay.

You can avoid having a worker classified as a statutory employee if the worker does not:

- Perform services personally for you. Sign a written agreement with the worker stating that the worker has the right to subcontract or delegate the work out to others. This way, you make clear that the worker doesn't have to do the work personally.

- Make a substantial investment in your equipment or work facilities. Encourage the worker to invest in outside facilities, such as her own workspace.

- Have a continuing relationship with your crafts business. A continuing relationship means working for the hiring firm on a regular or recurring basis. Avoid a continuing relationship with the worker by assigning single projects, not ongoing tasks.

Firing Workers

A crucial distinction between independent contractors and employees concerns how long you must keep them around. You do not have an unrestricted right to fire an independent contractor as you do with most employees.

Strictly speaking, you can't fire an independent contractor. If the contractor fails to perform the services—that is, breaches the agreement—you can terminate your arrangement. But if the contractor has performed and you terminate your agreement without a legal reason, the independent contractor can sue you. If he wins, he can get an order requiring you to pay a substantial amount of money in damages. In short, your right to legally terminate an independent contractor's services is limited to situations where the independent contractor breaks the terms of your written or oral agreement.

You can fire at-will employees. Most employees are considered "at will," which means just about what it sounds like: At-will employees are free to quit at any time, for any reason; and you are free to fire them at any time and for any reason—unless your reason for firing is illegal. I cover these illegal reasons to fire, including discrimination, bad faith, and public policy violations, below.

Generally, however, you may fire an at-will employee for even the most idiosyncratic reasons—for example, you simply want to hire someone else as a replacement. You are also free to change the terms of employment—job duties, compensation, or hours, for example—for any reason that isn't illegal. Your workers can agree to these changes and continue working or reject the changes and quit. In other words, the employment relationship is voluntary. You cannot force your employees to stay forever, and they cannot require you to employ them indefinitely.

You cannot arbitrarily fire an employee if it is forbidden by:

- **An employment contract.** Whether written, oral, or implied, an employment contract can limit your right to fire the employee. For these employees, the language or nature of the contract usually spells out the terms of employment, including when and for what reasons the employees can be fired.
- **State or federal laws.** You're prohibited from firing, disciplining, or demoting an employee in bad faith, in violation of public policy, or for a discriminatory or retaliatory reason.

Works Made for Hire

As explained in the Sister Hummel case (at the beginning of this chapter), the copyright in an artwork is sometimes owned by the person who paid for it rather than by the artist. When this occurs, the resulting work is called a work made for hire (or simply, a "work for hire"). The basis for this principle is that a business that authorizes and pays for a work should own the rights to the work. This issue is relevant for your crafts business because there are instances in which you may pay a worker to create a copyrightable work and the worker—not you—will own the right to reproduce it. Keep in mind the "ownership" that I'm discussing here has to do with creative work—for example, where a worker comes up with the design or appearance of your crafts. I'm not talking about the assembly of crafts items under your direction.

In general, the rules for works made for hire are as follows:

- You own the copyright in any work created by an employee in the course of employment.
- You may—depending on the circumstances—own the copyright in a commissioned work created by an independent contractor for your business.

If a work was in fact made for hire, the person paying for the work (the hiring party) is considered to be the copyright owner and is named as the creator (or "author") on an application for copyright registration. The work-for-hire status of a work also affects the length of copyright protection and termination rights. Works made for hire created after 1977 are protected for a period of 95 years from first publication or 120 years from creation, whichever is shorter. Therefore, a work made for hire created in 2002 but not published until 2003 would be protected until 2098 (95 years from the date of publication). (For a discussion of copyright principles, including what constitutes "publication," see Chapter 6.)

Every copyrightable work created by an employee within the scope of his or her employment is automatically a work made for hire. The term "scope of employment" does not refer to whether the work was created during business hours or at home; it refers to whether the work is within the "scope" or range of activities expected from the employee. As one court stated, the question is whether it is the kind of work the employee was employed to perform. If a work is created by an employee within the scope of employment, there are no other requirements and no need for a written agreement—it is a work for hire. It is for this reason that, when sorting out ownership issues, courts first look at whether an employer-employee relationship exists as opposed to an independent contractor relationship.

It's quite unusual for a crafts work created by an independent contractor to qualify as a work made for hire. That doesn't mean the person paying for the work can't acquire copyright ownership—I'll discuss that, below—but the method of acquiring ownership is different from the work-made-for-hire method.

That said, a copyrighted work created by an independent contractor (unlike a work created by an employee) is not automatically classified as a work made for hire. For an independent contractor's work to qualify as a work made-for-hire, three requirements must be met:

- the work must be specially ordered or commissioned—for example, the hiring party must request that the work be created; it cannot already be in existence

- the work must fall within a group of specially enumerated categories (outlined below), and
- a written agreement must be signed by both parties indicating it is a work made for hire.

A work-for-hire agreement should be signed before the independent contractor commences work. However, at least one court has held that the agreement can be executed after the work is completed, provided that at the time the work was created, the parties intended to enter into such an agreement. However, the facts of the case must clearly show the parties' intent.

IC (Not Employee) Work-Made-for-Hire Categories

The work of an independent contractor crafts artist will be a work made for hire only if it falls within one of several enumerated categories. Many work-made-for-hire categories are inapplicable to artists—for example, a translation, atlas, or test or answer material for a test. Below are those categories that may have some relation to crafts works:

- a contribution to a collective work—for example, creating a pewter chess set for a book featuring many chess sets
- a part of a motion picture or other audiovisual work—for example, creating a tapestry for the set of a television show
- a supplementary work—a work prepared for publication as a supplement to a work by another artist for the purpose of introducing, concluding, illustrating, explaining, revising, commenting upon, or assisting in the use of the other work—for example, a publisher is producing a book featuring famous quilts and asks you to diagram a pattern for one of them, and
- an instructional text used in teaching—for example, a book demonstrating how to create crochet works, provided that it is designed for use in day-to-day teaching activity. If it is not intended as part of a regular teaching program, it will not qualify.

Any work created by an independent contractor that does not fall within one of the above categories *cannot* be a work made for hire. (As you can see, most crafts work will not qualify.) This is so even if the parties have signed a written agreement stating that the work is a work made for hire.

> **EXAMPLE:** A fiber artist is commissioned to create a work for a school auditorium. The artist signs an agreement entitled "Work Made for Hire." Even though an agreement was signed, the artist (not the school) owns the copyright in the fiber work because these textile and fiber works are not included among the enumerated categories of works by independent contractors that can be works made for hire.

Work-Made-for-Hire Agreement

Below is a simple work-for-hire agreement. Remember, it is always necessary to use this agreement with an independent contractor—for example, if you pay an artist to create a design for your jewelry. Strictly speaking, it is not necessary to use this agreement when a work is to be created by an employee. The employer automatically owns an employee's work created within the course of employment, regardless of whether there is a written agreement. However, employers often prefer to use written agreements to make it clear to employees that the employer owns copyright.

FORM ON THE CD-ROM
You can find the Work-Made-for-Hire Agreement on the CD-ROM at the back of this book.

Completing a Work-Made-for-Hire Agreement

In the "Services" section, insert the work that the contractor is supposed to perform, for example, "Create a series of Gothic fabric designs." Insert the amount to be paid to contractor in the "Payment" section.

The section titled "Works Made for Hire—Assignment of Intellectual Property Rights" establishes that the work is made for hire. However, if the work does not meet the requirements of copyright law, a backup

Work-Made-for-Hire Agreement

This Work-Made-for-Hire Agreement (the "Agreement") is made between _____
_____ ("Company"), and
_____ ("Contractor").

Services. In consideration of the payments provided in this Agreement, Contractor agrees to perform the following services: _____
_____
_____

Payment. Company agrees to pay Contractor as follows: _____
_____ .

Works Made for Hire—Assignment of Intellectual Property Rights. Contractor agrees that, for consideration that is acknowledged, any works of authorship commissioned pursuant to this Agreement (the "Works") shall be considered works made for hire as that term is defined under U.S. copyright law. To the extent that any such Work created for Company by Contractor is not a work made for hire belonging to Company, Contractor hereby assigns and transfers to Company all rights Contractor has or may acquire to all such Works. Contractor agrees to sign and deliver to Company, either during or subsequent to the term of this Agreement, such other documents as Company considers desirable to evidence the assignment of copyright.

Contractor Warranties. Contractor warrants that the Work does not infringe any intellectual property rights or violate any laws and that the Work is original to Contractor.

General Provisions

Entire Agreement. This is the entire agreement between the parties. It replaces and supersedes any and all oral agreements between the parties, as well as any prior writings. Modifications and amendments to this agreement, including any exhibit or appendix hereto, shall be enforceable only if they are in writing and are signed by authorized representatives of both parties.

Successors and Assignees. This agreement binds and benefits the heirs, successors, and assignees of the parties.

Notices. Any notice or communication required or permitted to be given under this Agreement shall be sufficiently given when received by certified mail, or sent by facsimile transmission or overnight courier.

Governing Law. This agreement will be governed by the laws of the State of _____ .

Waiver. If one party waives any term or provision of this agreement at any time, that waiver will only be effective for the specific instance and specific purpose for which the waiver was given. If either party fails to exercise or delays exercising any of its rights or remedies under this agreement, that party retains the right to enforce that term or provision at a later time.

Severability. If a court finds any provision of this agreement invalid or unenforceable, the remainder of this agreement will be interpreted so as best to carry out the parties' intent.

Attachments and Exhibits. The parties agree and acknowledge that all attachments, exhibits, and schedules referred to in this agreement are incorporated in this agreement by reference.

No Agency. Nothing contained herein will be construed as creating any agency, partnership, joint venture, or other form of joint enterprise between the parties.

[*Optional*]

☐ **Attorney Fees and Expenses.** The prevailing party shall have the right to collect from the other party its reasonable costs and necessary disbursements and attorney fees incurred in enforcing this Agreement.

☐ **Jurisdiction.** The parties consent to the exclusive jurisdiction and venue of the federal and state courts located in _____ [*county*], _____ [*state*], in any action arising out of or relating to this agreement. The parties waive any other venue to which either party might be entitled by domicile or otherwise.

☐ **Arbitration.** Any controversy or claim arising out of or relating to this agreement shall be settled by arbitration in _____ [*county*], _____ [*state*], in accordance with the rules of the American Arbitration Association, and judgment upon the award rendered by the arbitrator(s) may be entered in any court having jurisdiction. The prevailing party shall have the right to collect from the other party its reasonable costs and attorney's fees incurred in enforcing this agreement.

Signatures

Each party represents and warrants that on this date they are duly authorized to bind their respective principals by their signatures below.

COMPANY:

_____

Signature

_____

Typed or Printed Name

_____

Title

_____

Date

CONTRACTOR:

_____

Signature

_____

Typed or Printed Name

_____

Title

_____

Date

provision is added that converts the arrangement to an assignment. This type of provision is commonly used by businesses seeking to make sure that ownership rights have been acquired.

The "Warranty" provision provides an assurance that the Contractor owns the work and that the work is not an infringement. This is necessary to provide an assurance that the work is not taken from another source.

This agreement includes some miscellaneous provisions ("Entire Agreement," "No Joint Venture," and so on). For a detailed explanation of these provisions, see Chapter 9.

Acquiring Ownership of Works for Hire

As explained above, it is unlikely that you will acquire initial copyright ownership of a crafts work created by an independent contractor under work-made-for-hire principles. If you would like to get the copyright transferred to you, you can do so by executing an assignment agreement or by inserting an assignment provision in your independent contractor agreement. You cannot do this with an oral agreement. An assignment must be in writing.

An assignment is a transaction in which a copyright is permanently transferred. Assuming you execute the assignment prior to the performance by the independent contractor, the payment to the independent contractor is sufficient compensation for the copyright. Sometimes, in return for the transfer, the independent contractor might also either get a lump sum or a continuing payment known as a royalty. Two examples of assignments are provided in Chapter 6. The second example, the artwork assignment, can be used with an independent contractor crafts artist.

Works Made for Hire & Design Patents

If you pay someone to create a design that's patentable, the rules are a little different than they are for copyrights. The rules discussed here are for design patents—the type of patent most likely to apply to crafts works. (See Chapter 7 for more on design patents.) However, the same rules would apply for utility patents, which are for functional, not ornamental innovations.

- You will automatically own any patentable rights in a design if it was created by an employee (not an independent contractor) who was hired to design.
- You can alternately gain ownership of patentable rights in a design if the worker (whether employee or independent contractor) signs a written agreement transferring the rights to you.

An employer may also obtain more limited rights, known as shop rights, to employees' designs in certain specific circumstances.

- **Employed to design.** If you hire someone to create designs, or if designing is one of the worker's job functions, you will own the patent rights to any designs created by the worker during the course of the employment. Despite this principle—known as the "hired to invent" rule—most businesses prefer to use a written agreement because it is easier to enforce.
- **Assignment agreements.** You can assure ownership of any patentable designs by requiring employees or independent contractors to assign these rights to you. When these arrangements are used with employees, they are sometimes called "preinvention" agreements, because the worker is agreeing to assign patent rights before the design is actually created. Below is an example of a preinvention clause that assigns an employee's rights to the employer:

For an example of a patent assignment that can be used for independent contractors, see the Artwork Assignment provided in Chapter 6. Five states (California, Illinois, Minnesota, North Carolina, and Washington) have laws that limit preinvention assignments to employers. These laws prevent an employer from claiming ownership of a patentable creation if the creation is created with employee resources, doesn't result from work performed for an employer, and does not relate to the employer's business.

Assignment of Innovations. Employee agrees that any design, invention, process, system, or patentable creation (Innovation) conceived, originated, discovered, or developed in whole or in part by Employee: (1) as a result of any work performed by Employee with Employer's equipment, supplies, facilities, trade secret information, or other Employer resources; or (2) on Employer's time, shall be the sole and exclusive property of Employer, provided that the Innovation either relates to Employer's business or anticipated research. Employee agrees to sign and deliver to Employer (either during or subsequent to his employment) such documents as Employer considers desirable to evidence: (1) the assignment to Employer of all rights of Employee, if any, in any such Innovation; and (2) Employer's ownership of such Innovations. And in the event Employer is unable to secure Employee's signature on any necessary document, Employee appoints Employer (and each of its duly authorized officers and agents) as his agent and attorney-in-fact, to act for and in his behalf and to execute and file any such document. Employee agrees to promptly disclose in writing to Employer all such designs or discoveries made or learned by Employee during the period of employment that are related to Employer's business, that result from tasks assigned to Employee by Employer, or from the use of facilities owned or otherwise acquired by Employer.

- **Shop rights.** Even though you may not acquire ownership of a patent or trade secret created by an employee or independent contractor, you may acquire a limited right to use these innovations, known as a shop right. With a shop right, the worker retains ownership of the patent or trade secret, but the employer has a right to use it without paying the worker.

A shop right can only arise if the worker uses the employer's resources (materials, supplies, time) to create an innovation. (Other circumstances may be relevant, but use of employer resources is the most important criterion.)

When Workers Learn Your Crafts Secrets

Does your crafts business have valuable information that you reveal to workers but that you'd like to keep under wraps from competitors? It could be your customer list, a unique method for affixing beads to metal, or a secret formula used to create a fabric dye. This confidential information is a form of property whose value could drop to zero if other companies got their hands on it. In legal terms, these are your business's trade secrets, and you want to prevent your employees or independent contractors from disclosing these secrets to the public.

> **TIP**
> **Who owns employee-created trade secrets?** If an employee creates a trade secret for your business, the rules regarding ownership of that secret are the same as for design patents—that is, you will own it if the employee was hired to create such secrets, or the employee signed an agreement assigning such secrets.

Nondisclosure Agreements

When it comes to trade secrets, the primary concern for most crafts businesses is that an employee or independent contractor will walk away with this valuable information. To protect the confidentiality of such information, use a nondisclosure agreement (or NDA). In a nondisclosure agreement, one or both parties agree to keep certain information specified in the agreement confidential. A person who reveals or misuses your protected information after signing a nondisclosure agreement can land in serious legal trouble. You can seek a court order barring further disclosure or misuse of your information, and you can also sue for financial damages.

It is not essential to use an NDA with employees. State laws prohibit employees from improper disclosure of your trade secrets, even without a written agreement. But using an NDA does give you additional benefits if you have to sue an employee who has disclosed or misused your trade secrets. These benefits can include larger financial damages, payment of lawyer fees, a guarantee about where the dispute will be resolved (your headquarters state, for example), and what mechanism will be used to resolve it (arbitration vs. lawsuit).

Keep in mind that nondisclosure agreements won't protect just any business information; the information must qualify as a trade secret. To qualify as a trade secret and be protected by an NDA, your business information must meet three criteria:

- the information can't be generally known or readily ascertainable
- the information must provide economic value or a competitive advantage, and
- the information must be treated with secrecy—that is, you must take reasonable steps to protect it.

The minimum safeguards you should take to protect your trade secrets include keeping your secrets out of sight when not in use, marking documents containing secrets as confidential, and, of course, using NDAs. An example of a basic NDA is provided below.

FORM ON THE CD-ROM
You can find the Nondisclosure Agreement on the CD-ROM at the back of this book.

Noncompetes and Nonsolicitation: When an NDA Is Not Enough

A noncompetition agreement (also known as a "noncompete" or "covenant not to compete") is a contract in which someone agrees not to compete with you for a certain period of time. Noncompetition and nondisclosure agreements both have the same goal: to prevent a competitor from using valuable business information. The difference is that a nondisclosure prohibits disclosure to a competitor, while a noncompete prohibits even working for a competitor or starting a competing business. In other words, the noncompete is broader and can be more heavy-handed in its

Nondisclosure Agreement

This Nondisclosure Agreement (the "Agreement") is made between _____
_____ (the "Disclosing Party") and
_____ (the
"Receiving Party"). The Parties agree to the following terms and conditions. Receiving
Party acknowledges that the following information constitutes confidential trade
secret information ("Confidential Information") belonging to Disclosing Party: _____
_____ .

In consideration of Disclosing Party's disclosure of its Confidential Information to
Recipient, Receiving Party agrees that it will not disclose Disclosing Party's Confidential
Information to any third party or make or permit to be made copies or other
reproductions of Disclosing Party's Confidential Information.

This Agreement does not apply to any information which:

   (a) was in Receiving Party's possession or was known to Receiving Party, without
       an obligation to keep it confidential, before such information was disclosed to
       Receiving Party by Disclosing Party

   (b) is or becomes public knowledge through a source other than Receiving Party and
       through no fault of Receiving Party

   (c) is or becomes lawfully available to Receiving Party from a source other than
       Disclosing Party, or

   (d) is disclosed by Receiving Party with Disclosing Party's prior written approval.

This Agreement and Receiving Party's duty to hold Disclosing Party's trade secrets in
confidence will continue until the Confidential Information is no longer a trade secret
or until Disclosing Party sends Receiving Party written notice releasing Receiving Party
from this Agreement, whichever occurs first.

If any legal action arises relating to this Agreement, the prevailing party will be entitled
to recover all court costs, expenses, and reasonable attorney fees.

This is the entire agreement between the parties regarding the subject matter. It
supersedes all prior agreements or understandings between them. All additions or
modifications to this Agreement must be made in writing and must be signed by both
parties to be effective.

This Agreement is made under, and will be interpreted according to, the laws of the State of _____ .

If a court finds any provision of this Agreement invalid or unenforceable as applied to any circumstance, the remainder of this Agreement will be interpreted so as best to effect the intent of the parties.

Dated: _____

DISCLOSING PARTY

_____
Name of Business

_____
Signature

_____
Printed Name and Title

_____
Address

_____

RECEIVING PARTY

_____
Name of Business

_____
Signature

_____
Printed Name and Title

_____
Address

_____

effect—so heavy-handed, in fact, that some states refuse to enforce (or limit enforcement of) noncompetes signed by employees.

States with restrictions include Alabama, California, Colorado, Florida, Louisiana, Montana, Nevada, North Dakota, Oklahoma, Oregon, South Dakota, and Texas. In general, you should consult with an attorney before entering into a noncompete agreement, because noncompete agreements are a potential minefield. Many courts are averse to enforcing them, and employees dislike being asked to sign them.

I recommend you avoid using noncompetes, except perhaps for a key employee—someone with an intimate knowledge of your crafts business and clients—that is, an employee who realistically could hurt your business by competing with it.

A nonsolicitation agreement prohibits a former employee from soliciting your customers or employees for a period of time. Most states will generally enforce nonsolicitation agreements that don't:

- unfairly restrict an employee's ability to earn a living, or
- unfairly limit a competitor's ability to hire workers or solicit customers through legitimate means.

Customer Lists as Trade Secrets

For many crafts artists, their primary trade secret is customer information. But trade secret law may not protect your customer list. If a dispute over a customer list ends up in court, a judge generally considers the following elements when deciding whether or not the list qualifies as a trade secret:

- **Is the information in the list ascertainable by other means?** For example, can someone using a search engine or email directory create a similar customer list? A list that's readily ascertainable can't be protected.
- **Does the list include more than names and email addresses?** For example, if your customer list includes purchasing information or special needs for online customers, it's more likely to be protected, because this information adds value.

- **Did it take a lot of time or effort or did you create a special system for assembling your list?** A customer list that requires more effort is more likely to be protected under an NDA.
- **Is your customer list long-standing or exclusive?** If you can prove that a customer list is special to your business and has been used for a long time, the list is more likely to be protected.

Hiring Sales Reps

My sister, Barbi Jo (or "BJ" as her friends call her), built her crafts business, Barbini, with the help of sales reps. "My business really took a leap when one of my sales reps wrote orders for Nordstrom's East Coast stores," says Barbi Jo. "That really opened the door for my other sales reps to get me into the Nordstrom in their territories." As Barbi Jo's business expanded, so did her use of sales reps. At one time she had no fewer than four regional reps working to sell her jewelry.

Now, 20 years later, she's severed all ties with reps. "They were helpful when I started, but I don't have the time—you have to prepare a complete line for the rep and replace it whenever you have a new line—and if the rep is carrying ten other artists, which is pretty common, then you may find you're not getting the attention you expect.

"It gets more complicated if you're doing trade shows," she adds. "Let's say you're at the Philadelphia [BMAC] show and you sell to a New Jersey store. Is your New Jersey rep entitled to a cut? That depends on the arrangement, but usually, yes, the rep expects a cut for every sale in her territory, or at least a cut of the reorders. After a while I found that it wasn't worth the effort.

"Reps can be very valuable," says BJ. "But when you're choosing your reps, do some research. Don't rely on the rep's promises; reps always promise they're going to do fabulous things with your work. So, get references. For example, find out what other lines they carry, and talk to those artists. Don't ask about money, because most artists won't discuss their sales numbers. Ask about consistency of sales. Does the rep consistently perform well? Do you get along with the rep? And you definitely want a good personality match."

How can an artist find a rep? "They have booths at wholesale crafts shows, or they may approach you directly. They also maintain showrooms, for example, in New York City at 7 W. 34th Street (the 7W Gift Mart; www.7wnewyork.com) or 41 Madison Avenue (The New York Merchandise Mart; www.41madison.com). Also, if your rep has a showroom, you may be charged a monthly fee to exhibit work there.

"And one other rule," advises BJ. "Never pay the rep until you get paid. If you don't get paid, the rep doesn't get paid."

My sister raises some important concerns, many of which you'll have to weigh based on your current needs. However, once you've settled on using a particular rep, your best line of defense in case something goes wrong is a written agreement that defines both parties' rights and responsibilities. Many reps use their own agreement. If yours does, compare the provisions in that agreement with the model agreement in this chapter to better understand the commitments you and the rep will be making. All agreements can be modified, so don't be shy about asking for changes. If the rep doesn't have a preprepared agreement, use the agreement in this chapter and modify it to meet your needs.

Looking for a rep? try talking to artists in similar lines, checking classified ads in trade magazines, calling or visiting stores where you would like to sell your work, and attending trade shows.

Some crafts artists recommend giving each rep a binder containing your company history, business policies, and accounts.

The model agreement provided below covers the many activities that a sales rep might take on in marketing your crafts and increasing your revenues. These include:
- operating showrooms and making sales to the trade or to collectors
- traveling to shops and taking wholesale orders
- brokering licensing deals with manufacturers, and
- helping you earn special order commissions.

The agreement also offers various ways to split revenue and avoid disputes with your sales rep. I provide a detailed explanation of each provision of the model agreement.

Model Sales Representative Agreement

As you'll see below, the model agreement covers a good deal of ground. In fact, it may seem longer or more complex than you envisioned. Simply remove any provisions labeled "optional" that aren't relevant to your situation and you'll end up with a concise agreement.

If you're using the model agreement for comparative purposes, locate a provision in the rep's agreement and find one that's similar in the model agreement—this shouldn't be too difficult, as the subject headings are likely to be the same or similar. Then read my explanation for the model provision, below, to help you understand what the sales rep is attempting to do differently.

The model agreement is set out in a letter format. Although a letter agreement appears less formal than a traditional contract, it is just as enforceable. If you don't want to use the letter format, simply remove the date and salutation.

 FORM ON THE CD-ROM

You'll find the Model Sales Representative Agreement on the CD-ROM at the back of this book.

Completing a Sales Representative Agreement

Below, I translate, decode, and otherwise advise on how to handle the provisions of the model Sales Representative Agreement.

Introductory Paragraph. Insert the date, your name as Artist, and the name of the sales representative or the sales representative's company.

Appointment. This provision establishes whether your relationship with the sales representative is exclusive or nonexclusive, and establishes in what geographical areas the sales representative will represent your works. Exclusive means that while the agreement is in force, only the sales representative (not you or another sales representative) can represent the works: (1) within the territory you define, and (2) for those sources of revenue set out in the agreement. If the relationship is nonexclusive, then others (including you) could solicit potential deals within the territory and for those purposes.

Include the type(s) of representation you desire, for example, retail accounts, wholesale accounts, and so on. If you choose licensing rights, specify the type of licensing—for example, licensing for posters, postcards, T-shirts, buttons, caps, and whatever else you and the sales rep envision. You can be as broad or as narrow as you want in defining licensing rights, for example: "all forms of merchandise licensing" or "fabrics." Also choose "commissioned works" if your sales representative will represent you for purposes of getting you work on commission, for example, from collectors.

Territory. Insert a statement in the Territory section to reflect the regions in which you have granted rights, for example, "New York," "New England," or "the world excluding North America."

If you already have accounts in these territories, you should exclude them from the agreement by checking the optional provision and listing the accounts on Attachment A.

Two other optional provisions are provided to deal with sales made by the Artist, not the rep, within the Territory. You should only choose these optional provisions if your arrangement is exclusive. If your agreement is nonexclusive within the territory, you don't need to account for sales that you make in the territory without the rep's help.

> **EXAMPLE:** Hans has a nonexclusive contract for wholesale accounts with Joanie, his rep, in the Southwestern United States. Hans solicits a wholesale account from a New Mexico gallery without Joanie's help. He does not have to account to Joanie for the New Mexico revenue. However, if the arrangement with Joanie were exclusive, Hans would have to account to Joanie, since she has exclusive rights to represent him in the Southwest.

If you and the sales rep agree on one of these optional choices, you'll need to figure out a method of accounting for this nonrep income. Depending on your negotiating leverage, you and the rep might agree on:

Sales Representative Agreement

Date: _____

Dear: _____

This letter sets forth the terms and conditions of the agreement (the "Agreement") between _____ ("Artist") and _____ ("Sales Representative"). Artist is the owner of all rights in certain crafts works (referred to as the "Works") and described more fully in Attachment A to this Agreement.

Appointment. Artist agrees to have Sales Representative serve as

[*Choose one*]

☐ an exclusive   ☐ a nonexclusive

sales representative for the Works in the Territory to

[*Choose one or more*]

☐ retail accounts   ☐ commissioned works, including: _____

☐ wholesale accounts ☐ licensing rights for the following markets: _____

☐ trade (wholesale) sales of crafts work

Territory. Sales Representative will represent Artist in the following territory: _____ _____ (the "Territory").

[*Optional*]

☐ The accounts and companies listed in Exhibit A are excluded from this Agreement, and Sales Representative shall not call on these accounts and shall not be entitled to income from such sources.

[*Optional (use only if Agreement is exclusive)*]

☐ Artist may advertise via ☐ Internet ☐ mail to accounts in the Territory. In that event, revenues from such sales shall be accounted for as follows: _____ _____ .

☐ Artist may attend trade shows or meet with accounts or collectors in the Territory. In the event that Artist obtains a sales order or agreement in the Territory from such solicitations, revenues shall be accounted for as follows: _____ _____ .

Obligations of Sales Representative; Disclaimer. Sales Representative shall use best efforts to contact and solicit sales or other sources of revenue, as described above, and present and communicate sales information between the parties. Nothing in this Agreement shall be interpreted by Artist or Sales Representative as a promise or guarantee as to the outcome of any solicitation or negotiation by Sales Representative on behalf of Artist or the Works. Any representations as to the likelihood of success regarding exploitation of the Works are expressions of opinion only. Sales Representative is free to conduct business other than on Artist's behalf, including business or agency relationships with other Artists.

[*Optional*]

☐ **Sales Representative Reimbursement.** Representative shall be reimbursed for the following expenses from any net revenue or net receipts as described in the "Payments" section, below (the "Work Income"). These reimbursements shall be deducted from Work Income before splitting the resulting revenues or receipts, provided that such expenses are solely for the purpose of promoting Artist:

[*Choose one or more*]

☐ promotional mailings   ☐ paid advertising   ☐ shipping

☐ insurance   ☐ travel   ☐ telephone

Artist's written approval is required for any individual expense over $_____ .

In the event that any such costs are incurred for the benefit of other clients of Sales Representative as well as for Artist, the expenses shall be prorated to reflect each client's actual expenses.

☐ Artist shall pay the following fees for showroom exhibit costs: _____

_____ .

Obligations of Artist. Artist will provide Sales Representative with:

[*Choose one*]

☐ _____ samples of the Works, which samples shall remain the property of Artist and shall be returned upon termination of this Agreement or upon thirty (30) days' notice from Artist. Sales Representative shall have the limited right to display, copy, and distribute the Works solely in conjunction with promoting the works and fulfilling obligations as set forth under this Agreement.

☐ printed materials as follows: _____

_____ .

Artist shall also perform the following duties: _____

_____ .

Payments. As compensation for the services provided above, Sales Representative shall receive the following compensation:

[*Choose one and fill in the percentage*]

☐ _____% of net receipts from all sales made by Sales Representative to retail accounts.

☐ _____% of net receipts from all sales made by Sales Representative to wholesale accounts.

☐ _____% of net revenues from any licensing agreements for the Works.

☐ _____% of net revenues from any commissions obtained by Sales Representative.

Artist agrees that all income paid as a result of any sales or agreements solicited or negotiated by Sales Representative for the Works (the "Works Income") shall be paid directly to Artist. Works Income shall include, but not be limited to, advances, guarantees, or license fees.

Artist shall issue payments to Sales Representative within ten (10) days of Artist's receipt of any Works Income along with any client accountings as provided by the licensee.

The party responsible for all billings and collections shall be:

[*Choose one*]

☐ Sales Representative

☐ Artist

Each party shall keep accurate books of account and records covering all transactions relating to this Agreement, and either party or its duly authorized representative shall have the right upon five (5) days' prior written notice, and during normal business hours, to inspect and audit the other party's records relating to this Agreement.

Rights. Artist represents and warrants that Artist has the power and authority to enter into this Agreement and is the owner of all proprietary rights, whether they are copyright or otherwise, in the Works.

Advertising. Sales Representative can use Artist's name, likeness, trademarks, and trade names in Sales Representative's advertising and promotions [*optional*: , but must obtain Artist's prior approval for every such use].

Assignment. This Agreement shall not be assignable by either party without the written authorization of the nonassigning party.

Termination. This Agreement may be terminated at any time at the discretion of either Artist or Sales Representative, provided that written notice of such termination is furnished to the other party thirty (30) days prior to such termination.

[*Optional*]

☐ If this Agreement is terminated by Artist, and within _____ (_____) months of termination Artist enters into an agreement for assignments, sales or licenses with any client or company for whom Sales Representative had entered into agreements on Artist's behalf during the term of this Agreement, Artist agrees to pay Sales Representative the fees established in this Agreement. This obligation shall survive termination of this Agreement.

No Special Damages. Neither party shall be liable to the other for any incidental, consequential, punitive, or special damages.

General Provisions

Entire Agreement. This is the entire agreement between the parties. It replaces and supersedes any and all oral agreements between the parties, as well as any prior writings. Modifications and amendments to this Agreement, including any exhibit or appendix hereto, shall be enforceable only if they are in writing and are signed by authorized representatives of both parties.

Successors and Assignees. This Agreement binds and benefits the heirs, successors, and assignees of the parties.

Notices. Any notice or communication required or permitted to be given under this Agreement shall be sufficiently given when received by certified mail, or sent by facsimile transmission or overnight courier.

Governing Law. This Agreement will be governed by the laws of the State of _____ _____ .

Waiver. If one party waives any term or provision of this Agreement at any time, that waiver will only be effective for the specific instance and specific purpose for which the waiver was given. If either party fails to exercise or delays exercising any of its rights or remedies under this Agreement, that party retains the right to enforce that term or provision at a later time.

Severability. If a court finds any provision of this Agreement invalid or unenforceable, the remainder of this Agreement will be interpreted so as best to carry out the parties' intent.

Attachments and Exhibits. The parties agree and acknowledge that all attachments, exhibits, and schedules referred to in this Agreement are incorporated in this Agreement by reference.

No Agency. Nothing contained herein will be construed as creating any agency, partnership, joint venture, or other form of joint enterprise between the parties.

[Optional]

☐ **Attorney Fees and Expenses.** The prevailing party shall have the right to collect from the other party its reasonable costs and necessary disbursements and attorney fees incurred in enforcing this Agreement.

☐ **Jurisdiction.** The parties consent to the exclusive jurisdiction and venue of the federal and state courts located in _____ _____ *[county]*, _____ *[state]*, in any action arising out of or relating to this Agreement. The parties waive any other venue to which either party might be entitled by domicile or otherwise.

☐ **Arbitration.** Any controversy or claim arising out of or relating to this Agreement shall be settled by arbitration in _____ _____ in accordance with the rules of the American Arbitration Association, and judgment upon the award rendered by the arbitrator(s) may be entered in any court having jurisdiction. The prevailing party shall have the right to collect from the other party its reasonable costs and attorney's fees incurred in enforcing this Agreement.

Signatures. Each party represents and warrants that on this date they are duly authorized to bind their respective principals by their signatures below.

SALES REPRESENTATIVE   ARTIST

_____   _____
Name of Business   Name of Business

_____   _____
Signature   Signature

_____   _____
Printed Name and Title   Printed Name and Title

_____   _____
Address   Address

_____   _____

- no payment to the rep
- full rep commission
- payment of a portion of the rep commission, or
- payment of the rep's commission for sales after the initial order.

Obligations of Sales Representative. This section establishes the sales representative's duties, namely evaluating opportunities, representing your work and negotiating deals. The "disclaimer" language is inserted to protect the sales representative from future claims that the sales representative promised or guaranteed that your work could be sold or licensed. This provision also guarantees that the sales representative is free to take on other clients.

Sales Representative Reimbursement. If you choose this optional provision, include only those expenses you will pay. If you must pay an exhibit fee to use the rep's showroom, indicate that fee and when it should be paid, for example, "$50 monthly." Insert an appropriate amount, for example, "$200," in the section indicating that your approval is required for expenses.

Obligations of Artist. This section establishes the artist's duties as well as the artist's ownership of the artwork samples. In the event that printed materials are required, indicate what materials should be provided. If any additional duties are required of the artist, write this in the blank space.

Payments. Under this provision, the sales representative receives a percentage of all "Works Income." This income is paid directly to the Artist, who then reimburses the sales rep within a fixed time period, for example, 30 days.

Rep commissions for sales range from 10%-25%, although they are commonly in the 15%-20% range. Commissions to licensing reps are typically between 20% and 33%.

The audit statement provides that each party can audit the other's books. That way, you can check to see what the rep has been doing with the accounts and vice versa. Normally, the artist is responsible for all billings and collections. However, if you and the rep have a different arrangement, make the agreement reflect your arrangement.

Rights. The rep will not want any surprises—such as someone claiming that you don't own the work or that your work infringes on someone's copyright. For this reason, you should provide a guarantee that you own the artworks and that you have the right to sell and license them. This won't completely prevent surprises, but it will help keep the sales rep free from liability if something unexpected does pop up.

Advertising. The rep may want to use your name, trademarks, or picture in promotional ads and at the rep's booth at trade shows. Check the second option if you and the rep have agreed to allow you prior approval of any such uses.

Assignment. This provision prevents you and the sales rep from transferring contract obligations to someone else. For example, if the rep sold her business to another rep and wanted to transfer your account as part of the sale, your permission would be required.

Termination. What happens if you terminate the sales representative agreement but want to continue your business contact with a company with which you had previously made a deal through the sales rep? Under this provision, if you enter into a sales or licensing agreement with such a company within a fixed period of time after termination, you will have to pay the sales rep a fee (three to six months is common). You can also alter the sales representative's fee for posttermination deals. For example, you can agree that the sales representative will get only one-half of the fees if any agreement is entered into after three months but before six months. The sales representative may insist that you change the agreement so that the sales representative is paid if you enter into a contract with anyone that the sales representative solicited. In that case, in order to be sure that the sales representative has solicited the client or company, request that the sales representative furnish you a list of persons who were solicited (and the dates of solicitation and the name of the person contacted). This list can be furnished at the time of termination, or you can request that the sales representative notify you periodically (say, every six months) of all solicitations during that period.

Miscellaneous Provisions. For information about the miscellaneous provisions—Entire Agreement, Relationships, Governing Law, Modification, Waiver, Severability, Arbitration, Attachments—read Chapter 9.

Attachment A. Write up a description of the works that the sales rep will be handling for you in the Attachment. As an alternative for listing specific works, you can include a statement such as, "All works created prior to and during the term of this Agreement" or "Any new artworks created during the term of this Agreement." Also, if you are excluding some accounts, list them in Attachment A, as well.

Business Forms & Legal Liability

Valerie Stainton always dreamed of opening a crafts gallery. One day, she took the plunge, gave notice to her employer of 22 years, and leased space for Valerie's Gallery (www. valeriesgalleries.com) in nearby Newburyport, Massachusetts. One of Valerie's biggest concerns was how to structure her enterprise—that is, as a sole proprietorship, partnership, corporation, or limited liability company (LLC). She knew something about business—she had been the business manager at her former job—and learned more by reading books and researching on the Net. (One helpful source was Score (www.score. org), where retired business persons counsel new businesses.)

Armed with this information, and with the help of an attorney, Valerie decided to form an LLC. "I'm a conservative person," says Valerie, "and one of [the LLC's benefits] is the protection of personal assets." In other words, creditors would be blocked from attempting to collect on business debts by reaching into Valerie's personal bank account or going after her house. By the way, in 2009, Valerie's Gallery was selected as "Retailer of the Year" by the local Chamber of Commerce.

Many crafts artists have the same nagging concern as Valerie Stainton. Will your personal savings, car, or house be at risk if your crafts business incurs a debt or causes an injury? In this chapter I'll discuss the three tried-and-true approaches to protecting your personal assets: (1) form a business entity that limits liability, (2) purchase insurance, and (3) simply act prudently—be careful, avoid risks, and use contracts wisely.

Personal Liability: What Is It?

Before talking about how to limit personal liability, let's define what liabilities are. They're basically debts—money you owe. Every crafts business carries some liabilities—for example, ongoing payments to suppliers, rent for your studio, compensation to employees, or booth fees at a show. Additional liabilities may arise if your business is devastated by a fire or flood or if you are the victim of a lawsuit—for example, someone is injured by your crafts product or in your studio and sues you for damages.

If you operate your business as a sole proprietorship—the most common business form for crafts businesses—then you will be personally liable for all business debts. The same is true for a partnership. A creditor can collect a partnership debt against any partner, regardless of which partner incurred the debt. That means that if your partner orders $50,000 worth of glass-blowing supplies (without telling you) and then moves to Venezuela, you could be on the hook. A written partnership agreement, discussed below, can apportion liability among partners, but it won't absolve you of personal liability.

The Business Entity as Shield

Corporations and limited liability companies (LLCs) are created to shield the owners from personal liability. For a dramatic example of how this shield works to deflect liability, consider the demise of People's Pottery, the 52-store chain that sold made-in-America crafts. The company filed for bankruptcy in 2001, owing millions to crafts businesses. However, the owners were not held personally liable, because they had created a corporate entity that owned the company. In short, if you operate as a corporation or LLC, creditors can—with rare exceptions—only collect their debts from the business's assets, not from the owners.

This protection comes at a price. To acquire corporate or LLC status, you need to pay fees and file paperwork with your secretary of state or other state filing office. And, regardless of the fees, LLCs and corporations require some continuing legal attention.

If your crafts business simply isn't going to run up many debts or run many risks you probably don't need to convert from a sole proprietorship to an LLC or corporation (18 million small businesses in the U.S. have not chosen to incorporate or form an LLC). These entities and corporations can shield your personal assets—your house and savings—from many business debts and court judgments, but they may not be necessary for businesses that are low on the liability scale. (Insurance may be a better method of protecting assets.)

Consider the cost. Forming an LLC or a corporation costs between $500 and $2,000 depending on who does it and in which state it's being formed. In many states there are annual fees (sometimes over $1,000 a year) for maintaining an LLC or a corporation. (California LLCs pay a minimum of $800 a year.)

Bottom line: if you're not that concerned about personal liability, or you believe that insurance can cover any liability, or you're just not that interested in paying the fees or dealing with the additional formalities, an LLC or a corporation is probably not the right choice for your crafts business.

Still not sure? Below, we provide a basic summary of sole proprietorships, partnerships, LLCs, and corporations.

What is a business form? A "business form" is the legal structure under which your business operates. Here's a snapshot of what distinguishes the four most popular business forms. I'll talk about each in more detail later in the chapter.

Sole proprietorship. One person (or a husband and wife) owns and operates the business and is personally liable for business debts.

Partnership. Two or more people own and operate the business, sharing expenses, responsibilities, and profits. Each partner is personally liable for all partnership debts.

Corporation. One or more persons own and operate the corporation and share corporate profits and losses (as shareholders). Each shareholder's personal liability is limited.

Limited liability company (LLC). One or more persons own and operate the LLC (as members), and profits and losses are shared in predetermined proportions. Each member's personal liability is limited.

Many crafts businesses also operate as cooperatives, discussed at the end of this chapter. Cooperatives—depending on state law—must choose to operate as either partnerships, corporations or LLCs.

Sole Proprietorship

If you're operating by yourself (or maybe with your spouse) and haven't incorporated or formed an LLC, you're a sole proprietorship. A sole proprietorship is the least expensive and easiest way to operate a crafts business.

Sole Propietorships at a Glance	
Taxation	A sole proprietorship is a pass-through entity. Your profits (and losses) pass through the business entity, and you pay taxes on any profits on your individual return at your individual tax rate. You report this business income on IRS Schedule C, *Profit and Loss From Business (Sole Proprietorship)*, which you file with your 1040 individual federal tax return.
Liability	As a sole proprietor, you're personally liable for all business debts and legal claims. Liability insurance may pay for some of your legal claims.
Formalities	A sole proprietorship is created automatically when you go into business. There is no fee to create one and no paperwork.

Can a Husband and Wife Be a Sole Proprietorship?

If spouses co-own and run a crafts business in a community property state (Arizona, California, Idaho, Nevada, New Mexico, Texas, Washington, or Wisconsin), they can operate as a sole proprietorship and report their business income as part of their joint tax return or they can operate as a partnership and file a K-1 partnership return. If spouses co-own and run a business in a non-community property state, they must operate as a partnership and file a K-1 partnership return.

In all states, if one spouse owns the business and the other works for it, the business is a sole proprietorship, and the owner will have to declare the spouse as an employee or independent contractor. If the spouse occasionally volunteers to help the business without pay, you won't have to declare the spouse as an employee or independent contractor.

Partnership

If you're operating with others and haven't incorporated or formed an LLC, then you're a general partnership.

General Partnerships at a Glance	
Taxation	A general partnership is a pass-through tax entity. The profits (and losses) pass through the business entity to the partners, who pay taxes on any profits on their individual returns at their individual tax rates. Even though a partnership does not pay its own taxes, it must file an "informational" tax return, IRS Schedule K-1 (Form 1065). In addition, the partnership must give each partner a filled-in copy of this form showing the proportionate share of profits or losses that each partner reports on an individual 1040 tax return. A partner pays taxes on his or her entire share of profits, even if the partnership chooses to reinvest the profits in the business, rather than distributing them to the partners.
Liability	Each partner is personally liable for business debts and legal claims. The partnership should have liability insurance that will cover most claims. What's more, a creditor of the partnership can go after any general partner for the entire debt, regardless of that partner's ownership interest. Any partner may bind the entire partnership (in other words, the partners) to a contract or business deal.
Formalities	You don't have to pay any fees or prepare any paperwork to form a general partnership; you can start it with a handshake. It makes far more sense, however, to prepare a partnership agreement. You may want to hire an accountant to manage the annual tax returns and documents.

How to Create a Partnership

If you're going into a crafts business with someone as partners, you should write a partnership agreement. Without an agreement, the one-size-fits-all rules of each state's general partnership laws will apply to your partnership. These provisions usually say that profits and losses of the business should be divided equally among the partners (or according to the partner's capital contributions in some states), and they impose a long list of other rules.

Without an agreement, the departure of a partner ends the partnership. Below is a sample partnership agreement.

> **FORM ON CD-ROM**
> You'll find the Partnership Agreement on the CD-ROM at the back of this book.

Completing the Partnership Agreement

The explanation below will help you when you and your partners sit down to think through and complete the partnership agreement.

Partners. Insert the names of all partners.

Partnership Name. Insert the name of the partnership. If you're going to use a business name for your partnership that's different from the names of the partners—for example, Miraculous Windchimes instead of Furry, Brown, and Nemir—it's wise to conduct at least a local name search to see whether some other business is already using the name. For more information on choosing a name, see Chapter 8.

Partnership Duration. Insert the date the partnership began or is to begin. Then indicate when the partnership will end. The second choice allows you to insert a date for the end of the partnership—for example, "June, 2010."

Partnership Office. Insert the address where partnership records will be kept. Usually this will be the partnership's main business location. If the partnership's mailing address is the same as the partnership office, include "the above address." If you have a separate mailing address—a post office box, for example—use the second option and fill in the mailing address.

Partnership Purpose. Insert the purpose of the partnership—for example, to manufacture and distribute handmade crafts and to operate one or more retail stores for the sale of crafts.

Capital Contributions. Insert the date when the partners are to contribute their start-up capital—the funds or property given to the partnership to enable it to begin operations.

If partners will be contributing cash, fill in their names and the amount each will contribute.

If partners will contribute property, insert the partners' names. Then describe the property and what value it will be given on the partnership's books.

Capital Accounts. You don't need to insert anything here. A capital account is a bookkeeping technique for keeping track of how much of the partnership assets each partner owns. Your capital account starts out with the amount you invest in the partnership. To that figure, you add your share of the profits and deduct your share of the losses. If you're getting bogged down on these calculations, consult an accountant.

Profits and Losses. Use the first option if you want the partners' shares of profits and losses to be proportionate to the capital they put into the partnership. Here are two examples of the results of making this choice.

> EXAMPLE 1: Three partners put in the same amount of capital: $10,000 each. All profits will be added equally to each partner's capital account (in other words, a $15,000 profit would result in a $5,000 addition to each partner's account), and losses will be equally subtracted.

> EXAMPLE 2: One partner puts in $20,000 and two partners put in $10,000 each. The profits and assets will be allocated 50%/25%/25%. (Therefore, a $15,000 profit would result in additions of $7,500 to one partner's account and $3,750 to the other two partners' accounts.)

Use the second option and insert a different formula if you don't want profits to be divided according to capital contributed. For example, if you agree that one partner will be spending more time than the others working on the partnership business, you may decide to allocate proportionately more profits to that partner.

> EXAMPLE: Since Linda Smith will be handling bookkeeping duties for the partnership in addition to her other partnership duties, she and her two partners decide that 40% of the net profits should be credited to her capital account and 30% of the net profits should be credited to the capital account of each of the other two. Net losses, however, will be charged equally against the partners' capital accounts.

Of course, this isn't the only way to recognize the contribution of a partner who's doing extra work. You could, for example, agree to pay this partner a salary for keeping the books, making it fair to simply allocate profits in proportion to contributions.

Salaries. You don't need to insert anything here unless you want to. Generally, a partner's reward for doing work for the partnership is a share of the partnership profits. But there's no legal or tax reason why the partners can't agree to hire one or more partners as employees who will receive a salary for their services. If you decide to follow such an arrangement, spell out the details in the partnership agreement.

Interest. You don't need to insert anything here. Again, the benefit a partner receives from investing money in a partnership is a share of partnership profits. If you agree that a partner is to receive interest, it's better to have the partner lend money to the partnership. Document the loan by creating a promissory note.

Management. Approach this section—describing how management decisions are made—with a healthy dose of skepticism. The reality is that for a small partnership to succeed, the partners need to have both shared goals and confidence in one another's judgment. Or, put more bluntly, if you don't trust your partners and enjoy working with them, don't bother creating a partnership in the first place.

It's difficult to define how day-to-day decisions will or should be made in a partnership. Certainly, talking the matter over with all the partners and respecting each other's opinions is wise. But unanimity on everything may be as unnecessary as it is hard to achieve—making it impractical to select the first option in this paragraph (agreement of all partners on all partnership decisions).

The second option—requiring a majority vote on routine decisions—allows you more flexibility. Unanimity is only required on the major business decisions specified.

Partnership Funds. Insert the name of the financial institution where you'll keep the partnership funds.

Then indicate who will be permitted to sign partnership checks. If you choose the last option, insert the number of partners who must sign a single check. In a three-person partnership, for example, you may want to require that all checks be signed by two partners.

The financial institution where you keep the partnership account will also have a form for you to fill out to indicate who has signing authority.

Agreement to End Partnership. You don't need to insert anything here. This paragraph makes it clear that the partnership can be ended if all the partners agree.

Partner's Withdrawal. This section deals with what happens if one of the partners wants to leave the partnership. It raises two major legal points for you to think about: First, unless your partnership has a written agreement stating otherwise, the law says your partnership will end if any partner decides to leave. Second, if your partnership has no agreement to the contrary, a partner isn't free to transfer his or her partnership interest to someone else. In short, unless you agree in writing to a different plan, if one partner leaves, the partnership assets will be liquidated, bills will be paid, and the partners will be cashed out. Choose the first option if this scenario is what you want.

Choose the second option if you want to give the remaining partners the chance to keep the partnership alive by buying out the interest of the withdrawing partner. Technically, this means the remaining partners will create a new partnership, but the business will continue as if there had been no change.

Partner's Death. As with a partner's withdrawal, a partner's death will end the partnership unless you agree to another outcome. Choose the first option if you want the partnership to end automatically after

Partnership Agreement

Partners. _____
(the "Partners"), agree to the following terms and conditions.

Partnership Name. The Partners will do business as a partnership under the name of

_____ .

Partnership Duration. The partnership [_choose one_] ☐ began ☐ will begin   on
_____ . It will continue:

[_Choose one_]

  ☐ indefinitely until it is ended by the terms of this agreement.

  ☐ until _____ , unless ended sooner by the terms of
    this agreement.

Partnership Office. The main office of the partnership will be at _____
_____ . The mailing address will be:

[_Choose one_]

  ☐ the above address.

  ☐ the following address: _____

Partnership Purpose. The primary purpose of the partnership is _____
_____ .

Capital Contributions. The Partners will contribute the following capital to the
partnership on or before _____ .

  A. Cash Contributions

   Partner's Name   Amount

   _____ $_____

   _____ $_____

   _____ $_____

  B. Noncash Contributions

   Partner's Name   Description of Property   Value

   _____   _____ $_____

   _____   _____ $_____

   _____   _____ $_____

   _____   _____ $_____

Capital Accounts. The partnership will maintain a capital account for each Partner. The account will consist of the Partner's capital contribution plus the Partner's share of profits less the Partner's share of losses and distributions to the Partner. A Partner may not remove capital from his or her account without the written consent of all Partners.

Profits and Losses.

A. The net profits and losses of the partnership will be credited to or charged against the Partners' capital accounts:

[Choose one]

☐ in the same proportions as their capital contributions.

☐ as follows: _____

_____

_____ .

B. The partnership will only make distributions to the Partners if all the Partners agree.

Salaries. No Partner will receive a salary for services to the partnership.

Interest. No interest will be paid on a Partner's capital account.

Management. Each Partner will have an equal say in managing the partnership.

[Choose one]

☐ All significant partnership decisions will require the agreement of all the Partners.

☐ Routine partnership decisions will require the agreement of a majority of the Partners. The following partnership actions will require the agreement of all the Partners:

[Choose one or more]

☐ borrowing or lending money

☐ signing a lease

☐ signing a contract to buy or sell real estate

☐ signing a security agreement or mortgage

☐ selling partnership assets except for goods sold in the regular course of business

☐ other: _____

Partnership Funds. Partnership funds will be kept in an account at _____

_____ , unless all Partners agree to

another financial institution. Partnership checks:

[*Choose one*]

☐ may be signed by any Partner.

☐ must be signed by all the Partners.

☐ must be signed by _____ Partners.

Agreement to End Partnership. The Partners may unanimously agree to end the
partnership.

Partner's Withdrawal

[*Choose one*]

☐ The partnership will end if a Partner withdraws by giving written notice of such
withdrawal to each of the other Partners.

☐ Upon the withdrawal of a Partner, the other Partners will, within 30 days, decide
either to end the partnership or to buy out the withdrawing Partner's interest
and continue the partnership. A decision to buy out the withdrawing Partner's
interest and continue the partnership requires the unanimous consent of the
remaining Partners.

Partner's Death

[*Choose one*]

☐ The partnership will end if a Partner dies.

☐ Upon the death of a partner, the other Partners will, within 30 days, decide
either to end the partnership or to buy out the deceased Partner's interest
and continue the partnership. A decision to buy out the withdrawing Partner's
interest and continue the partnership requires the unanimous consent of the
remaining Partners.

Buyout. If the remaining Partners decide to buy the interest of a withdrawing or
deceased Partner, the remaining Partners, within _____ days after that Partner's
withdrawal or death, will pay the withdrawing Partner or the deceased Partner's estate:

[*Choose one*]

☐ the amount in the capital account of the withdrawing or deceased Partner as of
the date of withdrawal or death.

☐ the fair market value of the interest of the withdrawing or deceased Partner as determined by the partnership's accountant.

☐ other: _____ .

General Provisions

Entire Agreement. This is the entire agreement between the parties. It replaces and supersedes any and all oral agreements between the parties, as well as any prior writings. Modifications and amendments to this agreement, including any exhibit or appendix, shall be enforceable only if they are in writing and are signed by authorized representatives of both parties.

Successors and Assignees. This agreement binds and benefits the heirs, successors, and assignees of the parties.

Notices. Any notice or communication required or permitted to be given under this agreement shall be sufficiently given when received by certified mail, or sent by facsimile transmission or overnight courier.

Governing Law. This agreement will be governed by the laws of the State of _____ _____ .

Waiver. If one party waives any term or provision of this agreement at any time, that waiver will only be effective for the specific instance and specific purpose for which the waiver was given. If either party fails to exercise or delays exercising any of its rights or remedies under this agreement, that party retains the right to enforce that term or provision at a later time.

Severability. If a court finds any provision of this agreement invalid or unenforceable, the remainder of this agreement will be interpreted so as best to carry out the parties' intent.

Attachments and Exhibits. The parties agree and acknowledge that all attachments, exhibits, and schedules referred to in this agreement are incorporated in this agreement by reference.

No Agency. Nothing contained herein will e construed as creating any agency, partnerhip, joint venture or other form of joint enterprise between the parties.

[*Optional*]

☐ **Attorney Fees and Expenses.** The prevailing party shall have the right to collect from the other part its reasonable costs and necessary disbursements and attorney fees incurred in enforcing this Agreement.

☐ **Jurisdiction.** The parties consent to the exclusive jurisdiction and venue of the federal and state courts located in _____ [*county*], _____ [*state*], in any action arising out of the ore relating to this Agreement. The parties waive any other venue to which either party might be entitled by domicile or otherwise.

[*Optional*]

☐ **Arbitration.** Any controversy or claim arising out of or relating to this agreement shall be settled by arbitration in _____ [*county*], _____ [*state*], in accordance with the rules of the American Arbitration Association, and judgment upon the award rendered by the arbitrator(s) may be entered in any court having jurisdiction. The prevailing party shall have the right to collect from the other party its reasonable costs and attorney's fees incurred in enforcing this agreement.

Date signed: _____

By: _____

Printed Name: _____

Address: _____

_____

By: _____

Printed Name: _____

Address: _____

_____

By: _____

Printed Name: _____

Address: _____

_____

a death. Once the partnership assets have been liquidated, the dead partner's share of the assets will be paid to that partner's estate.

Choose the second option if you and the remaining partners will want the chance to keep the partnership alive by buying out the interest of the deceased partner. (Technically, the remaining partners will then have a new partnership.)

Buyout. Complete this optional paragraph only if you've provided for a buyout of a withdrawing partner's interest (in "Partner's Withdrawal," above) or of a deceased partner's interest (in "Partner's Death," above). Include one of the first two options if it contains an acceptable formula for fixing the buyout price. If not, include the third option and fill in your chosen method of setting the buyout amount.

If you haven't provided for a buyout in "Partner's Withdrawal" or "Partner's Death," delete this paragraph.

Standard Clauses. The remainder of the agreement contains the standard clauses I discuss in Chapter 8. The only thing you'll need to fill in here is the name of the state whose law will apply to the contract, in the paragraph called "Governing Law."

Date and Signatures. Fill in the date the agreement is signed. Each of the partners must sign his or her name. Their respective names and addresses should be typed in.

LLC vs. Corporation—What's the Difference?

The LLC combines the best feature of corporations (limiting the owners' personal liability) without any changes in tax reporting (you file the same tax documents as sole proprietorships and partnerships). An LLC can be formed by one or more people. LLCs have largely replaced corporations as the favorite choice among small business owners.

Corporations are the most formal of the business entities. Owners hold shares (becoming shareholders) and elect a board of directors that directs management. If you incorporate your small business, you become an employee but still run it. Corporations are distinguished for tax purposes, as "C" corporations or "S" corporations. A C corporation is a regular for-profit corporation taxed under normal corporate income tax rules. (When I use the term "corporation" in this book, I always mean a C corporation.) In contrast, S corporations are taxed like partnerships—their income is passed on to the owners.

With LLCs, reporting and paying individual income taxes is easier than the corporate alternative. If you switch from sole proprietor or general partnership to an LLC, there won't be any changes in how you do your income tax reporting. That's because, like sole proprietorships and partnerships, most LLCs are pass-through entities. Pass-through taxation means that you report the money you earned from your business on your individual tax return and pay tax at individual income tax rates.

A corporation is not a pass-through entity; it's taxed as a separate entity, at a corporate tax rate. When the corporate profits are passed to the owners, they are taxed again on individual returns.

As a crafts business develops and income increases, however, some owners may prefer corporate taxation because the owners of a corporation can split business income between themselves and their business so that some business profits are taxed at the lower corporate tax rate. Small corporations can also offer employees fringe benefits, such as fully deductible group life and disability insurance, enhanced retirement plans, stock options, and other incentive plans. The owner/employees of corporations are not taxed on their individual tax returns for these benefits.

Finally, don't assume that forming an LLC or corporation will always shield all of your personal assets. Even if you operate as a corporation or an LLC, a creditor can still go after your personal assets if:

- You personally guarantee a loan or lease.
- You owe federal or state taxes.
- Your crafts business is subject to potential negligence claims—for example, someone trips over your extension cord at a crafts fair—or
- You fail to abide by corporate rules—for example, you mix corporate and personal funds and don't keep records of meetings and shareholders. In that case, a judge may strip away the asset protection feature of the corporation or LLC. It's called "piercing the veil."

LLCs and Corporations at a Glance		
	LLC	**Corporation**
Taxation	An LLC is taxed like a partnership—or, for a one-owner LLC, as a sole proprietorship. LLC income, loss, credits, and deductions are reported on the individual income tax returns of the LLC owners. The LLC itself does not pay income tax.	A corporation is a legal entity separate from its shareholders. The corporation files its own tax return (IRS Form 1120) and pays its own income taxes on the profits kept in the company.
Liability	The owner/members of an LLC are not personally liable for business debts and other liabilities. However, owners are liable for debts that they personally guaranteed, and tax debts.	The owners (shareholders) of a corporation are not personally liable for the business liabilities. However, as with LLCs, owners are liable for debts that are personally guaranteed, tax debts, and claims resulting from owners' negligence.
Formalities	To start an LLC, you must file articles of organization with the state business filing office. You and the other owners should also prepare an operating agreement to spell out how the LLC will be owned, how profits and losses will be divided, how departing or deceased members will be bought out, and other essential ownership issues.	To form a corporation, you pay corporate filing fees and prepare and file formal organizational papers, usually called articles of incorporation, with a state agency (in most states, the secretary or department of state). Directors must hold annual meetings and keep minutes, prepare formal documentation (in the form of resolutions or written consents to corporate actions) of important decisions made during the life of the corporation, and keep a paper trail of all legal and financial dealings between the corporation and its shareholders. The board of directors must appoint officers to supervise daily corporate business.

How to Create a Corporation

Each state's incorporation laws may differ. Therefore, providing detailed instructions for incorporating in your state is beyond the scope of this book. However, here are the basic rules followed in most or all states.

One person, or many, can incorporate a business. The process starts when an incorporator—any of the owners—prepares and files articles of incorporation with the state's corporate filing office, usually the secretary of state. Bylaws, rules that establish the voting, directors, equity, and other rules, must be prepared (but not filed).

Once the state certifies the articles of incorporation, the corporation's board of directors is chosen, the bylaws are adopted, and stock is issued to the owners (one person can own 100% of the stock). The directors manage the business and choose officers who manage the day-to-day operations.

All of this may sound frightfully complex, but rest assured, you can accomplish these tasks by yourself if you wish. Nolo, the publisher of this book, offers various books on the subject and provides incorporation services at its website, www.nolo.com.

How to Create a Limited Liability Company

You can form an LLC with just one member in every U.S. state. Like a corporation, creating an LLC requires formal filing procedures, and the rules differ from state to state. Again, I can only provide some basics.

Creating an LLC requires filing a document, called articles or certificate of organization, with the state's corporate filing office, usually the secretary of state. The owners (known as members) can manage the business or designate others to do so. In general, there is far less formality to maintaining an LLC than a corporation.

RESOURCE

Nolo, the publisher of this book, offers various books on the subject and provides LLC formation services at its website www.nolo.com.

The Cooperative

By 1844, the Industrial Revolution and its mechanized looms had devastated the British weaving trade. Weavers in Rochdale, England, worked 16-hour days for less than the modern equivalent of $1.25 a week. Unable to petition the government or organize labor unions or strikes, these crafts workers tried a radical experiment—creating a store to sell food and supplies. Unlike a traditional business that earned profits for investors, the Rochdale co-op was democratically owned and controlled. Its members—not outside investors—acquired benefits. The Rochdale experiment was a success, and the three principles it popularized became the tenets of modern cooperative business:

- **The user-owner principle.** Members own the business and provide the necessary financing.
- **The user-control principle.** Members control the business democratically, elect the board of directors, and approve changes in the business's structure and operation.
- **The user-benefit principle.** Members receive benefits—money, discounts, or goods—based on their contributions to the business.

American crafts workers, like their predecessors in Rochdale, often utilize the cooperative system to market their work, share studio space and expensive equipment, and save money when making bulk purchases.

Every Cooperative Needs a Business Form

The cooperative is a great way for crafts workers to participate together in a business. Unfortunately, the cooperative structure is not a distinct legal business form like the partnership, corporation, or LLC. In other words, it's not enough to band together and call your business a cooperative. Cooperative members must also adopt a traditional business form such as a partnership or corporation, and legal help may be needed during the organizing and formation stages.

Many cooperatives operate informally as partnerships without filing or preparing any written agreements. Some adopt a formal partnership agreement. Some cooperatives operate as corporations (either for-profit or nonprofit, depending on state law) or as LLCs.

State laws often permit (or require) incorporation in order to claim cooperative status. For example, in New Mexico five or more natural persons or two or more associations may incorporate as a cooperative association for any legal purpose to buy, sell, or produce goods or services.

It may seem odd to form a corporation or LLC when the underlying principles of corporations and cooperatives differ dramatically. But the union of these strange bedfellows is beneficial for cooperatives, because under corporation laws, the directors, managers, and members are generally shielded from personal liability for business debts. The same is not true in a partnership, where any partner may be individually liable for debts or liabilities of the partnership.

Just as with any incorporation, the cooperative must file articles of incorporation with the state government and must prepare bylaws (establishing voting, equity, refunds, and retained capital for each member or "patron"). Again, each state's laws may differ.

Decision-Making Practices

Whether a co-op chooses to be a partnership, corporation, or LLC, it typically opts for voting rights based on the Rochdale rule: one member, one vote. A small percentage of crafts co-ops make decisions based on a consensus (unanimity) of members.

The cooperative's voting system may establish rules for resolving conflicts, but sorting out disputes often depends more on the personalities than the paperwork. Earthworks Ceramics Cooperative in Berkeley, California, provides a good example. Founded 30 years ago, the members pool resources for rent, shows, and heavy equipment. "There are occasional squabbles," says potter Jiri Minarik, "but that's inevitable whenever people work together." For most of its history, Earthworks relied on consensus in its decision making, but two years ago it switched to a three-quarters majority. "So far we haven't had to use [the three-quarters majority]," points out Minarik.

An attorney (or accountant) may be needed for advice on other cooperative formation issues such as acquiring property, capitalizing the co-op (that is, getting money to start the business), and writing contracts with suppliers and members (see below). A co-op may also benefit by retaining an attorney's services to ensure continuing compliance with state laws.

Once the initial formalities are completed, the directors of the co-op, elected by the members, must chart a course of action. Even though co-ops are not run for profit in the traditional sense, some states require that they file as regular corporations; others require that they file as nonprofit corporations. Whatever money or assets the co-op accumulates (after its expenses and obligations have been paid) will ultimately be returned or distributed (as "patronage dividends") to members in proportion to the amount of work transacted by that member. For example, if you worked more days managing the store or more of your glasswork was sold at the co-op outlet, that might translate into a larger dividend.

Cooperatives receive an exemption under federal tax law, by excluding from their gross income any patronage dividend payments made to members. That's great for the co-op, but individual members must pay taxes on this income when preparing their individual income tax returns.

A Standard Membership Agreement

Although it's not mandatory, it's strongly recommended that each cooperative have a membership agreement—a document that is distinct from other business form documentation such as your articles of incorporation. This document establishes the legal relationship between the co-op and the member.

Under the agreement, the potential member:

- agrees to be bound by the co-op's rules
- appoints the co-op as its agent to sell crafts
- agrees to deliver products, and
- agrees to provide capital as required by the bylaws.

In return, the co-op:

- agrees to act as the agent for marketing the products, and

- agrees to account to the member in accordance with the co-op rules.

A lawyer should create or review the cooperative's standard membership agreement (sometimes referred to as a membership application). Most member agreements also describe what happens when members break the agreement. Often an agreed-upon payment (known as liquidated damages) must be paid for a breach. Courts have generally upheld these payments unless they don't accurately reflect the damage suffered by the co-op.

Membership agreements are usually open-ended in how long they last. Some extend for a year or two, after which either party can cancel by giving notice. In some states, the membership contract must be filed at the local county recorder's office.

Starting a co-op is a great way for craft artists to keep control of the selling of their work, but the legalities can be complicated.

While I recommend that you obtain legal and financial assistance from professionals when creating a cooperative, many online sources can also help you get started. See, for example:

- the National Cooperative Business Association (www.ncba.org)
- the Center for Cooperatives at UC Davis (www.sfc.ucdavis.edu), and
- the University of Wisconsin Center for Co-ops (www.uwcc.wisc. edu).

Should You Form a Nonprofit?

Any business created to benefit the public can be classified as a nonprofit corporation. The business can earn a profit, but the primary purpose has to be beneficial, like offering educational or charitable assistance. Most nonprofits incorporate because they thereby gain significant tax benefits. This book is written primarily for for-profit crafts businesses and I can't provide the in-depth information needed to start, manage and handle taxes for a nonprofit. However, Nolo (www.nolo.com), the publisher of this book, has an excellent collection of nonprofit books and resources, including *How to Form a Nonprofit Corporation*, by Anthony Mancuso .

Other Ways to Limit Liability

Many crafts businesses operate comfortably as sole proprietorships or partnerships because they have limited their liability in other ways. For example, you don't need to bother forming an LLC or a corporation if you:

Avoid incurring substantial debts. If you keep your debts to a minimum, you'll have gone a long way toward shielding yourself from creditor liability problems. In other words, take fewer business risks—don't rack up debts without having a good idea of how you'll pay for them.

> **EXAMPLE:** Sheila's GlassHouse receives an order for $300,000 worth of glass beads from KnickKnacks, a home furnishings chain (to be paid on a net-90-days invoice). In order to fill this mammoth order, Sheila would have to buy $80,000 worth of supplies. (KnickKnacks won't advance Sheila the cost of supplies.) Sheila decides not to accept the order because she believes her business is not prepared to carry an $80,000 debt for three months. By reducing her personal liability, she's also reduced the need for the protection of a corporation or LLC.

Maintain adequate insurance. Insurance can provide a suitable umbrella when creditor problems rain on your crafts business. Although insurance coverage will add to your ongoing costs, the addition will be regular and predictable, as opposed to the limitless costs that a natural disaster or a lawsuit could generate. (I'll talk more about insurance below.)

> **EXAMPLE:** Jack's pewter business has sufficient insurance to cover injury to visitors, loss of business property, and any legal costs related to common business lawsuits. Since Jack's insurance covers most of the predictable disasters, forming an LLC or corporation is probably not worth the hassle.

Use liability-shifting techniques when entering into contracts. Every agreement you sign makes you liable for something—for example, if you fail to pay rent, you're liable for the missing payments; if you wreck your rental car, you're liable for damages. You and your attorney may be able to negotiate changes to some agreements that shift or lessen your liability.

> **EXAMPLE:** Andrew is licensing his crafts doll design to a toy company. He receives a $20,000 advance, but the license agreement states that Andrew must refund his advance if the company is sued for copyright infringement over the design. Andrew and his attorney modify the agreement so that Andrew refunds the advance only if thelawsuit results in a final verdict—in other words, if infringement is proven, not just claimed. This substantially shifts the liability away from Andrew and makes him less likely to have to pay back the $20,000.

The Need for Basic Insurance

No matter how small your crafts business, there may be situation when you definitely need insurance. For example, a general liability insurer will defend you in court if an independent contractor, a customer, or any other nonemployee claims you caused or helped cause an injury. The insurer will also pay out damages or settlements, up to the policy limits. Although I don't want you to spend money insuring against disasters that will probably never strike, it's foolish to do operate crafts businesses without some basic insurance coverage. What's more, you may be required to have some types of insurance by law or by those you do business with (lenders, landlords, and others). The trick is to get only the coverage you really need—and to pay as little as possible for it. I'll explain the basics, below.

Key Insurance Terms	
Policy	Your policy is the written document or contract between you and the insurance company.
Premium	The premium is the periodic payment you pay to the insurance company for the benefits provided under the policy.
Rider	A rider is a special provision attached to a policy that either expands or restricts the policy.
Claim	A claim is your notification to an insurance company that you believe a payment is due to you under the terms of the policy.
Commission	This is a fee or percentage of the premium you pay to an insurance broker or agent.
Deductible	The deductible is the amount of out-of-pocket expenses that you must pay before the insurance payment begins. For example, if your deductible for business equipment loss is $1,000 per year and you suffer $1,000 in damages in one year, there will be no payment under the policy.
Endorsement	An endorsement is paperwork that is added to your policy and that reflects any changes or clarifications in the policy.
Exclusions	Exclusions are things your insurance policy will not cover.
Underwriter	This is the person or company that evaluates your business and determines what insurance you may qualify for.

If you decide to get insurance for your crafts business, you'll be faced with a few choices. Here's a brief description of some common forms of insurance protections.

Property Insurance

Business property insurance compensates you for damage or loss of your property—both the physical space where you work (your home office, for example) and the equipment and other furnishings of your business. If you operate a home business, you can probably take care of your property insurance needs through an endorsement to your homeowners' policy, particularly if you don't have much pricey business equipment. But don't assume that your homeowners' policy will cover business losses—most offer very limited coverage (if any) for business property.

If you rent commercial space—for example a studio for your jewelry business—your lease may require you to carry a specified amount of property insurance.

A "named peril" policy protects against only the types of damage listed in the policy—typically, fire, lightning, vehicles, vandalism, storms, smoke, and sprinkler leaks. A "special form" policy offers broader coverage, commonly against all but a few excluded risks (often including earthquakes), and is more expensive.

When you're buying property insurance, you'll have a choice between an actual cash value policy, which pays you whatever your damaged property is actually worth on the day it is damaged, or a replacement cost policy, which pays to replace your property at current prices. A replacement cost policy is always more expensive, but it's often worth the extra money. Business equipment, such as computers, fax machines, copiers, and so on, lose their value quickly. And if you're like most new business owners, you're probably using some equipment that's already out of date. If you suffer a loss, you'll need to replace this equipment and get back to work—not to go out to a fancy lunch on the $100 your insurance company thinks your old computer was worth.

Liability Insurance

Liability insurance covers damage to other people or their property for which you are legally responsible. This includes, for example, injuries to a customer who trips on your son's skateboard on the way to your home studio; damage caused by your crafts products (called product liability coverage); and harm caused by your errors in providing professional services (called professional liability coverage). Liability insurance policies typically pay the injured person's medical bills and other out-of-pocket losses, any amount you are ordered to pay in a lawsuit for a covered claim, and often the cost of defending you in such a lawsuit. If you have a home crafts business and are seldom visited there by clients or customers, you may be able to get a relatively inexpensive liability endorsement to your homeowners' policy.

Car Insurance

If you have a car, you probably already have insurance that covers your personal use. However, your personal insurance policy may not cover crafts business use of your car. If it doesn't, you'll want to get business coverage to protect against lawsuits for damage you cause to others or their vehicles while using your car for business.

If you don't do much business driving—and particularly if you don't often have business passengers, such as clients or customers—then you can probably get coverage simply by informing your insurance company of your planned business use (and paying a slightly higher premium). Many insurance companies simply factor in occasional business use of a vehicle, along with commuting miles, driver experience, and many other factors, in setting your insurance premium. If you use a commercial vehicle (such as a van or delivery truck) or put most of the miles on your car while doing business—for example, traveling to crafts shows—you will probably have to get a separate business vehicle insurance policy.

Business Interruption Coverage

If your crafts business becomes your primary source of income, I recommend that you obtain business interruption insurance—a policy that replaces the income you won't be able to earn if you must close, rebuild, or relocate your business due to a covered event, such as a fire or storm. These policies typically provide both money to replace your lost profits, based on your business's earnings history (as shown by its financial records), and money to pay the operating expenses you still have to pay even though you can't do business (like rent and overhead). (If you are not dependent on your crafts business, you may not wish to spend money on this type of policy.)

When you're shopping for this type of insurance (or any other, for that matter), always check the exclusions and coverage. For example, some policies may provide an "extended period of indemnity," which kicks in after you reopen, to cover your continuing losses until you are fully back on your feet. If your customers don't immediately flock back to your new location, your policy will pay for the business you're still not getting during this transition period.

Web Insurance

Some insurance companies offer Web insurance policies, which protect businesses with websites against a variety of risks, including theft, copyright infringement, and interruptions of service. Today, you can get insurance for a simple site for anywhere from $500 to $3,000 a year. An insurance professional can help you decide whether your cyber-risks are great enough to justify this expense.

Package Deals

Many insurance companies offer package policies geared to the needs of small businesses. If you run a home crafts business, you may be able to get less expensive coverage through an in-home business policy. These policies typically also cover business property and liability, and some also provide business interruption protection. According to the Insurance Information Institute, an in-home business policy will cost something in the range of $250 to $400 a year for about $10,000 of coverage. However, your business will have to meet the insurance company's requirements for coverage, which may include having very few employees, bringing few business visitors to your home, or purchasing your homeowners' insurance from the same company.

If your home crafts business can't meet these requirements, or if you run a business outside of your home, you can consider a business owners' policy or BOP. These packages typically include business property insurance, liability protection, and some business interruption protection. According to Chad Berberich, director of Executive Products at RLI Corporation Insurance (www.rlicorp.com), a "mom and pop" home-based business with revenues up to the low six figures can expect to pay an annual premium of anywhere from $1,500 to $4,000 for a BOP.

Typically, neither a BOP nor an in-home business policy provides coverage for professional liability (malpractice), employment practices liability (often referred to as EPLI) to protect you from lawsuits brought by current or former employees, workers' compensation, or other employee benefits (health or disability insurance, for example). Also, you will almost certainly have to pay separately for automobile coverage if you use your car for business.

Insurance for Employees

Do you have any employees? Keep in mind that when you hire employees, you take on some financial obligations. In addition to paying wages and Social Security and Medicare taxes for each employee, you'll also have to pay for unemployment insurance and, in a handful of states, disability insurance. And if you have more than a few employees, you'll probably have to purchase workers' compensation insurance.

Even if you don't have employees, you may have to pay for workers' comp insurance to cover your own work-related injuries. This often comes up for business owners who perform services at a client's location—for example, plumbers and contractors. Particularly if your work creates a risk of injury, clients may insist that you have your own workers' compensation coverage to make sure that you won't make a claim against their policy—and that they don't have to pay extra to cover you on the policy they carry for their own workers.

Workers' compensation insurance. This insurance pays your employees for work-related injuries and reimburses them a portion of lost wages if they cannot work due to injury. You buy it either by paying into a state fund or by buying a policy from a private insurer. Some states don't require employers that have only a few employees to get this coverage; contact your state insurance or labor department to find out your state's rules.

Unemployment insurance. If you have even one employee, you will probably have to pay for unemployment insurance (UI). UI is a joint program of the state and federal governments. It's funded by a payroll tax on employers, which goes into a fund from which workers who are laid off or fired for reasons other than serious misconduct can draw money while they're unemployed. The amount you have to pay will depend on how many employees you have and how many unemployment claims your former employees have made (if any). For information, go to the website of the federal Department of Labor's Employment and Training Administration, at www.doleta.gov. Choose "Business & Industry" for a list of topics for employers, including UI.

Disability insurance. Five states (California, Hawaii, New Jersey, New York, and Rhode Island) provide temporary disability insurance to workers who are temporarily disabled and unable to work. In California and Rhode Island, employees pay the cost of this insurance through payroll deductions; in Hawaii, New Jersey, and New York, employers pay into the plan. If you do business in one of these states, go to your state labor department's website to find out more about your obligations.

RESOURCE

The Insurance Information Institute (www.iii.org) offers lots of free information on insurance and a glossary of common insurance terms. The Federal Small Business Administration offers a free primer on business risk and ways to transfer that risk (including insurance) at www.sba.gov. Type "business risk" into the site's search box. Insure.com offers extensive insurance information for small businesses, at www.insure.com/articles/businessinsurance.

Tips for Saving Money on Insurance

Besides keeping your coverage up to date—be sure to set aside a time once a year to consider whether you need to increase your coverage—there are many ways to make sure you're not wasting money on insurance.

Work with the right insurance professional. Try to find someone who will help you figure out what coverage you need and offer you a competitive price. There's no magic formula for finding the "right" insurance professional—you need to find someone who: you trust to do a good job for you; who will periodically provide you with information about new policies you might want to consider; give you quotes from other companies from time to time; and help you if you have to file a claim.

Start your shopping with required insurance. If you are legally required to carry certain types of insurance (such as workers' compensation), make sure you set aside the money for it.

Prioritize your greatest risks. Once you've dealt with required coverage, spend your money where you need it the most. If you face a serious risk of a loss that could wipe you out, put your insurance dollars there first.

Consider higher deductibles. When you purchase a policy with a higher deductible, you'll pay lower premiums. This can be a financial lifesaver if you need insurance and you're struggling to get off the ground.

Don't duplicate the coverage you already have. Take time to review your homeowners' or renters' insurance policy.

Consider riders to your existing policies. Home-based crafts businesses that have few business-related visitors can get a relatively inexpensive liability endorsement. You can also add an endorsement to increase coverage for business equipment. If you use your personal car for business and your existing auto insurance policy doesn't cover business use, you may be able to get the coverage you need through an endorsement. However, if you use a car solely for business, you'll have to buy a separate business/commercial auto policy.

Always read the fine print. Before you write your premium check, make sure you understand exactly what you're getting for your money. Check the terms, exclusions (what isn't covered), limits, and so on.

Make sure you can collect if you need to. If you need to make an insurance claim, you'll have to prove the extent of your loss. For property, you should photograph and keep records of the value of your business equipment, inventory, and so on. If you have very valuable items—for example, if you sell fine art or antiques—consider having them valued by an independent appraiser.

Combining Insurance and Limited Liability Business Forms

There is a reason why so many businesses—even those that have elected the protection of a corporation or LLC—purchase insurance coverage. Insurance allows your business to take a licking and keep on ticking.

> **EXAMPLE 1:** Leslie operates his Western-inspired jewelry business as an LLC. While at a show, his studio burns to the ground, causing the loss of $90,000 in supplies and $30,000 in inventory. At the time of the fire, Leslie owes creditors some $45,000. Because he has an LLC, Leslie's business can declare bankruptcy and avoid paying the $45,000 in debts. His personal assets are unaffected. Still, he has lost the tools of his livelihood, his workspace and goodwill among suppliers, who are now wary of offering him credit.

> **EXAMPLE 2:** If Leslie had instead maintained fire insurance, he would receive compensation for his supplies and possibly rental costs for a temporary studio. He would be able to return to work and hopefully repay creditors without declaring bankruptcy.

Insurance has its drawbacks: periodic payments, annoying deductibles, and hard-to-read policies. But insurance is the best way to protect against business disasters such as fire, theft, injury to visitors, workplace injuries, injuries resulting from the use of your crafts goods, and even claims that you stole someone else's design.

Sometimes your business must get insurance—for example, because state laws require obtaining workers' compensation coverage, or because you sign a lease requiring you to have business and personal property coverage. In other cases, insurance may prove too expensive and you'll have to forgo it. A good insurance agent can help you make the right decisions. Here are some additional tips on choosing and using your insurance wisely:

- Maintain enough property and liability coverage to protect yourself from common claims—for example, fire, theft, or accidental injury.

- Buy insurance against serious risks, that is, those that would cost you the most if they occurred (so long as the insurance is reasonably priced for your business).
- When possible, keep insurance costs down by selecting high deductibles.
- Do your best to reduce hazards or conditions that can lead to insurance claims.

Assess and Reduce Your Risks

Aside from incorporating or obtaining insurance, there is one final (and free) step you can take to reduce your personal liability: assess and lower your business risks.

Assess your true risks. By assessing your risks, you can determine if you need to be concerned. Assessment can also guide you as to how much protection is needed. Ask yourself the following questions:

- How much business property do you own? The more you own, the greater your loss in the event of a setback or disaster.
- Do you sell products? If so, what are the chances that they might cause someone injury? (See my discussion of product liability, below.)
- Do you carry a large inventory of completed products or valuable raw materials? The larger your inventory, the more of a financial loss from damage. If your raw materials are hazardous, you may face additional risks.
- If you sell services, could a client suffer harm (physical or financial) if you made a mistake? If so, you may want to consider malpractice insurance.
- Will you have employees? Employees increase your risks and liabilities.
- Are you a target? The wealthier you are, the more likely you will appear as a target for those who are injured.

Reduce your risk. Minimize your risks. Doing so may eliminate your need to form a separate business entity and it may bring your premiums down.

Consider your list of possible risks (above) and think about what you can do to eliminate them or reduce the potential for danger. Sometimes risk prevention requires investigation—learning about customers, suppliers, and people you employ. Sometimes, it's just a matter of common sense—if you're offering lessons to crafts artists about using propane, be sure you have a selection of safety goggles for students who have forgotten to bring their own.

You can transfer risk to others, as well. For example, don't store a lot of supplies or finished products on your premises, but leave them at your rented studio space. (Of course, this strategy will work only if the person or company where you store things is adequately insured.)

Product Liability

In general, handmade crafts are not often subject to personal injury lawsuits because they are commonly used for decorative purposes and are less likely to result in injuries—as compared to products such as cars, foods, cosmetics, etc. In addition, handmade crafts are usually less likely to have defects since their production often requires a higher degree of care (than mass-produced goods).

However, some crafts—for example, toys or furniture—may result in injuries. As the maker of the product you may be held liable for the injuries that are caused (referred to as "product liability"). Product liability, for the most part, is based on commonsense principles. You have a duty as a crafts artist to exercise reasonable care in the production of your goods. You also have an obligation to sell safe products. Finally, if there are inherent risks—for example—your handmade soaps contain a fragrance formulation that may trigger allergic reactions—you have a duty to warn consumers.

Product liability actually is an umbrella term that encompasses several legal theories including:

- negligence (failing to exercise a duty of care to customers)
- strict liability (placing defective products into commerce)
- breach of warranty, (breaking a promise of quality or performance associated with the goods), and

- various consumer protection claims (state laws aimed at protecting consumers).

You don't need to learn about the legal intricacies that differentiate these theories, but if you're concerned about this type of liability here are some things you can do to minimize product liability risks:

- **Obtain liability insurance** (see my discussion of insurance, above).
- **Provide adequate warnings.** It may seem obvious to you that a candle should not be left unattended or that wax should be kept free of matches, wick trimmings, or other flammable materials, but it doesn't hurt to include a warning sticker (some crafts supply stores offer preprinted warnings for various items).
- **Be careful what you promise.** Avoid language in brochures or signs that guarantees or promises standards that you cannot keep—for example, that your bookshelf will support unlimited books, when in fact it may buckle from more than 100 pounds.

Pay attention to design standards. Design defects are one of the leading causes of product liability claims. Follow industry standards—if you design lamps, for example, abide by the standards of the Underwriters Laboratories (www.ul.com).

Use reliable components. If you're making quilts or children's pajamas, be sure that the fabrics you purchase meet the safety standards regarding flammability. Read labels carefully.

Pay attention to legal requirements in your product area. Different industries may have special requirements. For example, in 2008, Congress passed the Consumer Product Safety Improvement Act which set out mandatory safety standards for products for children under 12—a law that set very difficult standards for handmade toy makers. (As this book went to press in 2010, the Handmade Toy Alliance was fighting to modify the law.) Talk to others in your field or join a crafts guild to learn industry requirements.

Protecting Appearances With Copyright

I n 1995, Lisa Graves sued a major catalog retailer, claiming that the company had stolen her copyrighted design for Bird's Nest napkin rings. The retailer's lawyer denied the company's made-in-India napkin rings were copies. He also argued that Graves' work was not entitled to copyright, claiming her design was based on real-life bird's nests. After all, he contended, no one can claim legal rights to something created in nature.

As Lisa's attorney, I contacted an ornithologist, Kimball Garrett, at the Natural History Museum of Los Angeles County. Mr. Garrett examined Lisa's napkin ring and stated that the design was not similar to any existing bird's nest, and that without a bottom, the design could never function as a nest anyway. In other words, Lisa had created something artistic, not copied something from nature. Soon after, Pottery Barn settled, paid Lisa for lost sales and stopped selling copies of her napkin ring.

One lesson from Lisa Graves's battle with Pottery Barn is that it's not enough to *claim* you have a copyright; sometimes you must enforce your rights by filing a lawsuit and proving that your work meets copyright standards.

In the last decade, many crafts workers have had to take a crash course in copyright law. For example, makers of quilt patterns found themselves in a Napster-like controversy as their work was widely circulated online without permission. Chat rooms exploded with debates on the subject. Was it really wrong, some quilt makers asked, to take designs without permission? Wasn't sharing part of the crafts tradition?

Copyright disputes became more prevalent as chain stores and catalog companies stepped up their manufacture of crafts knock-offs. These companies brazenly copied works, knowing that crafts artists can't afford to fight long legal battles. When crafts workers do challenge the big retailers—as in the case of jeweler Paul Morelli, discussed, below—the results are sometimes disappointing.

This chapter focuses on copyright ownership, registration, and avoiding typical copyright problems. (I discuss the works-made-for-hire rule—a copyright principle affecting ownership of employee-created works—in Chapter 4.)

Getting Copyright Protection Without Registering

You don't have to file an application and register with the U.S. Copyright Office to get a copyright on your crafts work. You get it once you create the work. In other words, once you finish a bracelet, wood sculpture, or glass candelabra—you have a copyright! However, there are two occasions when you don't get this automatic copyright after creating a work:

- the work is not copyrightable (discussed below), and
- someone hired you to create the work, and it was "work made for hire" (discussed in Chapter 4).

How a Copyright Protects You

Although you acquire copyright automatically, I recommend registering with the Copyright Office as well, particularly for those crafts works that are more likely to inspire copies. Registration provides advantages and creates helpful presumptions and it assists in doing two valuable copyright activities:

- **Chasing people who rip your work off.** If someone uses your copyrighted work without your permission—or, in legal terms, infringes your copyright—you can go after them, make them stop, and perhaps collect a financial payment for the damage they've done. You can take these actions against anyone who, without your permission, copies your work, displays your work, makes photos of it, broadcasts it on television, or makes variations or miniatures of it.
- **Earning money by licensing or selling your rights.** You can also make money by giving your rights to someone else, either temporarily (a license) or permanently (an assignment). For example, the artists who created Cabbage Patch Dolls have earned millions from licensing their creation. In return for letting a company "use" their copyrighted designs, they earn a royalty based upon each doll sold.

Copyright Lasts a Long Time

Copyright protection begins once a work is created and generally lasts for the life of the artist plus 70 years (for works created by a single author). Works made for hire are protected for 120 years from their date of creation or 95 years from their first publication, whichever is longer. The same duration of copyright will apply regardless of whether the work is registered.

What Type of Work Qualifies for Copyright

Start with the assumption that your original crafts work is protected under copyright law. As a general rule, if you didn't copy it from someplace else and it has some artistic expression, you can claim copyright. However, some crafts works—particularly functional and minimal works—may not come under copyright's blanket of protection. In these cases, you may find that the Copyright Office or a potential infringer will challenge your rights. Generally, claiming copyright becomes more difficult if:

- your designs are minimal and use common shapes, or
- it's difficult to separate the art from the function in your work.

TIP

When in doubt, register with the Copyright Office. Don't conclude, based on the information in this section, that you can't get a copyright. Let the Copyright Office be the judge. Regardless of your opinion about your work's functionality or minimalism, attempt to register it. (Your judgment may be more critical than that of the Copyright Office.) Getting a registration doesn't guarantee you can stop others—your copyright can still be challenged in a court battle—but it creates a presumption of validity that's tougher to beat.

Problems Protecting Minimal Designs and Common Shapes

If your crafts work is minimal—that is, you avoid artistic statements in favor of pure craftsmanship—or if your work uses common geometric or natural shapes, you may have difficulty claiming copyright protection.

Since copyright protects originality, not craftsmanship, even the most beautifully stitched leather goods or stunning glassware may not qualify for protection. In short, the more ornate work is more likely to acquire copyright.

Consider the dilemma faced by Paul Morelli, a jewelry maker whose works are offered in upscale stores like Neiman Marcus and Bergdorf Goodman. In 1987, he created a jewelry line called "Sprinkled Diamond." The first piece was a heart-shaped pendant with a zigzag pattern of inlaid diamonds flush to the surface.

Within a few years, Tiffany & Co.—after reviewing slides of Morelli's work—began selling a similar line of jewelry. Unfortunately, Morelli was not able to register his work with the Copyright Office, normally a prerequisite for filing a lawsuit. The Copyright Office claimed Morelli's minimalist designs lacked sufficient originality. In other words, because they were primarily basic geometric shapes, they lacked the creativity necessary to qualify for copyright. Morelli sued Tiffany & Co. anyway, under a rarely used law that permits an artist to file a lawsuit without a registration.

In his lawsuit, Morelli argued that the Copyright Office had erred. At the trial, a Justice Department attorney, John Fargo, explained why the government rejected Morelli's work:

"Common shapes—a heart, the square shape of a pillow earring, a circular shape of a ring or a bracelet—those are not copyrightable by themselves. They're geometric shapes that are free for all to use. The problem with minimalist work is it doesn't leave a lot in the way of expression."

Morelli's expert witnesses testified that his designs were the result of great creativity and were innovative, but it was not enough to overcome the jury's belief that the jewelry lacked copyrightable expression. The result was a major win for Tiffany & Co., which was able to continue selling its $30-million-a-year Etoile line.

Separating Art From Function

Copyright law won't protect a functional object like a lamp or a shoe. These "useful articles," if they are novel, may be protected under patent law. Their names and appearance can sometimes also be protected under trademark law. But copyright only protects expressions of ideas, not useful objects.

This doesn't mean you can't get a copyright for your elephant-shaped cup or your flower-patterned casserole cozies. You can usually claim copyright protection for the arty aspects of your work—the elephant shape and your original flower pattern—but not for the functional features.

> EXAMPLE: Daniel creates a whimsical hand-painted jewelry box. Daniel can stop others from copying his whimsical design on any other media—for example, on toy chests, puzzles, pot holders, or websites. But he cannot claim copyright in the functional aspects of the jewelry box—the way it closes, the system of storage, or the hinge mechanism on the back.

Sometimes, it's difficult to conceive of the art separate from the function—that is, the art and function seem to merge so completely that one cannot exist without the other. When that happens, it's hard to get copyright, because the design is considered necessary to the function.

This issue is resolved in legal disputes by asking the question, "Can this crafts work be created in many alternate ways and still function?" If there are many alternate designs, then the design is not crucial to the function.

Consider the bird's nest napkin rings discussed at the beginning of this chapter. There are many ways to make napkin rings other than with a bird's nest design. In fact, there are many alternative types of bird's nest designs that can be used to create napkin rings. (In preparation for her case, Lisa Graves demonstrated several other ways a wire napkin ring could be created.) Since there were so many alternative ways to express a napkin ring with a bird's nest motif, the function (holding napkins) and the design (the unique wire and solder design) were not inseparable. In short, Lisa Graves could not stop a retailer from creating a bird's nest napkin ring, but she could stop them from making a napkin ring with the same shape, same number of windings, and similar use of solder.

Below are more real-life cases that grappled with these same issues.

The Koosh Ball. The KOOSH ball is a sphere-shaped object with floppy, wiggly, elastic filaments radiating from a core. The Copyright Office denied copyright registration for the KOOSH ball because the ball's function could not be separated from any artistic expression. (*OddzOn Prods. v. Oman*, 924 F.2d 346 (D.C. Cir. 1991).) (Despite the lack of copyright protection, the KOOSH ball is protected under patent and trademark laws.)

The Belt Buckle. Jewelry designer Barry Kieselstein-Cord sued a company that copied his belt-buckle designs. (*Kieselstein-Cord v. Accessories by Pearl, Inc.*, 632 F.2d 989 (2d Cir. 1980).) At first, the court held that the belt buckles were not copyrightable because it was not possible to physically separate the sculptural work (the jewelry design) from the functional object (the belt buckle). However, a higher court reversed that decision and found that the artistic features of the belt buckle were conceptually separable, and Kieselstein-Cord was able to claim copyright protection.

The Motorcycle Kickstand. In 1995, the manufacturer of stylized chrome motorcycle parts attempted to register some of the company products (for example, kickstand mount, speedometer visor) as sculptural works. The Copyright Office refused to register these items, claiming that their function could not be separated from their claimed aesthetic worthiness. A court upheld this decision, agreeing that the sculptural or artistic aspects were not conceptually separable. (*Custom Chrome Inc. v. Ringer*, 35 U.S.P.Q.2d 1714 (D. D.C. 1995).)

Why were the results different in the belt buckle and motorcycle cases? The stylish beauty of the motorcycle parts was inseparable from their function. Alternatively, there may not have been suitable alternatives for expressing the kickstand mount or visor.

As you can see, the function/art issue is similar to the minimalism issue. Again, the more ornate the design, the more likely it is that the Copyright Office or courts will see how the design is separate from the function.

Clothing Designs—Can't Get No Respect

If you're wondering why you see so many fashion knockoffs in retail stores it's because clothing designs do not qualify for copyright protection. The Copyright Office steadfastly maintains that the art cannot be separated from the function in clothing designs. It's not as if clothing designers haven't tried for protection. Some clothing designers unsuccessfully petitioned Congress for a new type of legal protection. One costume designer attempted to sneak her work through the Copyright Office by claiming it was a "soft sculpture"—but the Copyright Office later rejected it. Although you can't protect the design, you can protect unique artwork featured on clothing, and you can protect arrangements of fabric—for example, quilt designs used on clothing.

Photographs of Your Crafts Work

Photographs or slides of your crafts products consist of two copyrights— the copyright in the photograph (owned by the photographer) and your copyright in the underlying crafts product. If you took the picture, then you own both copyrights. If not, the photographer must give you permission to reproduce the image. Usually, this isn't an issue since the photographer grants you—either explicitly or implicitly—carte blanche to use the photographs. Most crafts workers don't bother with the issue, and photographers rarely haggle over it.

But if you're concerned about your right to use photographs and want to guarantee a broad range of uses for the photos—for example, to be able to reproduce them on your website, on postcards, or in a crafts magazine—have the photographer assign all rights in the photographs to you. You don't need a full-blown agreement—although I provide an assignment agreement, below. Instead, you can just include the statement, "Photographer assigns all copyright in the photographs to [your name]" on the photographer's invoice and ask the photographer to sign it. Sometimes a photographer may be willing to assign copyright but wishes to retain the right to reproduce copies for a portfolio. That's okay. Just write out your understanding.

The dual copyrights in a photograph of crafts also work in your favor. Since you control the reproduction of your copyrighted crafts design, the photographer would need your permission to reproduce photos of your crafts. In other words, you could halt the photographer's unauthorized use of photos of your copyrighted work.

Do You Need to Register With the Copyright Office?

Although you do not need a copyright registration to claim copyright, I recommend that you apply for one. From a practical point of view, having a copyright registration sometimes speeds up resolution of copyright disputes. It lets the other side know you're serious, it frightens some pirates, and, because of the potential for an award of attorney fees and statutory damages discussed below, it may help you attract a lawyer to take your case. Here's a summary of some registration benefits:

- If you register your artwork within five years of publication, you are presumed to be the owner of the artwork and to have a valid copyright.
- If you register your artwork prior to an infringement, or within three months of its publication, you may be entitled to special payments known as "statutory damages" and to attorney fees from the person you sued.
- You can only file a copyright infringement lawsuit if you've registered your artwork first.
- The filing fee for registration is currently $45, and the registration process takes approximately six months. It's possible to expedite

the registration for an added fee, in which case it can be acquired within five working days. Expediting a copyright registration is not for convenience; it is only allowed in urgent cases (see below).

RESOURCE

The U.S. Copyright Office website (www.copyright.gov) is your one-stop source for all things copyright. You can download copyright application forms or copyright circulars (special publications that explain copyright laws and rules in plain language). (You can also write to the agency: Copyright Office, Library of Congress, Washington, DC 20559-6000.)

Choosing Whether to Register Your Works in Groups

You don't necessarily have to register each of your works one by one. To save time and money, it's possible to register a group or collection of your crafts works—depending on whether the conditions described, below, have been met. The registration requirements and process will depend also on whether the works are unpublished or published.

When is your crafts work published? The word "publication" has a broader meaning than you might expect in the copyright world. A work is considered to be published under copyright law if you sell, distribute, or offer to sell or distribute copies of your artwork to the public. Artwork displayed in a competition is not a publication, but when you display it for sale at a trade show, that's considered to be a publication. Posting artwork on a website may—or may not—be a publication. Neither the courts nor the Copyright Office has issued any definitive rulings on this. Take a conservative approach and consider website uses—particularly if you're offering the items for sale—as constituting publication.

There is one drawback to registering a group of works. If several of the items in your group registration are infringed, you may recover less money than if each work had been registered separately. Unsure of whether to register separately or in groups? Register your most popular works individually, and register the rest in collections.

Registering a Group of Unpublished Crafts Works

A group of unpublished works may be registered as a collection if all of the following conditions are met:
- you've organized the images of the works that you want copyrighted into an orderly collection (for example, each image is glued to a page within a bound book or loose-leaf volume)
- the collection has a single title identifying it as a whole (for example, "Hannah's Summer 2010 Crochet Collection"), and
- one person has created all of the works in the collection or has contributed to all of the works (for example, one artist does a series of collaborations with different artists).

Registering a Group of Published Works

You can register a published work that contains various works—such as a published book of your crafts works, a bound collection of postcards of your work, or a poster containing several of your crafts items. For example, a crafts artist who creates a collection of sculptured chess pieces, a playing board, and an ornate box to hold the pieces can claim a single copyright in the set. In order to register a published work containing many works, one person must have created all of the works.

Filing a Copyright Application

There are two ways to file a copyright application:
- file online (using the Copyright Office's electronic eCO system), or
- file the all-purpose Form CO (unveiled in 2008), which can be used for any copyrightable work.

Which is right for you?
- If you're comfortable with electronic filing—that is, preparing and filling out forms online—the eCO system is less expensive ($35 instead of $45) than using paper forms, and will likely result in faster turnaround.

- If you want to use paper and are eager to obtain your registration, use Form CO, because it will be processed faster than the traditional print application due to the incorporated 2-D bar code technology.

Regardless of which type of application is used, the information required for an application is the same. The primary difference between the types of applications is how and in what order the information is collected.

The Copyright Office provides extensive help for the application process. There are downloadable circulars that explain registration procedures and the eCO electronic system is heavily documented with online guidance.

Registering Your Crafts Work Using Form CO

The all-purpose Form CO can be used for registering any work and may be downloaded from the Copyright Office website. The download is in PDF format (the Adobe Acrobat format) and each downloadable application form is considered "fillable," meaning that you can type information directly into the form visible on your screen. Although you can print the completed form, you can't save the data. So, once you close the PDF form (or turn off your computer), you'll lose any information you typed into the form.

After you print it out the form, do not alter it by hand. That's because the information used by the Copyright Office is primarily stored in the barcodes on the form. If you want to register a series of similar works, keep the form open after you print it; then make the necessary changes and print the subsequent version, as well.

Once you complete the form, you must mail the completed application, your $45 fee (payable to the Register of Copyrights), and your deposit materials (two copies if the work is published; one if it is unpublished). Send all three elements of your crafts work copyright application in the same envelope or package to:

UNITED STATES COPYRIGHT OFFICE
Form CO · Application for Copyright Registration

APPLICATION FOR COPYRIGHT REGISTRATION VA

* **Designates Required Fields**

1 WORK BEING REGISTERED

1a. * Type of work being registered (*Fill in one only*)

☐ Literary work   ☐ Performing arts work

☒ Visual arts work   ☐ Motion picture/audiovisual work

☐ Sound recording   ☐ Single serial issue

1b. * Title of this work (*one title per space*)

Hayden Dolls

ApplicationForCopyrightRegistration

WorkTitles

1c. For a serial issue: Volume _____ Number _____ Issue _____ ISSN _____

Frequency of publication: _____

1d. Previous or alternative title

1e. * Year of completion | 2 | 0 | 0 | 9 |

Publication (*If this work has not been published, skip to section 2*)

1f. Date of publication 01/01/2009 (*mm/dd/yyyy*) **1g.** ISBN _____

1h. Nation of publication   ☒ United States   ☐ Other

1i. Published as a contribution in a larger work entitled

1j. If line 1i above names a serial issue   Volume _____ Number _____ Issue _____

On pages _____

1k. If work was preregistered   Number PRE- | | | | | | | |

UNITED STATES COPYRIGHT OFFICE
Form CO · Application for Copyright Registration

For Office Use Only

WorkBeingRegistered

2 AUTHOR INFORMATION

2a. Personal name   *complete either 2a or 2b*

First Name	Middle	Last
Margaret		Zimet

2b. Organization name

2c. Doing business as

2d. Year of birth 1 9 8 7   **2e.** Year of death

2f. * ☒ Citizenship ☒ United States ☐ Other
☐ Domicile

2g. Author's contribution: ☐ Made for hire ☐ Anonymous
☐ Pseudonymous

Continuation of Author Information

2h. * This author created *(Fill in only the authorship that applies to this author)*

☐ Text/poetry   ☐ Compilation   ☐ Map/technical drawing   ☐ Music
☐ Editing   ☐ Sculpture   ☐ Architectural work   ☐ Lyrics
☐ Computer program   ☐ Jewelry design   ☐ Photography   ☐ Motion picture/audiovisual
☐ Collective work   ☐ 2-dimensional artwork ☐ Script/play/screenplay ☐ Sound recording/performance

Other: 3D cloth doll

For Office Use Only

AuthorInformation

UNITED STATES COPYRIGHT OFFICE
Form CO · Application for Copyright Registration

3 COPYRIGHT CLAIMANT INFORMATION

Claimant   *complete either 3a or 3b* - If you do not know the address for a claimant, enter "not known" in the Street address and City fields.

3a. Personal name

First Name	Middle	Last
Margaret		Zimet

3b. Organization name

3c. Doing business as

3d. Street address *

950 Parker Street

Street address (line 2)

City *	State	ZIP / Postal code	Country
Berkeley	CA	94710	United States

Email	Phone number	
tz@nolo.com	510-555-1234	(Add "+" and country code for foreign numbers)

3e. If claimant is **not** an author, copyright ownership acquired by: ☐ Written agreement ☐ Will or inheritance ☐ Other

For Office Use Only

CopyrightClaimantInformation

4 LIMITATION OF COPYRIGHT CLAIM   Skip section 4 if this work is all new.

4a. Material excluded from this claim *(Material previously registered, previously published, or not owned by this claimant)*

☐ Text ☐ Artwork ☐ Music ☐ Sound recording/performance ☐ Motion picture/audiovisual

Other:

UNITED STATES COPYRIGHT OFFICE

Form CO · Application for Copyright Registration

4b. Previous registration(s)

Number		Year	
Number		Year	

4c. New material included in this claim (*This work contains new, additional, or revised material*)

☐ Text ☐ Compilation ☐ Map/technical drawing ☐ Music

☐ Poetry ☐ Sculpture ☐ Architectural work ☐ Lyrics

☐ Computer program ☐ Jewelry design ☐ Photography ☐ Motion picture/audiovisual

☐ Editing ☐ 2-dimensional artwork ☐ Script/play/screenplay ☐ Sound recording/performance

Other: _____

For Office Use Only

LimitationOfCopyrightClaim

5 RIGHTS AND PERMISSIONS CONTACT

☒ Check if information below should be copied from the **first** copyright claimant

First Name	Middle	Last
Margaret		Zimet

Name of organization

Street address
950 Parker Street

Street address (line 2)

City	State	ZIP / Postal code	Country
Berkeley	CA	94710	United States

Email	Phone number	
tz@nolo.com	510-555-1234	(*Add "+" and country code for foreign numbers*)

UNITED STATES COPYRIGHT OFFICE
Form CO · Application for Copyright Registration

For Office Use Only

RightsAndPermissionsContact

6 CORRESPONDENCE CONTACT

☒ Copy from **first** copyright claimant　☐ Copy from rights and permissions contact

First name *
Margaret

Middle

Last *
Zimet

Name of organization

Street address *
950 Parker Street

Street address (line 2)

City *
Berkeley

State
CA

ZIP / Postal code
94710

Country
United States

Email *
mz@nolo.com

Daytime phone number
510-555-1234

(Add "+" and country code for foreign numbers)

For Office Use Only

CorrespondenceContact

7 MAIL CERTIFICATE TO:

* Complete either 7a, 7b, or both

☒ Copy from **first** copyright claimant　☐ Copy from rights and permissions contact　☐ Copy from correspondence contact

7a. First Name
Margaret

Middle

Last
Zimet

UNITED STATES COPYRIGHT OFFICE

Form CO · Application for Copyright Registration

7b. Name of organization

7c. Street address *

950 Parker Street

Street address (line 2)

City *	State	ZIP / Postal code	Country
Berkeley	CA	94710	United States

For Office Use Only

MailCertificateTo

8 CERTIFICATION

17 U.S.C. § 506(e): Any person who knowingly makes a false representation of a material fact in the application for copyright registration provided for by section 409, or in any written statement filed in connection with the application, shall be fined not more than $2,500.

I certify that I am the author, copyright claimant, or owner of exclusive rights, or the authorized agent of the author, copyright claimant, or owner of exclusive rights, of this work, and that the information given in this application is correct to the best of my knowledge.

Sign Here

8a. Handwritten signature

Margaret Zimet   2/15/2010

8b. Printed name   **8c.** Date signed

8d. Deposit account number   Account holder

8e. Applicant's internal tracking number (optional)

Library of Congress
Copyright Office
101 Independence Avenue, SE
Washington, DC 20559-6233

Below are instructions for completing Form CO. Much of this information is taken verbatim from the instructions provided by the Copyright Office.

Section 1. Work Being Registered

NOTE: *   indicates a required field
         ** indicates required alternate fields (one of two fields required).

Understanding the lingo: For copyright purposes, a crafts artist is an "author," and the crafts being registered is the "work."

1A.* Type of work being registered. Check the appropriate box for the type of work—most likely visual arts work. If your work contains more than one type of authorship, choose the type for the predominant authorship in the work.

1B.* Title of work. Enter the title. Give the complete title exactly as it appears on the material about the crafts work. If there is no title copy, give an identifying phrase to serve as the title or state "untitled." Use standard title capitalization without quotation marks; for example, *Turn the Love Around*. If you want to include additional title(s)—for example, titles of individual works in an unpublished collection or works owned by the same claimant, click the "additional title" button.

1C. Serial issue. A serial is a work issued or intended to be issued in successive parts and intended to be continued indefinitely. You can leave this blank.

1D. Previous or alternative title. If the crafts work is known by another title, give that title here.

1E.* Year of completion. Give the year in which creation of the crafts work was completed—the date you stood back and said, "I'm done." If the crafts work has been published, the year of completion cannot be later than the year of first publication.

1F–1H. Date of publication. Give the complete date, in mm/dd/yyyy format, on which the crafts work was first published. If you're unsure, get as close as reasonably possible. Do not give a date that is in the future. Leave this line blank if the crafts work is unpublished.

When Is Your Crafts Work Published?

The word "publication" has a broader meaning than you might expect in the copyright world. A work is considered to be published under copyright law if you sell, distribute, or offer to sell or distribute copies of your artwork to the public. Artwork displayed in a competition is not a publication, but when you display it for sale at a trade show, that's considered to be a publication.

Posting crafts artwork on a website may—or may not—be a publication. Neither the courts nor the Copyright Office has issued any definitive rulings on this. Take a conservative approach and consider website uses—particularly if you're offering the items for sale—as constituting publication.

1G. ISBN. You can leave this blank.

1H. Nation of publication. Give the nation where the crafts work was first published. If the crafts work was first published simultaneously in the United States and another country; you can list the United States. Leave this line blank if the crafts work is unpublished.

1I. Published as a contribution in a larger work entitled. If this crafts work has been published as part of a larger work—for example, it's one crafts work from a collection—enter the title of the larger work.

Section 2. Author Information

2A** or 2B. Personal name/Organization name. Complete either 2A or 2B but not both. Copyright law refers to you—the person who created the work—as "author." Provide your name, unless you wish to be anonymous or pseudonymous. A coauthor is someone who, at the time the work was created, made a copyrightable contribution.

> **EXAMPLE:** While sitting in your booth at a trade show, you and your five-year-old son decide to modify one of your intricately carved wooden jewelry boxes. You draw a damsel in a castle. Your son draws on a crude image of a dragon. To your surprise, a buyer from a chain store walks by the booth, sees it and orders 100. The design—combining your intricate woodwork and his dragon image—is a work of coauthorship.

Complete section 2B only if the crafts work is made for hire, in which case the hiring party is the author.

2C. Doing business as. You can leave this blank unless you've transferred crafts work ownership to a company using a DBA.

2D. Year of birth & 2E. Year of death. Give the year the author was born (and deceased, if applicable). The year of birth is optional but is very useful as a form of author identification because many authors have the same name. Your birth date will be made part of the online public Copyright records and cannot be removed later.

2F. Citizenship/domicile. Check the U.S. box if applicable, or if the author is a citizen of another country, enter the name of this nation. Alternatively, identify the nation where the author is domiciled (resides permanently). If you wish to remain anonymous and your name is given in line 2A, it will be made part of the online public records produced by the Copyright Office and accessible on the Internet. This information cannot be removed later from those public records.

2H.* This author created. Here you check the appropriate box(es) that describe this author's contribution to this crafts work. Hopefully, you will be able to use one of the boxes—sculpture, jewelry design, two-dimensional artwork, or photography. If not, give a brief statement on the line after "other" and be specific. The Copyright Office recommends against using terms such as idea, concept, title, or name.

Section 3. Copyright Claimant Information

3A and 3B.** Personal name/Organization name.** Again, as with Section 2A and 2B, complete one or the other, but not both. Here we are listing the person or entity who owns the copyright—either the crafts artist who created it, or the person or organization to which the copyright has been transferred by an author, or other authorized copyright owner.

3C. Doing business as. You can leave this blank unless you've transferred crafts work ownership to a company using a DBA.

3D. Address, email, and phone. The claimant postal address will be made part of the online public Copyright records and cannot be removed later. However, the email address and phone number will not appear in the public record unless it is also included in section 5, Rights and Permissions Contact.

3E. Copyright ownership acquired by. If the claimant (the person claiming copyright ownership) is the author of the crafts work, skip this line. Transfer information is required if the claimant is not an author but has obtained ownership of the copyright from the author or another owner. In that case, check the appropriate box to indicate how ownership was acquired. When you check "Written agreement" that includes a transfer by assignment or by contract. "Will or inheritance" applies only if the person from whom copyright was transferred is deceased. If necessary, check "other" and give a brief statement indicating how copyright was transferred.

Section 4. Limitation of Copyright Claim

You do not need to complete this section unless the work contains or is based on previously registered or previously published material, material in the public domain, or material not owned by this copyright claimant. The purpose of section 4 is to exclude such material from the claim and identify the new material upon which the present claim is based.

4A. Material excluded from this claim. Check the appropriate box or boxes to exclude any previously registered or previously published material, material in the public domain, or material not owned by this claimant. For example, if you were registering a fabric print that contains some public domain images, you would enter "public domain image of Sigmund Freud" in the "Other" box.

4B. Previous registration. If the crafts work for which you are now seeking registration, or an earlier version of it, has been registered, give the registration number and the year of registration. If there have been multiple registrations, you may give information regarding the last two. If you are registering the first published version of a crafts work that is identical to a previously registered unpublished version (contains no new material not already registered), check the "other" box in line 4a and state "First publication of work registered as unpublished." In this case, skip line 4c.

4C. New material included in this claim. Check the appropriate box or boxes to identify the new material you are claiming in this registration. Again, you are only filling in this section if your work contains material by someone else. In section 4C, your goal is to indicate what you contributed. Give a brief statement on the line after "other" if it is necessary to give a more specific description of the new material included in this claim or if none of the check boxes apply.

The Compilation box. A compilation is a collection of material—for example, a book titled "The Crafts Report's 100 Greatest Crafts Artists"— in which someone assembled, selected, or organized the preexisting materials without transforming them. The author of a compilation seeks to protect the collection, not the individual works. A collection of your crafts works is not a compilation, since you're seeking to protect all of the individual works, not the manner in which they are arranged or selected. A claim in "compilation" does not include the material that has been compiled. If that material should also be included in the claim, check the appropriate additional boxes.

Section 5. Rights and Permissions

Here is where Form CO differs from previous copyright applications. Form CO asks for a listing of the person to contact for permission to use the material. If this is the same as the first copyright claimant (see above), you can simply check the box and the information will be generated to complete this section. Again, all the information given in this section, including name, postal address, email address, and phone number, will be made part of the online records produced by the Copyright Office and cannot be removed later from those public records.

Section 6. Correspondence Contact

This is the person that the Copyright Office should contact with any questions about this application. If this is the same as the first copyright claimant or the rights and permissions contact, simply check the appropriate box. (Information given only in this space will not appear in the online public record.)

Section 7. Mail Certificate To

This is the person to whom the registration certificate should be mailed. If this is the same as the first copyright claimant, the rights and permissions contact, or the correspondence contact, simply check the appropriate box. (Information given only in this space will not appear in the online public record.)

Section 8. Certification

8A.* Handwritten signature. After you print out the completed application, be sure to sign it.

8B.* Printed name. Enter the name of the person who will sign the form.

8C.* Date signed. Choose "today's date" or "write date by hand." In the latter case, be sure to date the application by hand when you sign it. If your application gives a date of publication, do not certify using a date prior to the publication date.

8D. Deposit account. Leave this line blank unless you have a Copyright Office deposit account and are charging the filing fee to that account.

8E. Applicant's internal tracking number. If you have an internal tracking number, enter it here.

Preparing an Electronic (eCO) Copyright Application

The electronic copyright (eCO) application process has three parts. The applicant:

- completes the online interview
- pays the fee (payment can be made by credit/debit card, ACH, or by setting up a deposit account), and

- uploads or mails copies of the work. Unpublished crafts works and crafts works published only electronically (for example, digital photos used for your website) can be uploaded. All other works must be sent by U.S. Postal Service (USPS). You will be instructed to print out a shipping slip to be attached to the work for delivery by the USPS.

In order to use eCO, the user must disable pop-up blockers, and third-party toolbars. Not all browsers are supported by the eCO system.

RESOURCE

Need help? The Copyright Office (www.copyright.gov) has done a nice job of explaining the process and making it user-friendly with a tutorial and FAQs. The eCO process is peppered with helpful drop down menus, as well as hypertext links that provide pop-up explanations for each aspect of the application process. The explanations for paper forms provided earlier in this section should aid you answering the online interview—for example, how to respond to questions regarding the nature of work, title, date of publication, etc.

You will need to create a user account and password. The eCO system includes a special "Save for Later" feature which will preserve your work in the event you sign off and then sign on at a later time.

Below are some screenshots with explanations to give you an idea of how eCO functions.

Expediting Copyright Applications

For an expedited handling fee of $805 ($760 plus the $45 filing fee), the Copyright Office will process an application within five working days. You cannot choose this service for mere reasons of convenience; it is only allowed in urgent cases. You can request it using the form "Request for Special Handling," included in Copyright Circular 10. As an alternative to using this form, you can prepare a cover letter answering the following questions:

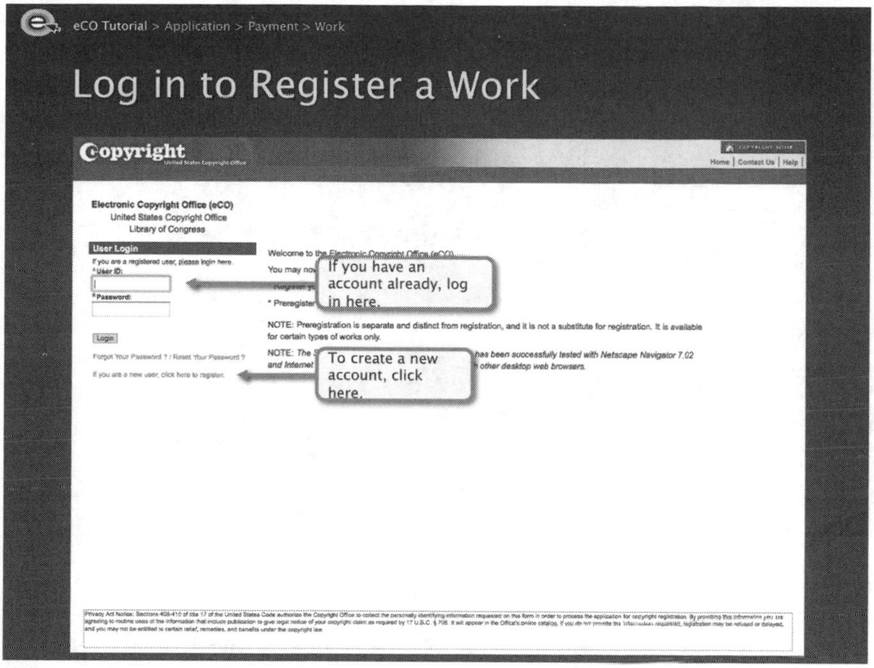
eCO Tutorial > Application > Payment > Work
Log in to Register a Work
Copyright
Electronic Copyright Office (eCO)
United States Copyright Office
Library of Congress
User Login
If you have an account already, log in here.
To create a new account, click here.

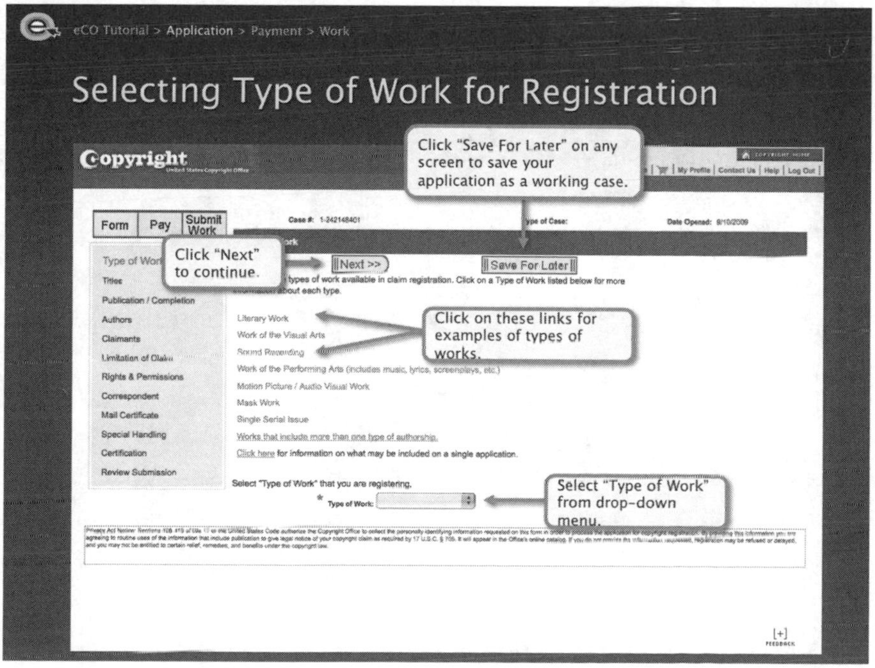
eCO Tutorial > Application > Payment > Work
Selecting Type of Work for Registration
Copyright
Click "Save For Later" on any screen to save your application as a working case.
Form
Pay
Submit Work
Click "Next" to continue.
Next >>
Save For Later
Click on these links for examples of types of works.
Literary Work
Work of the Visual Arts
Sound Recording
Work of the Performing Arts (includes music, lyrics, screenplays, etc.)
Motion Picture / Audio Visual Work
Mask Work
Single Serial Issue
Select "Type of Work" from drop-down menu.

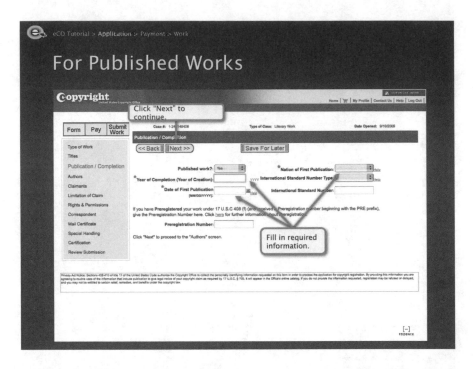

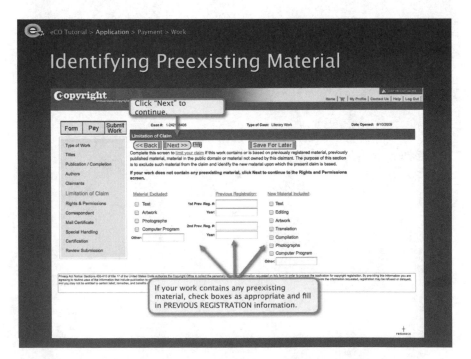

Why is there an urgent need for special handling? Examples of an urgent need include: upcoming litigation, a pending customs matter, a looming contractual or a publishing deadline.

If you're requesting the rapid action in order to go forward with litigation: (a) Is the litigation actual (the suit will definitely be filed) or prospective (the suit may be filed)?; (b) Are you the plaintiff (the person claiming infringement) or defendant (the person accused of infringement) in the action?; (c) What are the names of the parties, and what is the name of the court where the action is pending or expected?

You must certify that the statements in the letter are correct to the best of your knowledge, and you must provide a mailing address and phone number for contact. The letter and the envelope should be addressed to Special Handling, Library of Congress, Dept. 100, Washington, DC 20540. Money orders or cashier's checks are recommended for the fee. A personal check will be accepted, but if the check bounces, the registration will be revoked. Expedited registrations can be sent by Federal Express or other overnight courier. It is wise to include a prepaid return envelope (for example, FedEx, Express Mail, and so on) for overnight mailing of the Certificate of Registration back to you.

Posting a Copyright Notice on Your Work

Because of the automatic copyright on creative works, you don't have to wait until your work is registered to place your copyright notice on your work. Although not required for works published after March 1, 1989, it's still advisable to place the familiar copyright notice (for example, Copyright © 2010 Art Jones) on each published copy of your crafts work. This tells anyone who sees the work that the copyright is being claimed, who is claiming it, and when the work was first published. This notice prevents an infringer from later claiming that the infringement was accidental, and may provide additional benefits when you seek damages from an infringer. You can place the notice on the back of a work provided that it's visible from that angle. For example, if you can take a painting off the wall and read the information on the back or if you can lift up a vase and find the notice on the bottom, it's okay.

Getting Permission to Use Someone Else's Work

So far, my discussion has focused on your copyrights—what you get by creating and, if you choose to, registering a work. In this section, I'll discuss what to do when you want to use someone else's copyrighted work in connection with your own—for example, you'd like to reproduce someone's photographs on your pillowcases.

The consequences of failing to get permission can be expensive. In 1980, photographer Art Rogers took a photograph of a friend's eight puppies. Seven years later, artist Jeff Koons, without Rogers' permission, used the photograph as the basis of a series of wood sculptures. Rogers sued over the unauthorized use of his photo, and Rogers later was awarded several hundred thousand dollars in damages along with an order prohibiting Koons from making or selling any more of the sculptures.

If Koons had asked Rogers for permission before starting the sculptures, Rogers could have refused, or he could have asked for a payment, perhaps a percentage based upon the revenue from the statues. In either case, Koons would have saved over a half million dollars in damages and attorney fees.

This isn't to say that if you use something without permission you will suffer the same result as Jeff Koons. The risk of a lawsuit depends not just upon your particular use, but upon other factors such as the likelihood that the use will be spotted, whether you are a "worthy" target for litigation, whether permission is really needed (see below), and whether the other side is inclined to sue.

But even if you don't get sued, there's always a potential risk when you fail to ask for permission to use someone else's work. You may not have to pay damages, but you may have to destroy inventory, molds, or accompanying promotional material. The more successful your crafts business becomes, the more likely that a copyright owner will learn of your use and take action.

What does it take to acquire permission? The first step is to determine whether you can use the work without asking for permission. Permission is not always necessary, because copyright law does not protect all materials. For example, works published before 1923 in the United States are in the public domain and free to use. However, a work is not in the public domain simply because it has been posted on the Internet (a popular fallacy) or because it doesn't sport a copyright notice (another fallacy).

The second step in getting permission is to identify the owner of the work you want to use. Often, you can locate the rights owner just by looking at the copyright notice on the work. Sometimes, more detailed research is required, for example, searching the records of the Copyright Office.

The third step in getting permission is to identify the rights you need. Identifying the rights can be as simple as stating your intended use—for example, you'd like to reproduce a photograph on postcards. Generally, you will need to consider three common rights variables:

- exclusivity
- term, and
- territory.

Most permission requests are nonexclusive, meaning that others can use the material in the same way as you. An exclusive permission agreement means you are the only person who has the right to use the work as described in the agreement.

The length of time for which the use is allowed is often referred to as the "term." If there is no established limitation on the use, you are allowed to use the material for as long as you want or until the copyright owner revokes the permission. Your rights under a permission agreement may be limited to a certain geographic region, referred to as the "territory."

Once you identify the owner and the rights needed, it's time to contact the owner and ask for permission. The primary issue that arises when seeking permission is whether payment is necessary. Sometimes the owner of the work will not require payment if the amount being used is quite small or if the owner is eager for exposure. Sometimes, an owner may agree to suspend payment until your crafts project becomes profitable, or the owner may condition payment on other factors.

Finally, you need to formalize the arrangement. Oral permission agreements are legally enforceable. Moreover, even if you have no explicit oral agreement, you may still have a right to use a work if permission can be implied from the way the parties have behaved.

> EXAMPLE: Lou, a jeweler, asks for permission to reproduce Tom's photo within ten pendants. Tom responds that he will grant permission for $100. After receiving the payment, Tom sends the photographs to Lou. A permission agreement may be implied from Tom's conduct.

That said, relying on an oral or implied agreement is sometimes a mistake. You and the rights owner may have misunderstood each other or remembered the terms of your agreement differently. For that reason, written agreements are preferable. These need not be formal or in legalese. A simple statement of permission signed by the person granting permission is usually suitable.

It's also possible for you to hire an artist or other creative person to create a work for you. If the creative person qualifies as your employee, you will automatically own all rights to the work created on your behalf, and no permission will be required. If the person creating the work is not an employee, he or she is an independent contractor, and your ownership of the contractor's work is not automatic.

To guarantee your ownership of an independent contractor's work, you should use either a work-made-for-hire agreement (see Chapter 4) or an assignment agreement (see below).

In summary, a conservative approach to using material created by others will best protect your crafts business. Unless you are certain that the material is in the public domain or that your use is legally excusable, I advise you to seek permission. If you are not sure, you'll have to either make your own risk analysis or obtain the advice of an attorney knowledgeable in copyright or media law.

As a general rule, it is wise to operate under the assumption that all materials are protected by copyright law unless conclusive information indicates otherwise.

TIP

You may need other permissions. Permission is sometimes needed to reproduce a trademark or to use a real person's image. A trademark is any word, symbol, or device that identifies and distinguishes a product or service. Permission is generally needed if your use is commercial and is likely to confuse consumers or to tarnish the trademark's reputation (see Chapter 8). Your use of an individual's image or name may require permission if you are implying a commercial connection between the individual and your product. For example, you will need permission to include a celebrity's image on a belt buckle or in an advertisement. A sample model release is included, below.

Fair Use: When It's "Fair" for You to Use Pieces of Others' Works

In the previous section I mentioned a case in which the artist Jeff Koons failed to get permission and had to pay hundreds of thousands of dollars in damages. Twenty years after that decision Koons was at it again. He used another photographer's work without permission; this time he reproduced fashion photos of a woman's legs in a collage entitled, "Niagara." The photographer sued and this time Koons prevailed in his lawsuit. The court ruled that permission was not needed because Koons' reproduction was a "fair use." The two important factors that the court mentioned were that Koons' use was "transformative"—Koons was using the image to make a point about American materialism—and his use did not harm the fashion photographer's potential market for the photo.

Under a legal doctrine known as "fair use," there are times when you have the right to discuss, criticize, or poke fun at copyrighted works without seeking permission from the copyright owner. In general, fair use permits you to copy small portions of a work for "transformative" purposes such as parody, scholarship, or commentary. For example, a political cartoonist can freely copy an image of a copyrighted character for purposes of making an editorial cartoon.

The difficulty of applying fair use is that the standard is often subjective. That is, you can't guarantee that your use is a fair use until a judge says so at the end of a lawsuit—and at that point you may be bankrupt from legal fees. On the flip side, the problem with suing people over their "unfair" use of your work is that you can't know in advance whether you'll win and thus whether the legal fees will be worth it. The upshot is this: Tread carefully in the realm of fair use.

The First Sale Doctrine: Your Right to Resell Works

The first sale doctrine permits the owner of a copy of a copyrighted work to resell, destroy, or lend this copy. You can utilize the first sale doctrine for your own benefit. For example, if you're a frame maker, you can purchase copyrighted posters and resell them in your custom-made frames. Similarly, if you are a cabinetmaker, you can apply copyrighted postcards to the outside of a bureau. But beware—as the story below demonstrates, the first sale rules are sometimes confusing

The Public Domain: Free Stuff

Permission is not needed to reproduce artwork that is in the public domain: that is, anything that was published in the United States before 1923, or any copyrighted work that was published before 1964 and whose copyright was not renewed (it's estimated that only about 11% of copyrights issued before 1964 were renewed).

Determining whether a work is in the public domain requires research. The Copyright Office does not maintain a list of public domain works. Private companies can perform searches and furnish public domain reports, but this gets expensive. If you're interested in pursuing public domain works, I'd recommend you review the only authoritative text on the subject, *The Public Domain: How to Find & Use Copyright-Free Writings, Music, Art & More,* by Stephen Fishman (Nolo).

To Frame or to Mount?

As with many areas of copyright law, there is some confusion as to the boundaries of the first sale doctrine. Two cases involving the framing of artwork seem to have arrived at different results. In one case, a company purchased a book of prints by the painter Patrick Nagel, cut out the individual images and mounted them in frames for resale. The Ninth Circuit Court of Appeals in California held that this practice was an infringement and was not permitted under the first sale doctrine. (*Mirage Editions, Inc. v. Albuquerque A.R.T. Co.*, 856 F.2d 1341 (1988); and see *Greenwich Workshop Inc. v. Timber Creations, Inc.*, 932 F. Supp. 1210 (C.D. Cal. 1996).)

In a different case, however, a company purchased note cards and mounted them on tiles. (*Lee v. Deck the Walls, Inc.*, 925 F. Supp. 576 (N.D. Ill. 1996); and see *C.M. Paula Co. v. Logan*, 355 F. Supp. 189 (D.C. Texas 1973).) A federal court in Illinois determined that this practice was not an infringement and was permitted under the first sale doctrine. Under these rulings, a person in California cannot mount individual images from an art book, while a person in Illinois can mount individual note cards.

Should it matter whether the object that is mounted is from an art book or from a note card? Perhaps: In the California case, the justices felt that removing individual images from a bound collection altered the works. In other words, Nagel's estate did not intend for the works to be separated from the collection. Therefore, this framed use was considered a derivative work. In the Illinois case, the judge did not believe that mounting an individual note card, already separate, created a derivative work, since the image was not altered or modified.

Using Copyright Assignments

Let's say you create a portrait of a client using puka shells. The client loves it and wants to own all rights to the work—including the right to reproduce the image. The client makes you an offer you can't refuse, and you sell the copyright. This permanent transfer of copyright ownership is known as an "assignment." You're still the author of the work, but you're not the owner.

A work-made-for-hire arrangement differs from an assignment, because the person paying for the work is considered the owner *and* author of the work. For example, when the Disney Company employs animators who create a cartoon as works made for hire, the Disney Company is the author and owner of the cartoon.

An assignment is a transaction in which a copyright is permanently transferred. In return for the transfer, the copyright owner might get a lump sum or a continuing payment known as a "royalty." An assignment differs from a license agreement (discussed in Chapter 9), because under the terms of a license, the artist retains the copyright and grants only a temporary, conditional right to use the work. An assignment may also provide a method by which the rights are assigned back to the artist in the event of a certain condition—for example, if the person who purchased the copyright (the "assignee") stops selling the work.

An assignment may not last for the full term of copyright protection. The heirs of the author may reclaim rights 35 years from the date of the assignment. For example, an artist who assigned rights to you in 2003 can reclaim the rights in 2038. Since many works do not have a useful economic life of more than 35 years, this recapture right is often not important.

An assignment must be in writing. Notarization is not required. If there are multiple owners of the copyright, for example, the work was created by two artists, the signatures of all owners must be obtained for the assignment. Assignments can be recorded with the Copyright Office. There is no legal requirement that an assignment be recorded, but doing so provides public notice of the transfer and may provide advantages in the event of a dispute over ownership or infringement.

Copyright Assignments

Below are two copyright assignments that can be used for any type of completed artwork. The Basic Copyright Assignment is intended for a simple purchase of artwork rights for a lump sum—for example, you want to buy the copyright in an existing photograph. The Artwork Assignment Agreement is intended for hiring an artist to create a work to which you wish to own all rights or, vice versa, if someone is hiring you. This differs from the Commission Agreement in Chapter 1 because, in that case, the artist makes a crafts work for a client but retains copyright.

Basic Copyright Assignment

In the first two blanks of the first paragraph, insert the artist's name and the title of the work. In the next blank space, either describe the work or enter "See Attachment A" and attach a copy of the work to the assignment. If you attach a copy, be sure to label it "Attachment A."

In the next paragraph, insert the amount of the payment and the name of the assignee. The artist (or artists) must sign the agreement.

> **FORM ON THE CD-ROM**
> You'll find the Basic Copyright Assignment on the CD-ROM at the back of this book.

Artwork Assignment Agreement

The Artwork Assignment Agreement provides for assignment of your crafts design, photography, or artwork. It can be used if you are commissioned to create a work (or have completed a commission) and you have agreed that you will not retain any rights in the copyright—in other words, the "Company" will acquire all rights under copyright such as display, publication, duplication, and the ability to make derivatives. The assignment includes optional provisions for payment of expenses and for dispute resolution.

Basic Copyright Assignment

I, _____ ("Artist"),

am owner of the work entitled _____ (the "Work")

and described as follows: _____

_____ .

In consideration of $_____ and other valuable consideration, paid by

_____ ("Assignee"), I

assign to Assignee and Assignee's heirs and assigns, all my right, title, and interest in

the copyright to the Work and all renewals and extensions of the copyright that may

be secured under the laws of the United States of America and any other countries, as

such may now or later be in effect. I agree to cooperate with Assignee and to execute

and deliver all papers as may be necessary to vest all rights to the Work.

Signature(s) of Artist(s):

_____

_____

_____

Artwork Assignment Agreement

This Artwork Assignment Agreement (the "Agreement") is made between _____

_____ ("Company"),

and _____   _____ "Artist").

Services. Artist agrees to perform the following services: _____

_____ and create the following artwork (the "Art") entitled:

_____ .

The Art shall be completed by the following date: _____ .

During the process, Artist shall keep the Company informed of work in progress and shall furnish test prints of the Art prior to completion.

Payment. Company agrees to pay Artist as follows:

$_____ for performance of the art services and acquisition of the rights provided below.

Rights. Artist assigns to the Company all copyright to the Art and agrees to cooperate in the preparation of any documents necessary to demonstrate this assignment of rights. Artist retains the right to display the work as part of Artist's portfolio and to reproduce the artwork in connection with the promotion of Artist's services.

Expenses. Company agrees to reimburse Artist for all reasonable production expenses including halftones, stats, photography, disks, illustrations, or related costs. These expenses shall be itemized on invoices, and in no event shall any expense exceed $50 without approval from the Company.

Credit. Credit for Artist shall be included on reproductions of the Art as follows: _____

_____ .

Artist Warranties. Artist is the owner of all rights to the Art and warrants that the Art does not infringe any intellectual property rights or violate any laws.

General Provisions

Entire Agreement. This is the entire agreement between the parties. It replaces and supersedes any and all oral agreements between the parties, as well as any prior writings. Modifications and amendments to this Agreement, including any exhibit or appendix hereto, shall be enforceable only if they are in writing and are signed by authorized representatives of both parties.

Successors and Assignees. This agreement binds and benefits the heirs, successors, and assignees of the parties.

Notices. Any notice or communication required or permitted to be given under this Agreement shall be sufficiently given when received by certified mail, or sent by facsimile transmission or overnight courier.

Governing Law. This Agreement will be governed by the laws of the State of _____ _____ .

Waiver. If one party waives any term or provision of this agreement at any time, that waiver will only be effective for the specific instance and specific purpose for which the waiver was given. If either party fails to exercise or delays exercising any of its rights or remedies under this agreement, that party retains the right to enforce that term or provision at a later time.

Severability. If a court finds any provision of this Agreement invalid or unenforceable, the remainder of this Agreement will be interpreted so as best to carry out the parties' intent.

Attachments and Exhibits. The parties agree and acknowledge that all attachments, exhibits, and schedules referred to in this Agreement are incorporated in this Agreement by reference.

No Agency. Nothing contained herein will be construed as creating any agency, partnership, joint venture, or other form of joint enterprise between the parties.

[*Optional*]

☐ **Attorney Fees and Expenses.** The prevailing party shall have the right to collect from the other party its reasonable costs and necessary disbursements and attorney fees incurred in enforcing this Agreement.

☐ **Jurisdiction.** The parties consent to the exclusive jurisdiction and venue of the federal and state courts located in _____ [*county*], _____ [*state*], in any action arising out of or relating to this Agreement. The parties waive any other venue to which either party might be entitled by domicile or otherwise.

☐ **Arbitration.** Any controversy or claim arising out of or relating to this Agreement shall be settled by arbitration in _____ [*county*], _____ [*state*], in accordance with the rules of the American Arbitration Association, and judgment upon the award rendered by the arbitrator(s) may be entered in any court having jurisdiction. The prevailing party shall have the right to collect from the other party its reasonable costs and attorney's fees incurred in enforcing this agreement.

Signatures

Each party represents and warrants that on this date they are duly authorized to bind their respective principals by their signatures below.

COMPANY	ARTIST(S)
Date	Date
Name of Business	
Authorized Signature	Signature
Printed Name and Title	Printed Name
Address	Address

The "Services" section should be used if the you have been hired to perform a specific job. If the artwork has already been completed and this provision is not needed, strike it or enter "N/A" for "not applicable."

The "Payment" section provides for one payment for services and assignment. If you plan to break this out as two payments, simply indicate that distinction and create a separate line for each type of payment.

Since you are assigning all rights in the work, the "Rights" section is as broad as possible, and you will not retain any rights to the artwork except for the limited right to display the work in connection with the marketing of your crafts business.

The "Expenses" section establishes that the company will reimburse you for reasonable out of pocket expenses, provided the company approves expenses that exceed $50.

The "Credit" section guarantees that your name or trademark will be included when the artwork is reproduced.

The "Warranty" section is an assurance that you own the rights being granted and a promise not to sue the company for legal claims such as copyright infringement. If you wish, you may include an arbitration or mediation section.

It's unusual that the artist would be a minor, but in that event, the artist and the artist's parent or guardian should sign a consent that states something to the effect of: "I am the parent or guardian of the minor named above. I have the legal right to consent to and do consent to the terms and conditions of this agreement."

 FORM ON THE CD-ROM

You'll find the Artwork Assignment Agreement on the CD-ROM at the back of this book.

What Rights Does the Customer Acquire When They Buy Your Work?

After buying your work, a customer acquires the limited right to display it at home (though not in a museum) and to lend it, rent it, and resell it (and in some cases, to destroy it—although certain fine art crafts works such as sculptures and limited edition prints and photographs are exempt from this rule; see my discussion about the Visual Artists Rights Act, below). The customer cannot make copies or otherwise reproduce it. You control all copyright in the work.

> **EXAMPLE:** Del purchases Eloise's handmade fabric. If Del wants to reproduce and sell the design as a computer screensaver, he must first get Eloise's permission.

Infringement of Copyright

An unauthorized reproduction, display, or derivative version of a copyrighted work constitutes an infringement, for example:
- making unauthorized copies of a jewelry design
- reproducing a fabric design without permission on paper products, or
- creating a sculpture based on a photograph.

Once you suspect infringement, you may file a lawsuit against the infringer for damages in a federal court, provided that the copyright has been registered with the U.S. Copyright Office. An expedited registration process is available for those who have not previously registered and need to get into court right away. The fact that the infringement began before the registration will diminish the rights and remedies available in court, unless the work was first published less than three months previously.

Whether or not your work will be found to have been infringed depends on three factors:

- **Is your work protected by copyright?** This is satisfied if the first work was independently created, shows enough creativity, and is fixed in a tangible medium.
- **Did the infringer copy the work?** In the absence of an admission that copying occurred, you need to show that:
  - **The infringer had access to your work.** One of the requirements of proving infringement is that the infringer had access to your work. Sometimes this can be proven by the fact that the similarity between the two works is so close that the infringer must have seen your work. For example, in a 1997 case, makers of Beanie Babies sued a company marketing a pig bean bag known as "Preston the Pig." Preston was nearly identical to the Beanie Baby known as "Squealor." Access was presumed. (*Ty Inc. v. GMA Accessories Inc.* 132 F.3d 1167 (7th Cir. 1997).)
  - **There is a substantial similarity between the two works.** The stronger the similarity, the greater the chance that a court will find infringement. Some courts use a three-step approach in deciding whether there's a substantial similarity between the two works (important for proving the second factor, above). First, they identify the aspects of the two works that are subject to copyright protection. That is, they first filter out the unprotectible aspects of a work such as those elements in the public domain. Then the court makes an objective comparison of these aspects to see how alike they are. If they are similar enough to warrant a suspicion of infringement, the courts then make a subjective determination as to whether the works are substantially similar enough to justify a finding of infringement.
- **Is there any reason to excuse the infringement?** Whether the lawsuit will be effective and whether damages will be awarded depends on whether the alleged infringer can raise one or more legal defenses to the charge. Common legal defenses to copyright infringement are:

- too much time has elapsed between the infringing act and the lawsuit (the statute of limitations defense)
- the infringement is allowed under the fair use defense
- the infringement was innocent (the infringer had no reason to know the work was protected by copyright)
- the infringing work was independently created (that is, it wasn't copied from the original), or
- the copyright owner authorized the use in a license.

In the event someone infringes your copyright, you can file a lawsuit in federal court asking the court to:

- issue orders (restraining orders and injunctions) to prevent further violations
- award money damages if appropriate, and
- in some circumstances, award attorney fees.

For advice on how to find an attorney to deal with the problem, read Chapter 11.

The Visual Artists Rights Act: Crafts Works and Fine Arts

Certain types of crafts works receive more rights than are normally granted under copyright law. The federal government has created a statute—the federal Visual Artists Rights Act (VARA)—that grants rights affecting reselling and destruction of artworks. Only some crafts works receive protection under VARA—paintings, drawings, prints, photographs, or sculptures in a single copy or limited edition of 200 copies or fewer (that are signed and consecutively numbered).

What happens if your wood sculpture is reproduced in a museum booklet or in a magazine review? Does that mass production remove the work from VARA status? No, you can still claim VARA rights as to the original.

When Crafts Become Fine Art: Preservation

The VARA statute protects you, as the creator of a work of visual art, from "intentional distortion, mutilation or other modification of that work which would be prejudicial to your honor or reputation." This is the most powerful right granted under the VARA provisions. For example, if a collector buys a limited edition silkscreen from you (fewer than 200 prints were made), the collector cannot destroy it without your permission. If the work is destroyed, you can sue under VARA and recover damages, provided you can prove that your reputation was damaged.

The rule regarding destruction does not apply if:

- the work was created prior to enactment of the VARA provisions on December 1, 1990
- you specifically waive the rights in a written statement, or
- the destruction or modification results from the passage of time or because of the materials used to construct the work. For example, certain works such as ice sculptures and sand sculptures by their nature self-destruct, and the owner would have no obligation to affirmatively prevent such destruction.

Length and Transferability of VARA Protection

Although copyright protection normally lasts for the life of the artist plus 70 years, the rights granted under VARA last only for the life of the artist. Once the artist dies, VARA protection no longer exists, and the work can be destroyed without seeking consent.

No VARA Rights If Work Is Made for Hire

Under certain circumstances, the person who employs an artist or commissions an artwork acquires copyright ownership. (This "work-made-for-hire" principle is discussed in Chapter 4.) If artwork is created as work made for hire, there are no VARA rights. That is, although normal copyright law applies to the work, neither the artist nor the person commissioning the work can claim rights under VARA.

Personal/Model Releases

In the event you are using a person's name and image in your work, you should probably get a personal release. (Note: Personal releases are often referred to as model releases, although the term "model" can be used for anyone, not just professional models.) There are two classes of personal releases: blanket releases and limited releases. The model release addresses certain rights that overlap with copyright—they are actually a separate area of law known as right of publicity—and I include them in this chapter because you may be taking photographs of people for, or using model images in, your copyrighted work.

A blanket release permits any use of the photographic image of the person signing the release and is suitable if the company or photographer needs an unlimited right to use the image. If you want all rights to the person's image for all purposes, use a blanket release. If the model is only consenting to a specific use—for example, in your crafts advertisement—then use a limited release that specifies the particular ways the image and name may be used. If a use exceeds what's permitted under the limited release, the person can sue for breach of the agreement. For example, a model who had signed a release limiting use of her image for a museum brochure sued when the photo appeared on a Miami transit card.

Get it in writing. Although oral releases are generally valid, you should always try to get a release in writing. This way, the model can't claim he or she never agreed to the release. In addition, the terms of an oral release can be hard to remember and even harder to prove in court if a dispute arises.

Make It Clear. When a release is sought for a specific purpose, do not hide or misrepresent facts to get the signature. A fraudulently obtained release is invalid. For example, a model was told that his image would be used by an insurance company and signed a blanket release based upon that statement. However, a viaticals company that pays cash for life insurance policies owned by AIDS victims used the photo. A Florida court permitted the model to sue.

Keep It Simple. Release agreements usually do not include many of the legal provisions found in other agreements in this book. Instead, releases are often "stripped down" in order to not trigger lengthy discussion or negotiation. So keep your release short and simple (see "Honey, I Shrunk the Release," below).

Honey, I Shrunk the Release

You may find it easier to obtain a signed release if you shrink the release information to the size of a 3x5 or 5x7 card. Photographers have found that photo subjects find the smaller documents less intimidating. Some photographers reduce the material to a font size that fits on the back of a business card. However, if you make the contract so tiny that it's difficult to read, a court will be less likely to enforce it.

Get it signed ASAP. It is sometimes difficult to track down a subject after a photo has been created. Also, there is less incentive for the subject to sign the release at a later date. Therefore, most photographers obtain releases prior to or directly after a photo session or when the model is paid.

Unlimited Personal Release Agreement

The Unlimited Personal Release Agreement is a blanket release agreement. It permits you to use the model's image and name in all forms of media throughout the world, forever. Explanations for the provisions are provided, below.

 FORM ON CD-ROM
You'll find the Unlimited Personal Release form on the CD-ROM at the back of this book.

Unlimited Personal Release Agreement

Grant. For consideration which I acknowledge, I irrevocably grant to _____
_____ _____ ("Company") and
Company's assigns, licensees, and successors the right to use my image and name in
all forms and media, including composite or modified representations, for all purposes,
including advertising, trade, or any commercial purpose throughout the world and
in perpetuity. I waive the right to inspect or approve versions of my image used for
publication or the written copy that may be used in connection with the images.

Release. I release Company and Company's assigns, licensees, and successors from
any claims that may arise regarding the use of my image, including any claims of
defamation, invasion of privacy or infringement of moral rights, rights of publicity, or
copyright. Company is permitted, although not obligated, to include my name as a
credit in connection with the image.

Company is not obligated to utilize any of the rights granted in this agreement.

I have read and understood this agreement, and I am over the age of 18. This
agreement expresses the complete understanding of the parties.

_____   _____
Signature   Witness Signature

_____   _____
Name

_____   _____
Address

_____
Date

[Include if the person is under 18]

Parent/Guardian Consent. I am the parent or guardian of the minor named above.
I have the legal right to consent to and do consent to the terms and conditions of this
model release.

_____   _____
Parent/Guardian Signature   Witness Signature

_____   _____
Parent/Guardian Name

_____   _____
Parent/Guardian Address

_____
Date

Limited Personal Release Agreement

The Limited Personal Release Agreement allows you to use the model's name or image only for the purposes specified in the agreement. An explanation is provided below.

 FORM ON CD-ROM
You'll find copies of the Limited Personal Release Agreement on the CD-ROM at the back of this book.

Completing the Personal Releases

The "Grant" paragraph establishes the rights granted by the person. In the unlimited agreement, a "blanket" grant is used. This grant is broad and intended to encompass all potential uses whether informational, commercial, or other.

In the limited agreement, the uses must be listed—for example, "for use on a postcard advertising the crafts business." This release also has limitations regarding territory and term. Insert the appropriate geographic region and term—for example, "North America with a two-year term."

A "Payment" section is included in the Limited version. If you would like to include this in the Unlimited version, copy and paste it.

A "Renewal" section is included in the Limited version. If you would like to include this in the Unlimited version, copy and paste it.

The "Release" is the person's promise not to sue the company for legal claims such as libel and invasion of privacy.

If the person is a minor, the parent or guardian should sign where it is marked Parent/Guardian Consent.

Since issues about release authenticity often crop up many years after a photo was made, a witness should sign the agreement to verify the person's signature or the signature of the parent. The witness should be an adult. An employee or assistant is suitable.

Limited Personal Release Agreement

Grant. For consideration which I acknowledge, I grant to _____

_____ ("Company") and Company's assigns, licensees, and successors,

the right to use my image for the following purposes:_____

_____in the following territory

_____ for a period of _____ year(s) (the "Term").

I grant the right to use my name and image for the purposes listed above in all forms
and media, including composite or modified representations, and waive the right to
inspect or approve versions of my image used for publication or the written copy that
may be used in connection with the images.

[*Select if appropriate*]

☐ **Payment.** For the rights granted during the Term, Company shall pay $ _____
upon execution of this release.

☐ **Renewal.** Company may renew this agreement under the same terms and conditions
for _____ year(s), provided that Licensee makes payment of $_____
at the time of renewal.

Release. I release Company and Company's assigns, licensees, and successors from
any claims that may arise regarding the use of my image, including any claims of
defamation, invasion of privacy or infringement of moral rights, rights of publicity, or
copyright. Company is permitted, although not obligated, to include my name as a
credit in connection with the image.

Company is not obligated to utilize any of the rights granted in this Agreement.

I have read and understood this agreement, and I am over the age of 18. This Agreement
expresses the complete understanding of the parties.

_____ _____
Signature   Witness Signature

_____
Name

_____
Address

_____
Date

[Include if the person is under 18]

Parent/Guardian Consent. I am the parent or guardian of the minor named above. I have the legal right to consent to and do consent to the terms and conditions of this model release.

_____	_____
Parent/Guardian Signature	Witness Signature
_____	_____
Parent/Guardian Name	
_____	_____
Parent/Guardian Address	
_____	_____
Date	

Protecting Appearances With Design Patents and Trade Dress

I n 1997, Alan Philipson and his son, Andre, patented a design for a decorative bead shaped like a woman's breasts. The Philipsons sold the patent to a New Orleans company, Superior Merchandise, and the design quickly became the best-selling bead in the company's line— especially popular during Mardi Gras, when celebrants on floats throw thousands of beads to parade watchers.

Superior later sued a competitor, M.G.I. Wholesale, that had begun selling a similar bead. In defense, M.G.I. argued that the U.S. Patent and Trademark Office (USPTO) made a mistake granting the design patent to the Philipsons. The human anatomy can't be appropriated by one designer, said M.G.I.'s attorneys, and anyway, the design was obvious. (This standard, known as nonobviousness, is discussed, below.)

The judge didn't buy M.G.I.'s argument. The Philipsons were not claiming rights in the human anatomy, said the judge, they were only claiming rights for their anatomical design on beads. There was no evidence of a previous bead with a similar design, and if it was obvious, the judge asked, why was M.G.I. copying the Philipsons' design? The judge upheld the patent and declared M.G.I. an infringer. (*Superior Merchandise v. M.G.I. Wholesale*, 52 U.S.P.Q.2d 1935 (E.D. La. 1999).)

Whether or not you believe that beads shaped like breasts are worth creating—or copying—this case graphically illustrates the power of a design patent. Of the four types of legal protection for crafts works— copyright, design patent, trade secret, and trademark—the design patent is probably the most potent. (It's been described as a "copyright with teeth.") Design patents have protected crafts artists for over a century. In one of the earliest reported cases, a jeweler in 1881 was awarded financial damages when a competitor copied his patented design featuring a bird on a twig with a diamond-studded leaf. (*Wood v. Dolby*, 7 F. 475 (1881).)

Comparing Design Patents and Copyright

Copyrights and design patents both do the same thing—protect your visual imagery—but they do it in different ways, and they sometimes do it for different subject matter. A design patent protects the visual appearance of a useful object—for example, the shape, proportion, and patterns that distinguish one doorknob from another. Copyright covers a broader palette and protects any original artistic expression—whether architecture, photography, music, writing, or dance. These two legal protections overlap when functional objects—for example, bronze bells, table tiles, clay pots, or candles—embody a distinctive or pleasing visual appearance.

The good news is that you don't have to choose one protection over the other. If your work qualifies for both copyright and design patent protection, you can—if it's worth the effort—claim both simultaneously. For example, the designers of the quilt design in Figure 7-1 or the puppet in Figure 7-2 have obtained both types of protection. The table below highlights the similarities and differences between the two forms of legal protection.

Figure 7-1: Quilt Design

Figure 7-2: Frankenstein Puppet

Copyright vs. Design Patent		
	Copyright	**Design Patent**
What types of crafts are hardest to protect?	**Minimal works are harder to protect than ornate ones.** The less ornate the design for your crafts work, the harder it is to obtain copyright protection. That's because the design must be conceptually separable from the object. For example, the glass in Figure 7-26 could probably acquire copyright protection; the glass in Figure 7-11 would have a very hard time. (Both designs acquired protection under design patent law.)	**Less "useful" crafts are harder to protect.** Design patents protect ornamentation on useful articles—and the USPTO has a limited view of what's "useful." For example, paintings, silk screens, sculpture, books, photographs, or two-dimensional surface ornamentation that is separable from the object (such as decals) are not "useful articles." In other words, any craft that is "art for art's sake" cannot get a design patent. (All of these examples could be protected under copyright law.)

Copyright vs. Design Patent (continued)		
	Copyright	**Design Patent**
What's the cost?	**Copyright protection is free.** However, if you choose to fortify your protection and register (recommended), the application fee is $35 to $45.	Total costs, including the application fee, will come to $700 to $3,000 depending on whether you use an attorney.
How long does it take to obtain?	**It's automatic.** You get copyright once you create the work. If you choose to register, the process can take up to 12 months.	**One to two years.** You have to register to obtain a design patent, and the examination process can take up to 24 months.
How long does it last?	Life of the artist plus 70 years.	14 years from the date the patent is issued.
How effective is it for stopping infringers?	**Copyright infringement is the harder to prove.** It's not enough that two works are substantially similar; you have to prove that the infringer had access to your work and copied it. The infringer can claim certain defenses—for example, the fair use doctrine, which allows limited copying for purposes of commentary.	**Design patent infringement is the easier to prove.** Design patent infringement is easier to prove than copyright infringement; you only have to prove the works are substantially similar. You don't have to prove that the infringer saw and copied your work.
Which should you choose?	**Copyright chooses you.** If your work qualifies for copyright, you obtain copyright protection automatically. To determine if your work qualifies, review Chapter 6. You can fortify your rights by registering with the U.S. Copyright Office.	**Choose design patent if:** (1) you don't qualify for copyright protection and you are concerned that someone will copy your work and deprive you of significant sales, or (2) you qualify for copyright but believe that the work will be one of your leading sellers and at high risk for copying.

The combined use of copyright and design patent protection is most effective in crafts works where the design can exist in another medium—for example, the design on a quilt could also be transferred to paper or fabric. A toy or a puppet may lend itself to animation or reproduction on merchandise. In that case, design patent law can effectively halt the copying of the craft, and copyright law can stop its being copied in other mediums.

> **EXAMPLE:** Consider the Frankenstein-style puppet in Figure 7-2. Imagine that, without permission of the designers, a movie studio creates an animated series based upon the puppet. The studio also sells copycat puppets, as well as merchandise containing the puppet's image. Under patent and copyright law, the designers can stop the movie studio from making, selling, or using substantially similar puppets. Under copyright law, they can stop the studio from making the animated series and related merchandise.

Design Patents: The Bottom Line

Although design patents offer broad legal rights, they haven't been widely accepted among crafts designers because of the time, expense, and legal hurdles involved in the registration process. The application, drawings, and filing fees can cost thousands of dollars depending on whether you use a patent attorney. In addition, your design must be new and not obvious to others in the crafts field. Finally, you must file your application within one year of any publication or offer for sale. Most importantly, your design patent is limited to the specific design. For example, if you obtain a design patent for an eagle-shaped belt buckle, you cannot stop others from creating original eagle-shaped belt buckles. You can only stop those that are substantially similar.

A design patent may be worth the effort and expense if you have a new design that is a likely to be a perennial seller and likely to be copied by competitors. Keep in mind that like a copyright, a design patent is a weapon, not a shield; in order to use it, you must sue or threaten to sue anyone who trespasses on your rights. You can do two things with a design patent:

- **Stop others who create substantially similar designs.** For 14 years from the date your design patent is granted, you can stop anyone from making, using, or selling your design or a substantially similar design on similar crafts goods. In order to stop an infringer, you must file a lawsuit in federal court. You'll have to show the court that an ordinary observer would be deceived into thinking that your item and the infringing item are the same. For example, the court in the ornamental bead case found that the beads were substantially similar even though they were not identical. Superior Merchandise sold a single flat-backed bead; its competitor sold a back-to-back (and anatomically impossible) bead. A design patent is interpreted through patent drawings that you file as part of your design patent application. These drawings define your rights and show the USPTO how the world will see your unique design. The design patent only protects what is disclosed in the drawings, so if you later change the design substantially, you can't protect it unless you apply for a new patent.

- **License, sell, or otherwise exploit your design.** Besides chasing infringers, you can earn money by exploiting your design—for example, another company might pay you to license your design for a salt and pepper shaker. In this case, you would retain the patent and the company would acquire a limited right to use the design and would pay out periodic royalties. You can also sell all rights ("assign") to the patent to a company in return for a lump sum or royalties.

How to Get a Design Patent

As you'll see from the illustrations in this chapter, design patent law protects a wide variety of crafts designs—virtually any new ornamentation that's intended for a useful object such as a table, hat, ring, belt buckle, and so on. You are eligible for a design patent if your design is new and isn't obvious to those in your crafts field. (An example of an obvious design would be a birdhouse in the shape of a standard, A-frame house.) You must file your application within a year of its publication or first offer for sale. If your application is approved by the USPTO, you'll become the proud owner of a design patent. These standards are explained in more detail, below.

If you don't want to do it all yourself, you'll have to pay between $1,500 to $5,000 for:

- an attorney to draft the design patent application
- a patent drafts person to create the drawings, and
- the fees for crafts artists operating a small business (as of 2010, a $110 filing fee, a $50 design search fee, a $70 design examination fee, and a $430 design issue fee.)

It is possible to save money and prepare and file your own design patent. Unless you pay for expedited (speedy) processing of your application, a design patent takes 12 to 24 months to obtain, and you cannot use it to stop others from copying until the patent has been granted. Design patents automatically expire 14 years after they're issued and cannot be renewed.

As the creator of the design patent, you will have the right to apply for the patent. The only exceptions are if you signed away your rights to someone else or you were employed to create the design. (For historical reasons, the USPTO often refers to the designer as the inventor, and refers to the design as the invention.)

If someone contributed to a new, nonobvious element of your design, they would be a coinventor, and you should reach an agreement as to your ownership of the patent. If you're employed to create designs, your employer may own rights in any potential design patents. Ownership depends on the contents of your employment agreement, employment manual policies, whether you used your employer's time and resources to create the design, and state laws regarding employee ownership rights. For more on employer ownership of rights, see Chapter 4.

What Qualifies for a Design Patent

In order to qualify for a design patent, you must create a new, original, ornamental, and nonobvious design. In addition, the design cannot have been published, sold, or offered for sale more than one year before filing your application. Below is a summary of these elements.

What Makes a Design Ornamental

A design patent is granted for the way something looks, not the way it works. As one judge stated, the design must be created for the purpose of "ornamenting" a functional object. Consider the design patent granted for the oval jewelry box in Figure 7-3. The patent only protects the appearance—the shape and proportions—of the box, not the way in which the box functions. The same is true for the jewelry box in Figure 7-4, the clock design in Figure 7-5, the glass-top coffee table in Figure 7-6, the combined high chair and rocking horse in Figure 7-7, and the candle in Figure 7-8. The designers acquire rights to prevent others from copying the form of these objects, not their function.

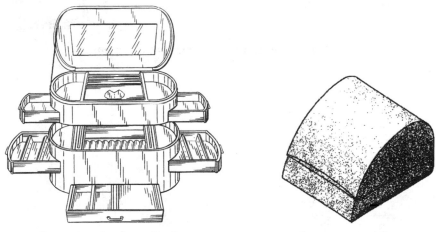

Figure 7-3: Oval Jewelry Box   Figure 7-4: Jewelry Box

Some crafts artists may find the term "ornamentation" puzzling, since it normally applies to superficial imagery. Under patent law, however,

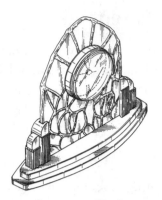

Figure 7-5: Clock

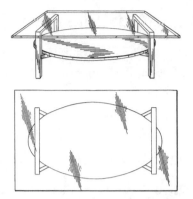

Figure 7-6: Glass-Top Coffee Table

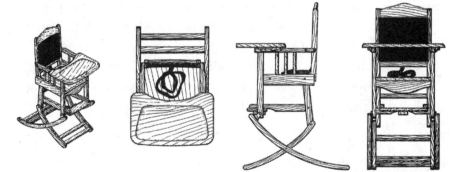

Figure 7-7: Combined High Chair and Rocking Horse

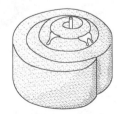

Figure 7-8: Candle

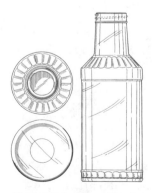

Figure 7-9: Glass Bottle

the meaning is broader. Ornamentation refers to the inseparable visual appearance of the functional object—for example, the shape and patterns of the glass bottle in Figure 7-9 or the patterns, inlay, and overall appearance of the double dresser with mirror in Figure 7-10.

Figure 7-10: Double Dresser With Mirror

This inseparable design has to create a unique appearance. Unlike copyright law, minimalism is not frowned upon. For example, the bowl with handles in Figure 7-11 and the glass in Figure 7-12 are minimal designs that were both granted design patents.

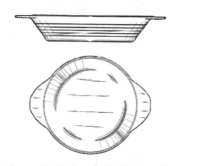

Figure 7-11: Bowl With Handles

Figure 7-12: Glass

If a design is purely functional, it won't be considered ornamental (and a design patent won't be granted). Generally, if there are several ways to achieve the same function with different designs, the USPTO will find the design to be ornamental.

> **EXAMPLE:** Apparently, there is no shortage of design ideas when it comes to creating shower caddies. There's the nautical approach (Figure 7-13), the feline angle (Figure 7-14), the fan style (Figure 7-15), the basic wire design (Figure 7-16), a variation on the basic design (Figure 7-17), the metal basket (Figure 7-18) the jazzy wire fashion (Figure 7-19), full frontal (Figure 7-20), industrial (Figure 7-21), and tubular (Figure 7-22). (And these are only a fraction of the design patents for shower caddies.) The wide variety of designs demonstrates that the function of these devices—to hold shower supplies such as soap and shampoo—is not limited by any one specific form.

Figure 7-13: Nautical Shower Caddy

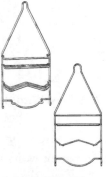

Figure 7-14: Kitty Shower Caddy

Figure 7-15: Fan Shower Caddy

Figure 7-16: Basic Wire Shower Caddy

Figure 7-17: Variation on Basic Shower Caddy

Figure 7-18: Metal Basket Shower Caddy

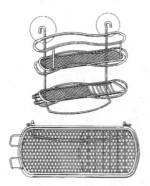

Figure 7-19: Jazzy Wire Shower Caddy

Figure 7-20: Full Frontal Shower Caddy

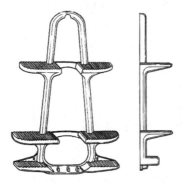

Figure 7-21: Industrial Shower Caddy

Figure 7-22: Tubular Shower Caddy

To be ornamental, the design should be visible during normal intended use or at some other commercially important time—for example, if the design is visible at the time of sale or in an advertisement.

EXAMPLE: The design of a waterbed mattress is not visible during normal use (see Figure 7-23), because it's hidden under the sheets and blankets. However, the unusual design is visible in advertisements and at the time of purchase. It's eligible for a design patent. (*Larson v. Classic Corp.*, 683 F.Supp. 1202 (N.D. Ill. 1988).)

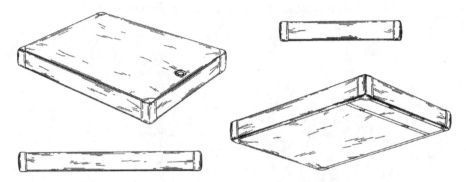

Figure 7-23: Waterbed Mattress

TIP

What's a useful article? Design patents only protect useful articles. Paintings, silk screens, sculpture, books, photographs, or two-dimensional surface ornamentation that is separable from the object (such as decals) are not considered "useful articles." These types of designs are more likely to be protected under copyright law.

What Makes a Design New and Original

In order to be new, your design must differ in some way from all previous designs. The USPTO refers to existing designs as prior art. Prior art consists of previously issued patents and other published materials. If your design differs visually in some way from the prior art, you have made it over this hurdle.

> **EXAMPLE:** Walter E. Durling obtained a design patent for a sectional sofa with a corner table and end tables (see Figure 7-24). A competitor with a similar design claimed that Durling was not entitled to a design patent because prior art existed—a sectional manufactured by another company—and therefore that the patent should be declared invalid. The federal court of appeals disagreed. The court acknowledged that the prior art "had the same basic design concept," but said that the two designs created different visual impressions. Therefore, Durling's design was new, original, and patent-worthy. *Durling v. Spectrum Furniture Co. Inc.* (Fed. Cir. 1996).

**Figure 7-24: Durling Design Sectional Sofa
With a Corner Table and End Tables**

One way of finding out whether someone else had your great design idea first is to conduct a search for prior art using the Internet. An Internet search has its limitations, though. It is not considered to be as thorough as searching at the USPTO, where you (or a professional searcher that you hire) can unearth all of the existing design patents in your classification (for example, tables, candle holders, and so on).

Considering the costs of a professional search at the USPTO, I would say that a basic Internet search combined with your own knowledge of the field is probably sufficient and cost-effective. That's because the cost of a search conducted by a patent professional will exceed, by several hundred dollars, the cost of your design patent application.

The downside is that if the USPTO uncovers prior art that you have not uncovered, the USPTO will reject your application. In that case, however, you will be out approximately $250 in government fees.

In addition to being new, your design must be original. USPTO guidelines state: "Clearly a design that simulates a well-known or naturally occurring object or person is not original as required by the statute. Furthermore, subject matter that could be considered offensive to any race, religion, sex, ethnic group, or nationality is not proper subject matter for a design patent application." (35 U.S.C. § 171 and 37 CFR § 1.3.)

These guidelines may seem at odds with the bead case discussed at the beginning of this chapter. In that case, a common anatomical shape was used, and it may have been offensive to members of the female sex and to members of some religious groups. Keep in mind that the standard for originality is often interpreted quite loosely and on a case-by-case basis. Although the USPTO and courts have, in the past, invalidated design patents that resembled human babies (*In re Smith*, 77 F.2d 514 (CCPA 1935)), it is rare that originality is a stumbling block to obtaining a design patent.

What Is Prior Art?

Prior art includes:
- any design used on a functional object in public use or on sale in the U.S. for more than one year before the filing date of the design patent application
- anything that was publicly known or used by others in this country before the date the design was created
- anything that was made or built in this country by another person before the date your design was created
- any work that was the subject of a prior design patent, issued more than one year before the filing date of your design patent or any time before the date you created the design, or
- any work whose publication occurred more than one year before the filing date of your design patent or any time before the date you created the design.

Searching for Prior Art

To search for prior art patents using the Internet, or to view images and text for the design patents mentioned in this article, I recommend two free patent search sites:

- the USPTO website (www.uspto.gov), and
- the Google patents website (www.google.com/patents).

Of the two, I prefer Google patents as it easier to use and in some ways, more comprehensive. On the Google Patents Home Page, choose Advanced Search and under Patent Type, make sure you choose "Design D." That will guarantee that your results only uncover design patents. To see images of any patent in your results, click "Read this patent." You can also download a PDF.

What Makes a Design Nonobvious

In order to qualify for a design patent, your design must not be considered obvious by others in your crafts field. The concept of non-obviousness was summed up by Albert Szent-Gyorgy as the ability "to see what everybody has seen and think what nobody has thought." Nonobviousness does not require great originality or craftsmanship; it only requires the ability to visualize things a little differently. For example, you can demonstrate nonobviousness by:

- the use of a familiar form in an unfamiliar medium—such as the use of a floral pattern as a candle holder (Figure 7-25)

Figure 7-25: Floral Pattern Candle Holder

- a slight change that produces a striking visual effect—such as alternating the position of hearts on a wedding ring (Figure 7-26)

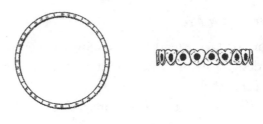

Figure 7-26: Wedding Ring

- the omission of a visual element commonly associated with similar designs—such as the waterbed design in Figure 7-23, which is distinguishable by the absence of visible seams on the top and sides of the mattress, or
- a juxtaposition of elements that creates an unexpected visual statement—such as embedding a poker chip in the bottom of a shot glass (Figure 7-27).

Figure 7-27: Shot Glass With Poker Chip

Indicators that help prove your design meets the "nonobvious" test include:

- it has enjoyed commercial success
- it has a visual appearance that's unexpected
- others have copied the design
- the design has been praised by others in the field
- others have tried but failed to achieve the same result, or
- you created a design that others said could not be done.

It is possible for a design to be novel but to be obvious as well. For example, a court determined that a design for an alcohol server that was shaped like an intravenous dispenser ("Combined Stand and Container for Storing Liquids" in Figure 7-28) was novel—no such design had been used for serving alcohol—but it was obvious and therefore not patentable. (*Neo-Art, Inc. v. Hawkeye Distilled Products Co.,* 654 F.Supp. 90 (C.D. Cal. 1987), aff'd 12 U.S.P.Q. 1572 (CAFC 1989).)

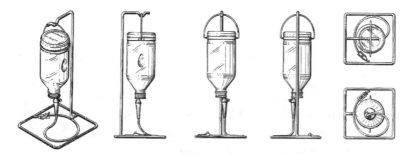

Figure 7-28: Combined Stand and Container for Storing Liquids

The difference between novelty and nonobviousness is that novelty is analyzed by asking whether someone has previously made a similar design, while nonobviousness is analyzed by asking whether your peers would have previously considered making the design. In practical terms, though, the two standards often overlap. For this reason, the lack of any prior art becomes important in demonstrating both nonobviousness and novelty.

Preparing a Design Patent Application

Patent attorneys and patent agents—professionals who have been licensed to practice before the USPTO—can analyze your design and properly advise you on whether pursuing a design patent is worthwhile. If so, the attorney or agent can prepare the application. If there is a problem at the USPTO—for example, an examiner challenges your application—the attorney or agent can respond and keep the application on track.

That said, if you're a self-starter with a do-it-yourself mindset, you can, with a bit of work, prepare your own design patent application and save approximately a few thousand dollars in fees.

Below, I present basic instructions for preparing a design patent application for filing by mail and electronically. Providing extensive details for this application is beyond the scope of this book. If you would like more information, read David Pressman's *Patent It Yourself* (Nolo), or read and download the design patent information provided at the USPTO website (www.uspto.gov).

Beware the One-Year Deadline

You cannot get a design patent if you wait more than a year after the design was publicly available to file your patent application. Another way to put this is that after one year following a sale, offer for sale, public or commercial use, or public knowledge about your design, that design will no longer be considered novel by the USPTO. If the USPTO is unaware of the public sale or use and issues a design patent, the patent will be declared invalid if it can later be shown that the design was publicly shown or sold. Therefore, the clock starts ticking once you post your design on your website, show your design at a crafts show, or print postcards with the design.

If you miss the one-year cutoff date, you can no longer seek patent protection for your design. However, you may still be able to protect it under other legal principles such as copyright or perhaps trade dress laws.

Filing by Mail

If you're filing with a paper application (and mailing the application by Express Mail), you'll need the following:

- The "specification"—a short written document
- drawing(s) showing the appearance of your design
- the Design Patent Application Transmittal—a cover sheet that accompanies your application
- the Declaration—an oath provided by the designer
- the Fee Application Transmittal Form, and
- a check for the filing fee ($110).

Mail Stop Box Design
Commissioner for Patents
P.O. Box 145
Alexandria, VA 22313-1450

PREAMBLE:

The petitioner(s) request that Letters Patent be granted to petitioners for the new and original design set forth in the following specification.

SPECIFICATION

Petitioners have invented a new, original, and ornamental design entitled "PIN" of which the following is a specification. Reference is made to the accompanying drawings, which are a part of the specification, the Figures of which are described as follows:

CROSS REFERENCES TO RELATED APPLICATIONS: None

STATEMENT REGARDING FED SPONSORED R & D: None

DESCRIPTION OF THE FIGURE(S) OF THE DRAWINGS:

Fig. 1 is a front view of my new PIN

Fig. 2 is a rear view of the PIN

FEATURE DESCRIPTION: My PIN is characterized by a rectangular sheet of metal loosely framed by wire wrapping.

CLAIM: I Claim: The ornamental design for PIN as shown and described.

Express Mail Label #

Date of Deposit _____

Figure 7-29: Specification for Pin Design

Specification

The specification is quite simple to prepare. I've provided a sample one for a pin design created by my sister (see Figure 7-29).

The elements of the specification are fairly straightforward. Here's a quick breakdown of how to approach them:

Preamble—one or two boilerplate sentences announcing that you're seeking a design patent.

Specification—the place to introduce your design by name. A basic title such as "glass bowl," "puppet," or "steel table" will work best.

Cross References to Related Applications—here, you indicate if you have filed a previous design patent application to which this one is related.

Statement Regarding Federally Sponsored R & D—indicate here if the design was prepared under a government grant or as part of government research.

Description of the Figure(s) of the Drawings—describe the view presented in each of your drawing sheets.

Feature Description—provide a short description of your design, for example, "My candle is characterized by a pinwheel effect that gradually slopes outward."

Drawings

As you can see from the drawings in this chapter, design patent drawings are technical and stylized. Each element—for example, the stippling (use of dots), the linear shading (use of lines), and the distinctive patterns (for indicating colors)—has a special meaning. You are allowed to provide informal drawings with your application, such as rough sketches or photographs, but your application will not be examined until you provide formal drawings similar to those shown in this chapter. For that reason, and to avoid delays, I recommend that you provide formal drawings. (The only reason to furnish informal drawings is that you are in a hurry to obtain an early filing date but you haven't had time to draft the drawings.)

Sheet 1 of 1

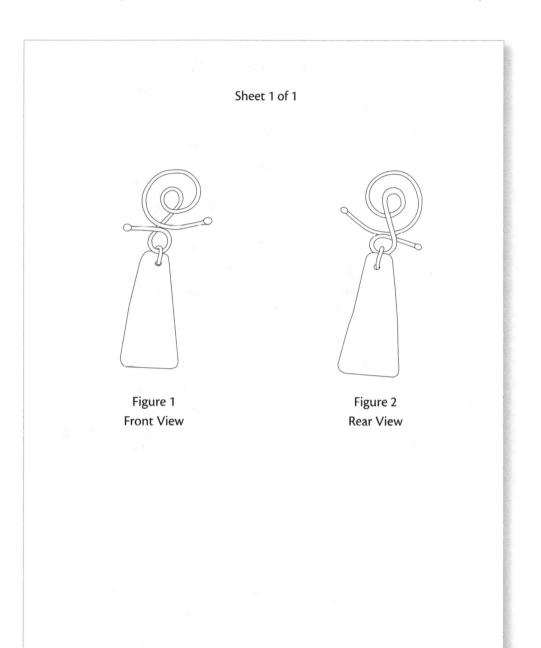

Figure 1
Front View

Figure 2
Rear View

Figure 7-29a: Drawing Sheet for Specification for Pin Design

With a little drawing skill or computer graphics knowledge, you can prepare formal drawings for your design patent application. In their book *How to Make Patent Drawings* (Nolo), David Pressman and Jack Lo explain how to prepare these drawings using computer software or pen and ink. One chapter is devoted solely to design patent drawing rules. If you prefer to have a professional draft your drawings, you can accomplish this relatively inexpensively (around $100 per drawing sheet; a sheet may contain one or two figures). You can probably find a suitable patent drafts person by typing "patent drawing" in your Internet search engine.

Designs are commonly depicted in different views or figures—for example, top views, side views, or disassembled views. You should present as many views as are necessary to demonstrate your design. Each view provides another way of "seeing" the design. Each view is given a discrete figure number (abbreviated as "Fig" in patent law).

The Design Patent Application Transmittal

You must submit a cover sheet with your design patent application. The USPTO has prepared one that I recommend you use. A sample is shown below. To obtain this form, go to the USPTO home page (www.uspto. gov) and click "Patents" on the left side of the screen. Click "Forms," then scroll down until you find Form PTO/SB/18. You must have a copy of Adobe Acrobat on your computer to download this PDF form. Save the form to your computer. That way, you can use it again without connecting to the Internet.

The cover sheet is a "fillable" PDF form, which means that if you have a current version of Adobe Acrobat, you can enter (but not save) information onto the form. If you don't have the technology to fill in the form on your computer, print out a copy of the form and fill in the blanks using a typewriter or pen.

First Named Inventor. At the top of the form, there's a box for supplying the First Named Inventor. Fill in the name of one of the designers.

Title. In this section, provide your design title as indicated in your specification.

Express Mail Label Number. Copy this number from the Express Mail label (the bottom page). You don't have to use U.S. Express Mail. If you wish, or if you're not in the United States, you can mail your design patent application by regular mail or by an overnight express service such as Federal Express. However, any document that you send by Express Mail that includes the Express Mail Number on the cover letter will be considered received on the day you mail it. (37 C.F.R. § 1.10.)

Application Elements. Check the "Fee Transmittal Form" box and check "Applicant claims small entity status." (You have small entity status if you are an independent designer, or if the company that owns the design is a nonprofit, or a for-profit company with 500 or fewer employees.) Check the "Specification" box and indicate how many pages you're sending in the box to the right. Check the "Drawings" box and indicate the number of drawing sheets in the box to the right.

Oath or Declaration. Check the "Newly executed" box. You will include a separate declaration.

Application Data Sheet. Do not check this box. (An Application Data Sheet is a voluntary submission that includes additional information about you and your design—there's no need to bother with it.)

Accompanying Application Parts. With the exception of the "Return Receipt Postcard," these choices will probably be inapplicable to you.

Correspondence Address. Provide an address where the USPTO can send correspondence regarding your design. If you have a USPTO Customer Number (many law firms and corporations do), mark the box and provide the number, or use a bar code sticker. Otherwise, mark the box "Correspondence address below" and write the name of the individual or company that should receive mail from the USPTO. If you fail to include something in your package, the PTO's Office of Preliminary Examination will send you a letter telling you what to do and what fees you will be charged for the error. Supply what is needed, following the instructions in the letter.

Declaration

The declaration, Form SB/01, is a two-page form that can be downloaded from the USPTO website. Check the box "Declaration Submitted with Initial Filing" and provide the title of your design. On page 2, list the designers and their addresses. Sign the declaration where it is marked "Inventor's Signature."

Fee Transmittal

The Fee Transmittal, Form SB/17, is a one-page form that can be downloaded from the USPTO website. Indicate your method of payment. Your choices are:

Check or Money Order. If you pay by check or money order, mark this box and include a check payable to Commissioner for Patents.

Deposit Account Number. Disregard this box unless you maintain a deposit account at the USPTO.

Payment by Credit Card. If you want to pay by credit card, check this box and download and complete an additional form (Form 2038: Credit Card Payment Form and Instructions). You cannot fill out Form 2038 on your computer; you'll need to print it and complete it by hand or typewriter. In the box titled "Description of Request and Payment Information" (in the section called Request and Payment Information), write Design Patent Application Fee. Leave the rest of this section blank. The remainder of Form 2038 is easy to complete—instructions are provided when you download the form.

In the box marked "Fee Calculation," write the fee in the box next to "Design filing fee." At the bottom of the form, provide your name, your telephone number, and the date. Sign the form on the indicated line.

It's important to include a return postcard with your application (and every document that you send to the USPTO). Once you get it back, tape it into your file. The postcard will be a permanent record that your application was received. (Your U.S. Express Mail tracking information and cancelled check also provide useful evidence of receipt—tape these into your file as well.)

Write your mailing address on the front of the postcard. On the back, write: "Design patent application of [*your name or names*] for [*title of design*] consisting of [*number of*] pages of specification, [*number of*] drawing sheets and filing fee of $ _____ received today: [*date*]."

Mailing

Assemble your completed cover sheet, specification, drawing sheets, return postcard, and check or Form 2038 if paying by credit card. Address your package to:

> Box Design
> Commissioner for Patents
> Washington, DC 20231

Enclose your materials and take the Express Mail to the Post Office. Don't deposit the envelope in a regular or even an Express Mail mailbox, since you won't immediately receive the Express Mail receipt. Instead, take the Express Mail directly to the Post Office and ask the clerk to date-stamp the sender's copy of the Express Mail receipt with her rubber stamp.

Filing Electronically

If you're filing electronically (using the EFS-Web system at the USPTO website), you'll need the following:

- an electronic file (in Adobe PDF format) of your specification (prepare it as described above),
- an electronic file (in Adobe PDF format) of your drawings (prepare it as described above), and
- a credit card for making the payment of your filing fee.

Start at the USPTO website (www.uspto.gov), click Patents, then "File Online in EFS-Web." Click, "EFS-Web Unregistered Filers," then sign on as an unregistered e-Filer. Choose "New Application," "Design," and then "Nonprovisional Application under 35 USC." (If you want to pay the extra fees for an accelerated examination, choose "Accelerated Exam," instead.)

Next provide the name of your design, the name of the inventor/ designers, and correspondence information. Next, choose Application Parts (on the "View All Categories" drop down) and choose Specification, and upload the PDF you prepared of your specification. Next choose Drawings and upload your drawings. Review the uploads and complete the fee calculations (choose the filing fee of $220) on the next page. Finally submit the application and make payment for the filing fee with your credit card.

If Problems Arise With Your Application

In a perfect world, your design application will sail through the examination process and you will, within 18 to 24 months, receive a notice that it's been approved. However, things don't always go this smoothly. An examiner may object to your application due to technical or substantive errors. It's beyond the scope of this book to advise you how to respond to examiner notices. If you run into a problem and want to handle it on your own, I would suggest reading David Pressman's *Patent It Yourself* (Nolo). Although the book primarily deals with utility patents, it provides a lot of helpful information on design patents and offers a thorough explanation of the USPTO examination process— including suggestions on responding to examiner objections.

Marking the Design Patent Number

Once you acquire a design patent, it's essential that you mark your crafts work with your design patent number. (You'll receive this number when the USPTO grants your patent.) Any placement is suitable, provided that the number can be located by an ordinary user. For example you can place the number on the back of an earring.

Failure to include the notice could cost you money if you later sue an infringer—even if you win. For example, in a case in which the Nike shoe company sued Wal-Mart, a court ruled that Nike could not collect a portion of Wal-Mart's profits or collect statutory damages (damages fixed by law) if it was proven that Nike had failed to mark the design patent number on one of its shoe designs. (*Nike Inc. v. Wal-Mart Stores*, 138 F.3d 1437 (E.D. Va. 1998).)

Are There Other Types of Protection?

In unusual cases, crafts works may qualify for protection other than copyrights or design patents. Below is a summary of additional types of legal protection.

Utility patents. Utility patents protect the way something works—for example, a novel clasp you created for a necklace or a unique mounting system to display glassware. Utility patents are granted for machines, processes, devices, or other useful objects. They are fairly expensive ($5,000 to $10,000) and last for approximately 17-18 years. For more information, visit the Nolo website (www.nolo.com) and click on "Patents and Trade Secrets," or visit the USPTO website (www.uspto. gov).

Trade secrets. A trade secret is any confidential information with economic value that gives a business an advantage over its competitors—for example, a method or process for affixing color to glass. Trade secrets are protected under state and federal laws and through the use of nondisclosure agreements. For more information on trade secrets, read Chapter 4.

Trademarks. A trademark is any word, symbol, design, device, logo, or slogan that identifies and distinguishes one product or service from another, like the unique name you use to identify your craft products. For more information on trademarks, read Chapter 8.

Trade dress. Trade dress is a subcategory of trademark law that applies to the packaging or total appearance of a product or service. As a result of a recent Supreme Court ruling, trade dress is less favorable as a source of protection for crafts. For more information on trade dress, see below.

Trade Dress

In 2000, the Supreme Court handed down a ruling that sent a chill through the hearts of crafts makers. The case, brought by Samara Brothers, a clothing company that manufactures a line of children's one-piece outfits appliquéd with hearts, flowers, and fruit, claimed that

Wal-Mart copied Samara's designs and sold the knock-offs at a lower price than offered by Samara.

Samara sued Wal-Mart, arguing that Wal-Mart had violated trade dress law. Trade dress is part of trademark law, and, like a trademark, it protects those aspects of a product that distinguish it from competing goods. Trade dress protects the appearance of a product or packaging but not its functional aspects. For example, in Samara's case, trade dress protection would extend only to the appearance of the hearts, flowers, and fruit, not to the functioning aspects or shape of the clothing. Trade dress does not require any form of government registration and does not require much originality.

Initially it appeared as if Samara was the victor when Wal-Mart was ordered to pay Samara $1.6 million for copying the product design. But the Supreme Court overruled that judgment, holding Samara's designs could not be protected under trade dress law unless Samara could prove that the designs were used to identify the source of the product (Samara) rather than the product itself.

In other words, in order for trade dress to apply, a customer seeing the arrangement of appliqués of hearts, flowers, and fruit on children's clothing would have to think of Samara as the source in the same way that a customer who sees the Nike logo on products associates those products with Nike. In the Wal-Mart case there was no evidence that customers associated the designs strictly with Samara.

The result of this Supreme Court decision is that your crafts product design will only be protected under trade dress law if you can demonstrate that its appearance serves to identify you as the source. In general, extensively exploited crafts items, for example, the Cabbage Patch Kids or Hummel figurines, are more likely to acquire the standard of customer association required by the Supreme Court.

Why does trade dress protection hinge on whether customers associate specific designs with the creators of those designs? The rationale is to prevent customer confusion in the marketplace. In other words, it's unfair for a customer to believe she is buying a polychromed wood sculpture from Wendell Castle when it is actually a knockoff made in Korea.

This customer association is known as secondary meaning, and there is no bright-line test for determining it. You can demonstrate secondary meaning by a showing of high sales volume, extensive advertising, a long period of use, unsolicited publicity such as newspaper articles or television shows, and customer surveys and other proof that customers associate the appearance with you. For example, one company proved secondary meaning in its lawn furniture designs with evidence of $1.2 million spent advertising the product line, gross sales of approximately $5 million, and testimony by customers stating they associated the design with the company.

The Supreme Court's ruling is a depressing shift in the law for crafts makers, making it easier for catalog companies and chain stores to knock off an item and sell it. However, the ruling emphasizes the importance of shoring up your rights under trade dress and trademark principles. Since trade dress protection for your craft design is difficult to get, you should consider the two alternatives discussed in this chapter: copyright and design patents.

To protect any rights you may have to trade dress protection, keep track of all publicity, advertising, and sales for your crafts products. These are the elements that demonstrate customer associations. Finally, keep track of any complaints by your customers who were confused by the knockoffs and thought they originated with you.

The trade dress rules we have discussed apply to product designs. You are more likely to qualify for trade dress for product packaging, product names, and product logos, for which the rules are different. For that reason, your packaging, name, and logo should be as distinctive as possible, and you should attempt to incorporate your trademark (your name or logo) into the work. If a competitor copies any of these elements, you will have better odds of stopping the theft.

What to Do If Your Work Is Ripped Off

It's your worst nightmare. A catalog company rips off one of your best-selling items and sells it at a lower price. You know the reality. If you sue, you may end up spending more on attorney fees than you lost from the rip-off—a fact that the company has probably considered. Grrr!!!

Suing a chain store or catalog company may cost anywhere from $5,000 to $100,000 in legal fees. Some infringers know that the cost of fees will exceed any victory in a lawsuit. They tend to take the attitude, "Sue me if you can afford it." In these cases, a lawsuit is a big gamble. However, if you have strong legal protection and a good case, pursuit of a big-time infringer will not be quite as risky, because you will be able to attract an attorney who will take your case on a contingency basis—that is, for a percentage of the judgment.

Unfortunately, there is no foolproof way to prevent someone from ripping off your crafts idea, and there is no guarantee of success in a legal battle. An article in the *Fortune Small Business Magazine* highlighted the rash of knockoffs by Target, QVC, Kmart, Wal-Mart, and Pottery Barn. In one particularly egregious case, the knockoff maker bought up all the available glass normally used by the glass artist for his picture frames. The more successful a crafts product becomes, the more likely another crafts business, a foreign manufacturer, or a catalog company will knock it off. Even though you cannot stop theft, there are laws that you can use to go after these thieves, and there are ways to use your legal rights to deter future thefts. Below, I provide some suggestions for dealing with infringers and thieves.

Gather evidence. The key to prevailing and to ending an infringement dispute quickly is often the evidence that's gathered. Your evidence should present a convincing story of how the work was created and stolen. Keep records of how you created your work in a crafts notebook. If you learn of a rip-off, buy a copy, and save the store receipt. If possible, obtain business cards or other contact information from buyers at a show or from anyone who wants to photograph your work. For example, in a case involving a major catalog retailer, a client was able to demonstrate that the buyer had seen and taken a copy of the work on the basis of a business card that the buyer left at the artist's booth.

EXAMPLE: Artist Lisa Graves had created distinctive heart-shaped earrings that were knocked off by two well-known retailers and three manufacturers. When she created her earrings, she left an incidental thumb mark in the back—a fingerprint. When the infringers copied the work, they simply threw it in a mold and reproduced it with the thumbprint included. As a result, it was difficult for the defendants in the case to claim (as they had) that the earrings were not copied—powerful evidence that helped us settle her case.

The Foundation for Design Integrity (www.ffdi.org) offers suggestions for relevant evidence at its website. These include documenting your design process, keeping accurate financial records, and maintaining an exhibition log.

Publicity helps. Publicity about your business, such as articles about your crafts or awards you've received, will help to demonstrate the legitimacy of your work (a factor for some judges). It can also aid in a trade dress case by demonstrating secondary meaning (in trademark disputes) or in a copyright case by demonstrating access to your work. You can also sometimes use publicity to shame an infringer into settling. For example, when I told one chain store that my client was preparing a press release about the fact that her made-in the-USA works were being knocked off by made-in-India imports, the store settled soon afterwards.

Don't say anything till you speak with an attorney. Never confront an infringer until you have spoken with an attorney. Accusing someone of being a thief, especially if you're wrong, can lead to legal claims against you.

Remember, not all crafts products qualify for legal protection. As you may have gathered after reading this chapter and the previous one discussing copyright, obtaining protection is a little like getting a bank loan: some crafts products qualify, and some don't. When a work is not protected, it is considered to be in the public domain, and anyone is free to copy it. Review Chapters 6 and 7 and follow the procedures for registering and protecting copyrights and design patents. Registration of copyright, for example, may enable you to claim attorney fees in the event of an infringement.

Names and Trademarks

For decades, three companies in the Black Hills of South Dakota manufactured and sold gold jewelry featuring three-color gold in a grape and leaf design under the trademark "BLACK HILLS GOLD JEWELRY." One day, a company from North Dakota began advertising its "BLACK HILLS GOLD JEWELRY" (also with a gold grape and leaf design) in South Dakota newspapers. The company's ads even included images of the Black Hills and pictures of Mount Rushmore. The South Dakota companies, unhappy with this northern invasion—sued to stop this interloper from using their trademark.

Under trademark law, a company can prevent a competitor from using a similar trademark if it is likely to confuse consumers as to the source of the goods. A federal court sorted through the matter and determined that the designation "BLACK HILLS GOLD JEWELRY" should only be used by jewelry manufacturers located in the Black Hills. On that basis, the North Dakota company was deceiving consumers by using the trademark. (*Black Hills Jewelry Manufacturing Co. v. Gold Rush, Inc.,* 633 F.2d 746 (8th Cir. 1980).)

This ruling highlights a basic trademark principle: If consumers have developed an association between a product and its name or designation, it's wrong to allow competitors to trade off that association by using a similar name. Your business may never be involved in a trademark problem—few crafts businesses run into conflicts with competitors over names—but in the event that you are choosing a name for your crafts products, gallery, or crafts services, or you are concerned about someone using your trademark (or your use of someone else's trademark), this chapter will help.

Trademark Basics

Few people are aware that this whole business of placing trademarks on goods was invented thousands of years ago by crafts artisans, eager to distinguish their works. Greek and Roman potters imprinted ceramic marks on their works, medieval papermakers invented watermarks to distinguish their papers, printers and furniture makers created unique marks identifying their crafts, and gold- and silversmiths used hallmarks—a series of markings stamped on gold and silver products—to signify the quality and maker of the product.

Trademarks still serve us in the same way as they did our crafts ancestors. You can claim exclusive trademark rights to any word, symbol, or device that identifies and distinguishes your crafts products or services. (When a trademark is used to identify services, for example FedEx for delivery services, it's sometimes referred to as a service mark. Both trademarks and service marks are referred to as trademarks throughout this chapter.)

The most popular types of trademarks are product names, for example, "Wilburton Pottery" or "One-of-A-Kind Weaver." However, there are other types of trademarks, including slogans, logos, domain names, and trade dress. There are also two offshoots of trademarks: collective marks that identify an organization, and certification marks that certify that a product or service has a certain quality, meets a certain standard, or is from a certain geographic location, discussed in more detail, below.

In order to stop a competitor who is using your trademark, you will need to file a lawsuit and obtain a court order. The government will not enforce your trademark rights for you. You may also realize after reading this chapter that many rules and decisions regarding trademarks seem arbitrary or are based on money and not fairness. Unfortunately, this is sometimes the case in trademark disputes, where big companies use trademark law to bully smaller competitors.

Crown and Initials logo used by Kiss My Ring Jewelry

Rule #1: First User Gets the Trademark

If you are the first crafts company to use a trademark in commerce, that is, the first to advertise or sell products or services under the mark, you acquire trademark rights and can stop others from using an identical or similar mark.

> **EXAMPLE:** A Spanish company was the first to use the trademark MAJORICA (on a ribbon or crest design) for its manufactured pearl jewelry. A second company later sought to use MAJORCA for its pearl jewelry (also in a crest design). A federal court prohibited the second user, because MAJORCA was phonetically and visually indistinguishable from MAJORICA and was likely to confuse consumers. (*Industria Espanola De Perlas Imitacion v. National Silver*, 459 F.2d 1049 (CCPA 1972).)

However, simply being the first user of a mark may not get you all the protection you need. Other factors that influence trademark rights are the geographical extent of your use, whether the mark is weak or strong, or whether you have abandoned your right to use the mark. I'll talk about these more, below.

Rule #2: Rights Are Limited to Your Goods and Services

One important feature of the early crafts marks—for example, ceramic marks and paper watermarks—was that they had the power to identify only a certain class of goods. For example, a hallmark for silver and gold products might have significance on a silver bowl, but it would have no meaning on the bottom of an earthenware bowl. The class of goods for the mark was limited to the type produced by the maker.

This rule is still a cornerstone of trademark law. You can only stop others from using a similar mark on goods or services with which the mark is used, intended to be used, or likely to be used.

ACC is a trademark for the American Craft Council, an organization that provides services including crafts shows, exhibitions, resources, and marketing services for crafts business. If another company wanted to use ACC as a trademark for cardiology and education services (American

ACC Trademark

College of Cardiology), sports services (Atlantic Coast Conference), insurance services (the Accident Compensation Corporation), or a musical group (Angel Corpus Christi), the American Craft Council would have difficulty stopping these uses because crafts, cardiology, insurance, basketball, and music are not competitive or related services or goods. They are not offered through the same channels of distribution or in the same retail outlets. However, if another company were to offer crafts shows and used the ACC trademark or logo, that use might confuse consumers as to their source. The American Craft Council could stop this competitive use. With a few exceptions (see below), noncompeting uses of a similar trademark cannot be prohibited.

Rule # 3: Creating a Trademark Doesn't Create Rights

Trademark rights do not arise because you create a trademark—for example, design a logo or coin a slogan. Trademark rights only occur if you use the trademark in commerce. You can reserve trademark rights—see below—but these rights will not vest unless you eventually use the mark in commerce.

Rule #4: Distinctive Trademarks Are Easier to Protect

Trademark protection is based around a "strength" classification system. Strong trademarks are distinctive, and you can immediately stop others from using similar ones. Weak trademarks are not distinctive and you cannot register one on the Principal Register—the best form of U.S. trademark protection—until you strengthen it by pumping up the mark with consumer awareness through advertising and sales (known as "secondary meaning").

To determine if a mark is "distinguishable" or "distinctive" start by asking whether a consumer associates the mark with a certain product or service, a certain quality, or a specific source. The more likely that there's a consumer association, the more likely than the mark is distinctive and strong.

The more that the mark describes the goods (for example, BEADS N THINGS), the weaker or less distinguishable the mark. Why? Because the mark describes the product, it doesn't distinguish it. Unfortunately, this classification system is not an exact science—there are no foolproof tests for determining if a mark is strong. A decision is usually made by a judge or trademark examiner who weighs the various factors described in the following sections. In reviewing decisions by judges or trademark examiners, you may well disagree with the reasoning as to whether a mark is distinctive. Many trademark decisions are simply subjective determinations, much like a referee's call at a football game.

Generally, a mark is strong if it is:

- born strong (so unique or clever that it is classified as "inherently distinctive"—for example, "SPLENDOR IN THE GLASS" for glassware), or
- made strong (it becomes distinctive through sales and advertising, as did the "PEOPLE'S POTTERY" mark).

Rule #5: Trademark Registration Helps

Trademark rights can be acquired without filing a federal or state trademark registration. However, federal registration will best protect your rights and provide the following benefits:

- Only the owner of a federally registered mark may use the symbol ® in conjunction with goods or services.
- The filing date of your trademark application gives you nationwide priority as of that date.
- The owner of a registered mark may, under some circumstances, recover lost profits, damages, and costs in a federal court trademark infringement lawsuit.

- The owner of a registered mark can deposit a copy of the registration with U.S. Customs in order to stop the importation of goods bearing an infringing mark.
- After five years of continuous use, a federally registered mark can, with some exceptions, become immune from challenge.
- A federal registration may serve as the basis for filing a trademark application in certain foreign countries.

If these benefits are important to your crafts business, and if you believe your trademark adds substantial value to your business, proceed with federal registration as described below. Registration takes approximately one a year and the fee ranges between $275 to $375 per class of goods. The fees are $275 if you register using TEAS Plus (the simplest system), $325 if you use TEAS (for more complex registrations), and $375 if you file a paper application. The United States Patent and Trademark Office (USPTO) administers federal registrations and can be accessed on the Internet at www.uspto.gov. Later in this chapter I explain the registration process.

Rule #6: No Trademark Protection If ...

There are some situations in which no trademark protection is available or possible. In these situations, the intended trademark cannot be registered, and the owner has no right to stop others using a similar mark. These include:

- **Nonuse (also known as "abandonment").** If you stop using a trademark and it appears as if you won't resume use, the mark is no longer protected and anyone can use it.
- **Generic terms.** If you attempt to use the name of the a class of goods—for example, you use the term "Leather" or "Jewelry" as the sole name for your leather or jewelry goods—the name will not be protected, because it is a generic term. You can, however, use these terms in conjunction with other terms—for example, Zen Woodwork or Genius Jewelry.

- **Weak marks** that have not achieved secondary meaning. As explained, above, a weak (or nondistinctive) mark cannot be protected without proof of consumer awareness.
- **Functional features.** A functional element of your craft or its packaging is not protectable as a trademark or trade dress (for more on the relationship between trade dress and trademarks see Chapter 7).

Rule #7: Beware When Using Your Surname as Your Trademark

Many crafts artists use their first name, last name, or both as a trademark, for example, "WEDEMEYER ORIGINAL WORKS" or "PERIE BROWN CREATIONS." Others use a variation on the name, for example, "ELLIE MAC DESIGN" (owned by Elenora Macnish) or "LUCYLAND" for a line of hand-milled soap. Using your own name makes sense. After all, crafts are a highly personalized occupation requiring unique skills, and historically crafts goods are known by the name of the creator, for example "Johnson Brothers" crockery. There are some advantages to using your own name:

- You have less chance of infringing on someone else's trademark.
- You won't have to file a fictitious business statement (sometimes known as a DBA) with your local county clerk when you create your business.
- You may have an easier time preserving your rights to a domain name.

The downsides. In the case of common names, for example, you may be surprised to find that someone else has preempted your field. For example, anyone with the family name Hummel will have a difficult time obtaining a trademark for figurines. And you may be surprised to learn that it's often difficult to register trademarks that use a family name, because the USPTO often considers family names to be weak trademarks. In the event you wish to register or assert rights to a family name, here are the rules:

- **Primarily a surname (weak).** A family name that is perceived primarily as a person's name is descriptive (weak) and can't be registered. The owners cannot stop others from using a similar mark without proof of secondary meaning. This is also true if the surname is used with other generic terms (for example, "STEINBERG GOURDS" or "O'NEILL GLASS ART"), or is used with initials. If the additional wording is more than a generic term, or if it creates a play on words—for example, Boyd Wright's "WRIGHT MADE PRODUCTS," the mark may be strong and registrable.

- **Not primarily a surname (may be weak or strong).** Some family names have a dictionary meaning, for example, Nathan Lefthand operates "LEFTHAND STUDIO." In these cases, the mark is not automatically presumed to be weak. You will have an easier time registering or protecting it.

- **Multiple surnames.** Generally, when a surname is combined with another surname (such as "BERNARD & SOKOLOFF ART GLASS"), it is not presumed to be weak, and you will have an easier time registering or protecting it.

- **Surnames combined with a design.** If the design is not particularly distinctive (for example, simple geometric shapes), the mark is considered weak. This is not the case if the design has some unique or distinctive features.

Trade Names and Trademarks

A trade name is the name of a business. It is not necessarily a trademark, but it can serve as one if it is used to advertise or sell a product or service. For example, not many consumers are aware of the Minnesota Mining and Manufacturing Company (a trade name), but most consumers are aware of its trademarked products such as Scotch Tape and Post-its. Your trade name (usually the name under which you register your business) will not become a trademark unless you use it in connection with the sale of your goods by putting that name on the tag of your products and advertising your products under that name.

Relationship of Domain Names and Trademarks

One consideration when choosing your trademark is whether the corresponding domain name is available. This search can be done for free at many sites on the Internet, located by typing "domain name" into any search engine. Trademark owners often vie for the same domain name. For example, the Arrow glass design company and the Arrow shirt company may both want the domain arrow.com. Although the term "Arrow" can function as a trademark for both companies since they have separate goods, there can be only one arrow.com. The first company to register the domain name acquires it. If a trademark owner wants to acquire rights from a legitimate domain name owner, the only solution is to negotiate to buy the rights.

Symbols Indicating a Trademark

Typically, the symbols ®, TM, or SM are used along with trademarks— as in The Crafts Report® or Cape Cod Crafters of New England™. The symbol ® indicates that a trademark has been registered at the USPTO. It is illegal to use the ® symbol if the trademark in question has no USPTO registration. There is no legal requirement that the ® be used, but the failure to use it may limit the amount of damages that the trademark owner can recover in an infringement lawsuit. If the trademark hasn't been registered, the TM symbol can be used. Similarly, the SM symbol can be used for service marks that have not been registered. The TM and SM have no legal significance other than to indicate the fact that the owner is claiming trademark rights.

Collective Marks and Certification Marks

Trademark law has two stepchildren: collective marks that signify membership in an organization, and certification marks that attest to a certain quality or standard. Collective and certification marks share some qualities and standards with trademarks, but they also have rules of their own.

Collective Marks

A collective mark signifies membership in an organization. For example, the collective mark "CROCHET GUILD OF AMERICA" signifies membership in this crafts organization. A collective mark can also function as a trademark or service mark, signifying that a product or service originates from an organization. If you are a member of a group or organization (for example, "THE MAINE CRAFTS GUILD"), you probably want to limit use of the name to members of the guild. You don't want nonmembers to use the name (that would undermine the group's standards), and you don't want another club to use the same name. In order to protect your group's right to the mark, you should federally register your group name as a collective mark.

The collective mark is owned by the organization (not by any particular member). The MAINE CRAFTS GUILD collective mark could be used to sell member products (selected crafts works) or offer services (knitting lessons). In other words, a collective mark can be used in two ways: to signify membership or as a trademark.

Certification Marks

A certification mark attests to some standard, quality, or origin of goods. For example, if you create ceramic lamps, you probably want to include the UL certification mark on your works indicating that Underwriters Laboratory has certified the safety of the product. As a purchaser of crafts supplies, you may seek a certain quality or standard, for example, 100% COTTON. Or perhaps you might want a certification that indicates the cotton was produced by an organic farm in California, for example, the CCOF certification mark (California Certified Organic Farmers). A crafts organization or a group of suppliers can organize to certify some standard, for example, that jewelry is manufactured in the Black Hills of South Dakota, by applying to the federal government for a certification mark.

Staying Out of Trouble

You've probably read about companies that have been told to stop using names, logos, or other marks because a competitor believes the mark infringes on theirs. If you receive a warning like this (known as a "cease and desist" letter), consult with an attorney (see Chapter 11 for information on finding an attorney). Below is information that will help you avoid trademark troubles and, in the event you do run into a problem, will help you evaluate your position.

Infringement

Trademark infringement occurs when one company uses another company's trademark (or a substantially similar mark) in a manner that is likely to confuse consumers into believing that there is some connection, affiliation, or sponsorship between the two companies. Usually this occurs when a trademark is used on similar goods.

> **EXAMPLE:** PLAY-DOH is the trademark for one of the most popular crafts products for children, a modeling compound that comes in various colors. (In the two-to-seven-year-old age group, one in every two children currently owns a PLAY-DOH product.) In the mid 1990s, a competitor, Rose Art Industries, began selling a modeling compound for children known as FUNDOUGH. A federal court determined that consumers were likely to be confused by the simultaneous use of FUNDOUGH and PLAY-DOH and prohibited Rose Art from using that trademark for its modeling compounds. (*Kenner Parker Toys v. Rose Art Industries,* 963 F.2d 350 (CAFC 1992).)

> **EXAMPLE:** "ARTCARVED" and "ART CREST," both used as trademarks for jewelry, were found not likely to infringe each other. A federal court determined that the two words were sufficiently different in pronunciation and meaning not to be confused by consumers. (*J.R. Wood and Sons v. Reese Jewelry,* 278 F.2d 157 (2d Cir. 1960).)

When determining likelihood of confusion, courts usually use several factors derived from a 1961 case, *Polaroid Corp. v. Polarad Elecs. Corp.*, 287 F.2d 492 (2d Cir.). These factors may vary slightly throughout the country but the important issues are commonly the strength of the senior user's mark (the senior user is the first user), the similarity of the marks and products, sophistication of the buyers, and evidence of actual confusion.

Trademark Dilution

Sometimes even if there's little likelihood of customer confusion, a company with a famous trademark can stop another company that commercially uses its famous trademark in a manner that blurs the two companies in the customers' minds. This is referred to as trademark dilution and occurs when the integrity of a famous trademark is "muddied" by an unwanted or insulting commercial association.

> **EXAMPLE:** Joshua designs a wooden holder for toilet paper rolls and names it ROLLS ROYCE. Consumers are not likely to think that the ROLLS ROYCE auto company produced the holder, but the auto company could stop Joshua from using the name by claiming that the association with toilet paper rolls dilutes its classy and famous trademark.

The alteration of a trademark in a comparative advertisement has also been found to be a dilution. In a television advertisement, an equipment manufacturer animated the John Deere "deer" logo and appeared to make it run from the competition. *Deere & Company v. MTD Prods. Inc.*, 34 USPQ 1706 (S.D. N.Y. 1995).)

When You Need Permission to Use a Trademark

Below are some rules in the event you want to use someone else's trademark in connection with your products or advertising.

Informational uses. Informational (or "editorial") uses of a trademark do not require permission from the owner. These are uses that inform, educate, or express opinions protected under the First Amendment of the United States Constitution (protecting freedom of speech and of the press). For example, permission is not required to use the Shell gasoline logo at your website when discussing the various ways that sea shells have been used in American crafts and art.

Comparative advertising. It's permissible to use a trademark when making accurate comparative product statements in advertisements. However, since comparative advertisements tend to raise the hackles of trademark owners, an attorney knowledgeable in trademark or business law should review the advertisement.

Commercial uses. Commercial uses of a trademark in your advertising, promotion, or marketing require permission (except for cases of comparative advertising; see above). For example, don't wear a T-shirt that says "Chanel" in a print advertisement for your jewelry.

Using trademarks in crafts products. Proceed with caution if you're using trademarks as part of your crafts art—for example, producing a fabric with a repeating image of the American Express card or producing earrings that feature the Apple computer logo. You may be able to argue that your use is informational (see above) and is protected by the First Amendment. However, this argument may be a loser if it looks like you're trading off the success of a trademark rather than commenting upon it. For example, a company that sold trading cards of collectible cars was prohibited from reproducing Chrysler trademarks and trade dress, because Chrysler licensed similar collectible products. (*Chrysler Corp. v. Newfield Publications Inc.*, 880 F.Supp. 504 (E.D. Mich. 1995).) Be aware that making a First Amendment argument means that you've already triggered a company's ire, and you will have to deal with the consequences. This isn't to discourage you from speaking out against corporate branding, just to alert you to the potential morass that awaits if you do.

Parodies. A trademark parody occurs when a trademark is imitated in a manner that pokes fun at the mark, for example, by selling caps printed with the words, "Mutant of Omaha." Bear in mind that offensive parodies are the ones most likely to trigger lawsuits. For example, lawsuits were filed over lewd photos of the Pillsbury Doughboy and of nude

Barbie dolls and imagery entitled "Malted Barbie" and "The Barbie Enchiladas." Although the artist in the case involving Barbie dolls eventually won his claim, it required substantial legal effort and expense. (*Mattel Inc. v. Walking Mountain Productions, Inc.* 2001 U.S. App. LEXIS 2610; (9th Cir. 2002).) Weigh the legal consequences carefully before proceeding. A trademark parody is less likely to run into problems if it doesn't compete with the trademarked goods and services and doesn't confuse consumers—that is, they get the joke and do not believe the parody product comes from the same source as the trademarked goods. Also keep in mind that not all humorous uses are parodies. To avoid trouble, the use should specifically poke fun at the trademark.

Trademark Disclaimers

A disclaimer is a statement intended to minimize confusion in consumer's minds or deflect liability. A disclaimer is only effective if it is prominently placed, permanently affixed, can be read and understood, and really minimizes confusion. A disclaimer, by itself, will not provide a shield against litigation. However, when properly done, a disclaimer can minimize confusion and prevent dilution.

> **EXAMPLE:** "FUR RENDEZVOUS" is the trademark for a winter festival held in Anchorage, Alaska. The trademark is owned by the Greater Anchorage corporation. Vernon Nowell, a private citizen with no affiliation to the festival, created and sold lapel pins with the words "FUR RENDEZVOUS." When Greater Anchorage objected to Nowell selling the pins, he consulted his attorney and developed a disclaimer, glued to the back of the pins, which states: "This pin, and V.L. Nowell, have no connection whatever with, nor has the pin been approved by, Anchorage Fur Rendezvous, Inc., or Greater Anchorage, Inc." In addition, the disclaimer explained that "Fur Rendezvous is a registered trademark of Greater Anchorage, Inc." When Nowell sold the pins, he handed out fliers explaining the history of the festival and the pin and explicitly stating that "This pin has no connection with nor has it been approved by

Anchorage Fur Rendezvous, Inc. or Greater Anchorage, Inc."
A federal court permitted Nowell to sell the pins as long as the
disclaimers were included. (*Greater Anchorage, Inc., v. Nowell*, 1992
U.S. App. LEXIS 22906 (9th Circuit 1992).)

Trademark Searching

The purpose of a trademark search is to determine if a similar name or
mark is being used on similar goods or services. The person performing
the search must delve into collections of trademarks (known as trademark databases) and search through business directories and news articles
describing names of products or services. With the advent of Internet
access, a competent search can be performed online. Professional search
firms perform these tasks and prepare written reports for a fee of several
hundred dollars.

A trademark search should locate substantially similar variations on
the mark. For example, if a crafts artist selling bird cages intends to use
the name BIRD MAN for his products, he would need to search for
that name as well as soundalikes ("BYRD"), plurals ("BIRD MEN"),
gender variations ("BIRD WOMEN" or "BIRD BOY"), and perhaps
foreign translations. The search would have to be broad enough to find
substantially similar terms for bird cages and for related product services
and goods such as bird food. Even though these are not the products or
services for which the mark is intended, these categories are considered
"related goods or services" and may result in potential conflicts.

If a search determines that the desired mark or a substantially
similar mark is already in use, it's time to rethink your choice of mark.
Frustrating though this is, it's better than closing your eyes to the
competition and hoping for the best. Failure to search—or to act on
what you discovered in a search—can have expensive consequences. If
you rush to market, blind to the fact that a similar trademark is already
being used by a competitor, the competitor may obtain a court order
preventing your use of the trademark, and you may also have to pay
monetary damages and attorney fees.

The most economical method of searching is to start with a prelimi-nary search on the Internet using Google and following that up with a search of the USPTO database (on the USPTO home page, click Trademarks, then click Search). If the preliminary search turns up similar marks, you can then narrow your choices before proceeding to a professional search report.

If your preliminary search does not turn up any similar marks (referred to as "potential conflicts"), you can, if you wish, hire a professional search firm to prepare a complete report of any similar federal, state, common law, or, if desired, international trademarks. Since these searches are expensive (often $300-$500), I would suggest bypassing this professional search unless you are either entering into a licensing agreement or distribution agreement in which you must promise your trademark does not infringe, or your crafts products are becoming successful and you need the peace of mind that comes with knowing you are not infringing any existing marks. Two companies that perform professional searches are Thompson Compumark (http://compumark.thomson.com/jsp/index.jsp) and Trademark Research Corporation, (www.cch-trc.com).

Federal Registration

Below is an explanation for how to prepare and file a federal trademark application. Before you begin your federal application, you'll need to figure out what theory it's based on. Most federal trademark applications are based on either "use in commerce" or an applicant's intention to use the trademark (referred to as an "intent-to-use" or ITU application).

RESOURCE

Nolo's Online Trademark Application Program. Nolo, the publisher of this book, also offers an online system for filing with the USPTO. For more information, visit the Nolo website and click "Online Legal Forms."

Preparing the Federal Trademark Application: The TEAS System

The preferred (and less expensive) method of preparing the federal trademark application is to use the online Trademark Electronic Application System (TEAS) located at the PTO's website (www.uspto.gov). TEAS is an interactive system in which the user is asked a series of questions. If a question is not answered or an essential element is not completed, the applicant is asked to correct the error. I recommend starting with the TEAS PLUS system, as it is the least expensive way to file.

Basis for Application

Using the online TEAS PLUS system, you will be asked the basis for your application. If you have already used the mark in connection with the sale of crafts goods or services, then you would check "Yes" under "Use in Commerce." As for dates of use, you will need to provide the date (or your best guess as to the dates) you first sold goods or services using the trademark, anywhere. You will also need to provide the date when you first sold your work or services outside your state (for example, through an Internet sale or during travel to a crafts fair). If you have not yet used the mark but have a bona fide intention to use the mark, check "Yes" under "Intent to Use."

Identification of the Class of Goods or Services

You will need to identify your class of goods. The USPTO uses the International Schedule of Classes of Goods and Services to group-related goods. This helps them make appropriate comparisons of the mark. For example, glassware, porcelain, and earthenware are in Class 21. You can register your work in many classes, but each class registration costs $275 or $325 (depending on whether you use TEAS PLUS or TEAS).

To identify the class for your goods, search the USPTO's goods and services manual online. Go to the home page, click "Trademarks" (on the left side of the page), then look under the heading "Manuals & Publications" and click "Acceptable Identification of Goods and Services Manual." Type in the crafts product that you sell in your search results, the class number is indicated after the letter G (for Goods) or S (for Services). For example, flower baskets, plant baskets and picnic baskets are all in Class 21.

Two sources for guidance in identifying goods are the *Trademark Examiners Manual of Procedure* (TMEP) and the U.S. Patent and Trademark Office *Acceptable Identification of Goods and Services Manual*, which lists appropriate choices of identification of goods and services in alphabetical order and by class. Both of these guides can be obtained in book form, on CD-ROM, or online at the USPTO website.

Description of the Goods or Services

Along with the class for the goods, you will need to provide a description of the goods or services. This description is different from the listing of the International Class. For example, if you are selling key rings (International Class 6, "non precious metal goods"), the listing should state "key rings," not "non precious metal goods."

The description should be precise. If your description is too broad, the USPTO's trademark examining attorney will negotiate an appropriate description with you. (According to a USPTO survey, the applicant's identification of goods and services was questioned in more than 50% percent of trademark applications.)

Again, two sources for guidance in identifying goods are the *Trademark Examiners Manual of Procedure* (TMEP) and the USPTO *Acceptable Identification of Goods and Services Manual*, both available online.

When using the TEAS system, choosing the proper description is simplified because the TEAS system is electronically linked to the USPTO *Acceptable Identification of Goods and Services Manual*. An applicant can type in a word related to the goods and examine sample descriptions and lists of goods and services.

Identification of the Mark

If the mark is a word or group of words, identification of the mark is straightforward. The mark may be identified simply as "JUST JULES" or "HOOKY WOOKY HATS." But if the mark is a stylized presentation of the word, a graphic symbol, a logo, a design, or any of the other devices permitted under trademark law, a statement must be provided that clearly identifies the mark. If you're using the TEAS system, type in the word mark or, in the case of a stylized mark, attach a graphic file (either JPG or GIF format) containing a black-and-white rendition of the mark. Insert a written description in the appropriate box.

> **TIP**
> **For the broadest protection for a word mark, register it free of any lettering style.** This will give you the ability to use the trademark in various fonts, rather than being restricted to your original presentation of the mark.

Information About the Applicant

The applicant—your crafts business—can be an individual, a partnership, a corporation, an association such as a union, social club, or cooperative, or a joint ownership by some combination of any these forms. If you are acting on behalf of a partnership, include the names and citizenship of the general partners and the domicile of the partnership. If you are representing a corporation, include the name under which the business or group is incorporated and the state or foreign nation under which it is organized.

Your own citizenship is required as well as a mailing address. If you are doing business under a fictitious name, that information should be provided, especially if it is included on any specimen furnished with the application. If the mark is owned jointly by two entities, that should be stated as well. Supplying this information online using TEAS is facilitated by typing the appropriate information into the form. Drop-down menus and online help screens are available to guide you.

Declaration

You are required to provide a declaration, a sworn statement, or other verification that the facts in the trademark application are true. You, or an officer of your corporation or association, should sign the declaration.

The TEAS application provides an all-purpose declaration that can be used for both ITU applications and for trademarks that are in use.

Disclaimers

Many trademarks include words or phrases that, by themselves, cannot be protected under trademark law. For example, no person can claim an exclusive right to the word "pottery" or "basket." To allow one person an exclusive right to use such terms would decimate the English language. Therefore, the trademark office usually requires a disclaimer as to certain portions of trademarks. For example, if an applicant wanted to register the mark Lucky Jewelry, the applicant would be required to disclaim "jewelry." This means that apart from the use as a part of the trademark, the applicant claims no exclusive right to use the word "jewelry."

Specimen

If your application is based on actual use of your mark in commerce, you'll need to enclose a specimen—that is, an actual example of the trademark being used on your goods or in your offer of services. In the case of ITU applications, the specimen must be filed later, together with a document entitled "Amendment to Allege Use." You'll see that the USPTO provides a means for uploading a digital photograph of the specimen. Since crafts works are goods, a label, tag, or container for the goods is considered to be an acceptable specimen of use for a trademark. A letterhead or business card is unacceptable as a trademark specimen because it doesn't follow the goods through the stream of commerce.

Completing the Process

You will complete the process by paying the fees, authorizing your electronic signature, and validating the application. After you click "Pay/Submit" and your transaction is successful, you will receive a confirmation.

Later, you will receive email acknowledging the submission of your application. Hold on to that email, because it is the only proof you'll have that the USPTO has your application. It is also proof of your filing date and contains the serial number assigned to your application.

After Filing

The USPTO filing receipt explains that you should not expect to hear anything about your application for approximately three months. If you have not heard anything in three and a half months, it is wise to call and inquire as to the status of your application. There are three ways to do this:

- Check TARR: The online Trademark Applications and Registrations Retrieval system page (http://tarr.uspto.gov) allows you to get information about pending trademarks obtained from the USPTO's internal database by entering a valid trademark serial number.
- TRAM automated system: TRAM stands for trademark reporting and monitoring. From any touchtone phone, Monday through Friday from 6:30 a.m. to midnight, eastern time, dial 703-305-8747. After the welcome message and tone, enter your mark's eight-digit serial number and the pound symbol. You should immediately hear the computer give you the current status of your mark along with the effective date of the status.
- If you want additional information or would prefer talking with a person, call the Trademark Assistance Center at 703-308-9400 and request a status check.

You will likely receive some communication from the USPTO within three to six months. If there is a problem with your application, you will receive what's called an "action letter." This is a letter from your examiner explaining what the problems are. Most problems can be resolved with a phone call to the examiner.

When the examiner approves your application for publication, you will receive a Notice of Publication in the mail. Your mark will then be published online in the *Official Gazette*. For 30 days following publication, anyone may oppose your registration. Only 3% of all published marks are opposed, so it is very unlikely you will run into trouble.

Once your mark has made it through the 30-day publication period, and you are filing on an actual use basis, you will receive a Certificate of Registration. The USPTO sometimes has a difficult time moving applications through this long process. As a result, it may take a year or more to process your application.

If you filed on an intent-to-use basis, your mark will not be placed on the trademark register until you file an additional document with the USPTO when you put it into actual use. This form, available on the TEAS system, is called "Statement of Use/Amendment to Allege Use for Intent-to-Use Application." It tells the USPTO the date you started using the mark and completes the registration process. You must also provide a specimen at that time, showing how you are using the mark.

Communicating With the USPTO

The chances are good that you will be communicating with the USPTO after you have filed your application. Few applications sail through completely unscathed.

You are required to be diligent in pursuing your application. If you are expecting some action from the USPTO (the ball is in their court) and more than six months have elapsed without your hearing from them, immediately check the TARR system or call the USPTO Status Line (the TRAM Automated System, described above). If you discover a problem, bring it to the USPTO's attention. If you fail to respond in a timely manner to a request from a USPTO examining attorney, your application may be considered abandoned. If that happens, you may petition the Commissioner for Trademarks within 60 days to reactivate your application.

If the examiner wants you to change your application, such as claiming a different description of services or goods, there is usually some room for negotiation.

An examiner with a brief question might call you and then issue and mail you an examiner's amendment. This is a form on which the examiner records in handwriting a phone conversation or meeting with the applicant. Read the amendment carefully to make sure it matches your understanding of the conversation. If you disagree, or don't understand the amendment, first call the examiner, and then, if necessary, write the examiner a letter with your concerns, explaining your point of view on the communication.

Licensing

Textile designer Rebecca Yaffe (www.rebeccayaffe.com) creates colorful hand-dyed and hand-painted fabrics using materials such as silk charmeuse and silk crepe. For eight and a half years, she sold clothing made from her fabrics. In 1999, she changed her strategy, stopped making clothes, and sold just the fabrics. Suddenly, Yaffe found herself thrust into a new market, with different customers, different competitors, and different trade shows. "I ended up with two types of new customers: small manufacturers such as clothing designers and lamp designers, and small fabric stores."

Yaffe also ended up with a third group of customers—licensees—companies that wanted to use her designs on their own products. The first licensee to approach her was a small decorative paper company. "They looked at my fabric and saw it translated into decorative paper. They said, 'We want you to design paper for us for a 5% royalty.'" Yaffe spent an intense week preparing designs. The company eventually manufactured 20 different versions of her paper. Later, a subsidiary of a large fabric company asked for the right to license 16 of Yaffe's designs. This time, Yaffe received an advance payment (to be deducted from future royalties).

The path to royalty payments is not always so easy. A licensor like Rebecca Yaffe must negotiate the license agreement, determine financial terms, examine and approve the licensed products, and develop personal radar to separate the trustworthy licensees from the troublesome ones. But the rewards can make it all worthwhile—for example, years after creating a design, Yaffe still earns royalty payments. "I recently had a cool experience in Seattle. I was in a store and my papers were hanging there. Two and a half years later and those designs are still making money."

In this chapter I help you grapple with the legal and business issues of licensing, provide explanations for all the key provisions of typical license agreements, and provide examples of two agreements—a long form license agreement and an abbreviated one.

The Artist Is the Licensor; the Manufacturer Is the Licensee

When you license your work, you are the licensor. The person or company who manufactures your work is the licensee. In addition to the traditional crafts artist/manufacturer arrangement, a crafts artist can also license from another crafts artist. I explain how that might happen, below.

Finding licensing opportunities is beyond the scope of this chapter. Crafts artists often locate licensing opportunities by talking to artists in similar lines, checking classified ads in trade magazines, or exhibiting their work at trade shows. You may also wish to use the services of a licensing rep.

Crafts Licensing Overview

When you license your crafts work or design to be manufactured, the agreement is usually referred to as a "merchandise license." You may find it crass to refer to your art as merchandise, but lawyers use this terminology to distinguish your arrangement from other licensing arrangements such as invention or trademark licenses. Merchandise refers to any common consumer product that has some utility or function, for example, a T-shirt, ceramic cup, handbag, or jewelry.

Deciding whether to pursue a licensing opportunity requires weighing its potential benefits against other business issues. Is the licensed merchandise the type you would normally make and sell? Will the licensed merchandise cut into your existing sales or make current clients unhappy? Will the license provide you with new opportunities or freedom from manufacturing and selling? Once you have considered these issues, you'll be much better prepared to field an offer.

How Much Will You Get?

You benefit from licensing because you retain legal ownership of the work—for example, you keep your copyright or design patent—but someone else makes and sells it or something using its image. In return for granting the license, you receive a percentage—known as a royalty—

of the profits. In addition, you may receive an advance payment secured by future royalties.

> **EXAMPLE:** National Jewelers licenses a design from Sarah and pays Sarah an advance of $5,000 against a royalty of 5%. National produces and sells $200,000 worth of the licensed jewelry. Sarah earns $10,000 in royalties, but National deducts $5,000 as compensation for the advance.

In addition to paying royalties, the licensee must meet obligations set forth in the license agreement governing quality control, timely payments, and continuing to offer the merchandise for sale. If the licensee fails to perform according to these obligations, the licensor can terminate the agreement. Termination should not be taken lightly, since it can cause great expense for both parties, including the loss of income for the licensor and the loss of a substantial investment for the licensee.

Royalty rates for merchandise licensing vary depending on the merchandise involved. Below are some royalty estimates:

- greeting cards and gift wrap—2% to 5%
- household items such as cups, sheets, towels—3% to 8%
- fabrics, apparel (T-shirts, caps, and so on), decals—2% to 10%
- posters and prints—10% or more.

These royalties are commonly a percentage of net sales—usually the total or "gross" income received, less quantity discounts and customer returns. Some companies, however, may deduct more sums from the income before paying royalties. This makes the allowable deductions virtually as important as the royalty rate in determining how much money ultimately comes your way. For example, a royalty rate of 2% of net sales (as defined above) with no deductions may earn you more than you'd get from a 5% royalty rate from which marketing, shipping, commissions, and related expenses are deducted.

Always Check Out the Licensee

The suggestions I provide about license agreements will help protect your interests—but keep in mind that every agreement is only as solid as the parties who sign it. Make an effort to learn about the licensee. Ask for names of other designers from whom the company has licensed works, and talk to them about their experiences with the company. Find out the company's record regarding payments, credits, and other issues that matter to you. Use the Internet to research any articles about the company—for example, check business websites to see if the company has been rated badly or has been the subject of lawsuits.

You Are Licensing Legal Rights?

Under a license agreement, you retain ownership of the legal rights to your crafts but, for a limited time, you "rent" these rights to someone else. That person or company then manufactures and sells the work. The right that you license may be a copyright, design patent, trademark, or even trade secret used to create your work. If you have no legal rights, a licensee does not have to obtain your permission or pay you to use the work. In other words, you will have difficulty licensing your work if there are no legal rights to protect in it.

Licenses Compared With Assignments

If you see the word "assign" in the proposed license agreement, watch out. An assignment means that a craft artist is selling legal rights in a work to someone else—for example, if you were to sell your copyright in a fabric design. This is far different from the "rental" arrangement I've been describing. If you assign all your rights in a work, then that's it—you can't reproduce and sell that work any longer. There may be an occasion where an assignment makes sense—for example, sometimes you can assign all rights for the term of the license and they will be assigned back to you after it's over, or you may receive a large sum of money for an assignment. Nevertheless, if the licensee seems to be angling for an assignment, have an attorney review the draft agreement to guarantee that you're not permanently giving up all rights.

Do You Need an Attorney?

If you're a savvy, confident businessperson capable of reading contracts, you can probably negotiate your own license agreement. Many licensors use an attorney for their first license but proceed on their own with subsequent agreements. Whether you need to use an attorney usually depends on the following factors:

- **The parties.** If the licensee is a large corporation represented by attorneys, you'll probably need the assistance of an attorney.
- **The license agreement.** You'll have less need for an attorney if the other side provides an easy-to-understand agreement.
- **The work.** If a company wants to license your best-selling or signature work, you may want to invest in an attorney's help to give that work the extra protection it deserves.
- **Your comfort level.** If legal agreements just make you nervous, you might as well secure some backup and retain a knowledgeable licensing attorney.

For more information on hiring attorneys, review Chapter 11. Even if you use an attorney, you'll save money and increase your licensing awareness by reading this chapter. That way, you won't have to pay the attorney to educate you about the common concepts I describe here.

Who Furnishes the License Agreement?

Generally, the licensee drafts, prepares, and presents you with the merchandise license agreement. Before it does so, however, the two of you should work out the financial terms—for example, the royalty rate, rights being transferred, length of time the agreement will last, and other similar issues. To help you prepare this information, I have included a Merchandise License Worksheet later in this chapter. Use it to keep track of the essential terms of your agreement. Sometimes these terms are included on an exhibit that's attached to the agreement. (The model agreement includes such an exhibit.)

Prior to signing, but after the terms are agreed upon and the license is furnished, one or both parties may need to ask for changes to the agreement. For example, the licensor may want to modify provisions about sublicensing or dispute resolution. Be prepared to make modifications, to cut and paste provisions, or to restructure and reorder the agreement. These types of changes are common.

When Crafts Workers Are Licensees

Lori Sandstedt's artfully embellished handbags and colorful bracelets (www.lorimarsha.com) have proven a commercial and critical success (two of her handbag designs were selected as finalists for the 2002 Niche Awards). Sandstedt has no shortage of creative ideas, but when she met a like-minded artist who painted images on tiles, she wondered: What if she could incorporate the other artist's work onto her handbags? Discussions about the project left Sandstedt with many questions. "I wondered what was the right amount to pay for a royalty, and I was also unsure whether royalties were paid on net sales or a percentage of the wholesale price. Do I pay per image used? What if I used more than one image on a handbag? And where can I find a license agreement?" Lori Sandstedt's questions are good, and below I've organized some other queries that a licensor should ask:

- How much will it cost per item to manufacture the work?
- How much will it cost to ship it?
- How much commission must you pay to distributors or agents?
- How long will it take you to get the product to market?
- What's your net profit from each item?

Once you know these numbers, you can get a rough idea what offer to make to a potential licensor. Bear in mind that many other variables may play into your offer, such as the fame of the artist or the economics of mass production.

Underlying Lori Sandstedt's questions is another, more philosophical issue: How can a crafts business earn a profit from someone else's work and still maintain integrity and credibility? The key to negotiating any license agreement—whether with a large company or a local artist—is your ability to justify your position and to understand the other party's point of view. To accomplish this, you must do a thorough economic analysis, and you must be flexible in your discussions.

Creativity and flexibility help when negotiating. If you run into an impasse over terms, consider a system that rewards increasing sales—for example, a sliding royalty scale that rises as sales targets are reached. If one party is nervous about the deal, try making the period short—say, one year—with a renewal if sales targets are reached.

Little People = Big Bucks

Consider the story of Georgia crafts artist Xavier Roberts. In the 1970s, Roberts created his soft-sculpture "babies" known as "Little People" and dressed them in old clothes found at local yard sales. A year later, Roberts and five college friends created Original Appalachian Artworks and began offering the creations as Cabbage Patch Kids. One unique feature of the Cabbage Patch Kids was that a purchaser "adopted" each creation (adoption papers were included with each sale). The dolls became popular throughout the southeastern United States. In 1983, representatives of the Coleco toy company entered into a license agreement with Original Appalachian Artworks to manufacture and sell the dolls.

In the two decades since the Coleco deal, Roberts's crafts have generated over $4 billion (selling over 100 million dolls). For Appalachian Artworks, licensing has proven to be a successful strategy. When Coleco's license terminated in 1990, Appalachian was able to license to another toy company, Hasbro. Later, in 1995, it licensed to Mattel. In addition, Appalachian Artworks has entered into other license agreements with other companies. For example, it has licensed the right to make Cabbage Patch Kids videos, recordings, and other merchandise.

Merchandise License Agreement

In this section I'll analyze the provisions of the standard merchandise license agreement included with this book. I'll assume that you, the crafts worker, are the licensor. So when I refer to "you" I am speaking about the person who owns the design and is licensing it to a manufacturer. When I refer to the licensee, I'm referring to the company who will manufacture the design. (Though it's also possible that you may license another crafts worker's work.)

The licensee may furnish a preprepared merchandise license agreement. In that case you will need to read and review it, comparing its provisions to the model agreement in this book. Unfortunately, there are no rules for the ordering and placement of provisions in a license agreement. Many agreements seem haphazardly organized. In order to analyze an agreement, be prepared to spend several hours, and follow these steps:

- Make a photocopy of the agreement.
- Locate the major provisions (as discussed below) and, in the margin, label them according to the titles—for example, "grant of rights" or "arbitration." That way, you can find them quickly when making comparisons.
- Compare each provision with the language suggested in this chapter.
- Underline everything in the licensee's version that you don't like or don't understand.
- Prepare a chart listing each provision and your concerns.
- Convert the chart into a response letter detailing your requested changes.

 FORM ON CD-ROM
You can find the full text of the Merchandise License Agreement on the CD-ROM at the back of the book.

Here I explain the provisions in the Merchandise License Agreement.

Introductory Paragraph

The introductory paragraph should identify the people or companies entering into the agreement, known as the "parties." The introductory paragraph may also include the parties' business structure (corporation, sole proprietorship, and so on) and business address. Insert that information, if desired, following the name of each party—for example, "Artco Manufacturing, a California corporation located at 434 W. Oakdale Avenue, Los Angeles, California."

Instead of Licensee and Licensor, the agreement can be drafted to use the names of the parties throughout the agreement or terms such as "Artist" for the licensor and "Manufacturer" for the licensee. But once you've chosen to use certain terminology such as this, make sure to use it consistently throughout the agreement.

SAMPLE

Introduction. This License Agreement (the "Agreement") is made between _____ (referred to as "Licensor") and _____ (referred to as "Licensee"). The parties agree as follows:

TIP

"Whereas" Provisions. In some license agreements, the introductory information is referred to as the "Whereas" provisions. For example, the agreement might read: "Whereas DTK Decorating Company (the licensee) desires to acquire rights." The use of the term "whereas" has no particular legal significance, and I have abandoned it in our model agreements.

The Work

Your crafts work (the design or crafts work) is referred to as the "Work." Any appropriate term can be substituted instead of "work"—for example, "the Design" or "the Jewelry"—as long as this terminology is used consistently within the agreement. If more than one work is being licensed from the licensor, each work can be identified separately, such as Work #1, Work #2, and so on. You don't need to go into great detail yet—it's customary to do this in the first attachment to the agreement,

"Exhibit A." There, you'll describe each work, or, if possible, reference a separate photocopy of the artwork or text that will also be attached to the agreement. (Exhibit A is further described below.)

SAMPLE

> **The Work.** The Work refers to the work described in Exhibit A. Licensor is the owner of all rights to the Work, and Licensee shall not claim any right to use the Work except under the terms of this Agreement.

The Licensed Product

A licensed product is any merchandise that incorporates the work. If the definition of the product is too narrow, the licensee may be precluded from certain markets. For example, if the licensed product is described as "T-shirts," other shirts like tank tops could not be sold. Similarly, the term "ceramic cups" precludes the sale of plastic cups. If, however, you want to keep the range of potential merchandise narrow, be sure to define your licensed product very specifically. For instance, instead of "upper body apparel," define your licensed product only as "T-shirts." The definitions should be inserted in Exhibit A.

SAMPLE

> **Licensed Products.** Licensed Products are defined as the Licensee's products incorporating the Work specifically described in Exhibit A (the "Licensed Products").

The Grant of Rights

The grant of rights (also known as the "grant") officially permits use of the work, describes the legal rights being licensed, and establishes whether the rights are exclusive or nonexclusive. In a merchandise license agreement, the grant must include the following rights:

The right to reproduce. This refers to the right to make copies of the work or merchandise. This is similar to the grant of rights for a regular license agreement that gives the right to make copies on various media such as print or film. This right is essential for the merchandise agreement. Without it, the licensee won't even get to square one. The right to reproduce is not unlimited. The agreement specifically limits it to the use of the material on "Licensed Products." In other words, the artwork can only be used on specific products as defined in the attached exhibit.

The right to distribute copies. This refers to the right to sell or give away the work.

Reproduction and distribution are closely related and every merchandise license agreement requires both rights. Other rights, however, are optional. Below, I discuss the difference between exclusive and nonexclusive rights, and what optional rights may be granted.

Exclusive vs. Nonexclusive Rights

Every merchandise license agreement is either exclusive or nonexclusive. Exclusive means that only the licensee will have the rights granted in the agreement—no one else can be given those same rights for as long as the agreement lasts. Nonexclusive means that the owner of the crafts can give the same rights to someone else—for example, two different companies could license your pottery designs. The primary reason a licensee wants exclusive rights is to prevent a competitor from using the same material.

An exclusive license is usually more expensive than a nonexclusive license, but not always. For example, the fee for an exclusive license to use an image on auto seat covers may be the same as a nonexclusive license simply because the seat cover market is limited and there are few manufacturers. However, an exclusive license for T-shirts or calendars may be two or three times the cost of a nonexclusive license.

Optional Rights

The following rights may be included in a merchandise agreement:

The right to adapt or create derivatives. This refers to the right to modify the work—for example, to alter a design so that only a portion is used. The result of the modification is referred to as a derivative work. If the licensee plans to create a derivative work, the grant of rights must reflect that permission has been granted to modify the original work. The language in the model agreement allows you to own any modifications or contributions the licensee makes to the work. If this language is not included, you and the licensee may become coauthors of any jointly created derivative work—a result you may not desire (for more on coauthorship, see Chapter 6).

The right to display publicly. This refers to the right to publicly exhibit or display a licensed product. Even without acquiring this right in the agreement, the licensee can, under copyright law, display the artwork (as it is included on the merchandise) in connection with advertisements.

SAMPLE

Grant of Rights. Licensor grants to Licensee:

[*Select one*]

☐ an exclusive license

☐ a nonexclusive license

to reproduce and distribute the Work in the Licensed Products.

[*Optional*]

The right to modify the Work to incorporate it in the Licensed Products provided that Licensee agrees to assign to Licensor its rights, if any, in any derivative works resulting from Licensee's modification of the Work. Licensee agrees to execute any documents required to evidence this assignment of rights and to waive any moral rights and rights of attribution provided in 17 U.S.C. § 106A of the Copyright Act.

[*Optional*]

The right to publicly display the Work as incorporated in or on the Licensed Products.

Sublicenses

A sublicense allows the licensee to turn around and license its rights to another company. For example, a licensee may want to grant rights to other companies in the United States or in foreign countries, where the licensee is not prepared to play an active role itself. The only problem with sublicensing is that a new company—one with which you had no chance to meet and negotiate—suddenly has the right to make your design. In addition, you may be apprehensive about having your work sublicensed, especially if it's going somewhere where it would be expensive for you to enforce your legal rights. (You can also limit foreign sublicensing by restricting the territory covered by the agreement to a particular country.)

The safest route is to give the licensee a very limited right to sublicense rights abroad—one conditioned on you giving your consent to the deal. That way, you can review each sublicense agreement to determine its relative advantages and disadvantages. If you are experienced at selling in foreign markets and can handle foreign licensing yourself, then you will probably want to prohibit foreign sublicensing and retain those rights. The model agreement provides three choices regarding sublicensing. You can either:

- not permit sublicensing
- permit sublicensing only with your written consent, or
- permit sublicensing with your written consent, while stating that your consent cannot be unreasonably withheld. This is the preferred option for most licensees, because it means that you can only withhold consent for a valid business reason.

SAMPLE

> **Sublicense.**
>
> *[Select one]*
>
> ☐ **Consent required.** Licensee may sublicense the rights granted pursuant to this Agreement provided Licensee obtains Licensor's prior written consent to such sublicense, and Licensor receives such revenue or royalty payment as provided in the Payment section below. Any sublicense granted in violation of this provision shall be void.
>
> ☐ **Consent to sublicense not unreasonably withheld.** Licensee may sublicense the rights granted pursuant to this Agreement provided Licensee obtains Licensor's prior written consent to such sublicense, and Licensor receives such revenue or royalty payment as provided in the Payment section below. Licensor's consent to any sublicense shall not be unreasonably withheld. Any sublicense granted in violation of this provision shall be void.
>
> ☐ **No sublicensing permitted.** Licensee may not sublicense the rights granted under this Agreement.

Reservation of Rights

Ordinary contract law says that if you do not grant a specific right, you have retained (also known as "reserved") that right. Although it makes no legal difference whether you state this fact in your agreement, most licensors prefer to include this statement.

SAMPLE

> **Reservation of Rights:** Licensor reserves all rights other than those being conveyed or granted in this Agreement.

Territory

You can geographically limit where the licensee can exercise rights, by defining a "territory" in your agreement. If the territory is to be the entire world, insert the word "worldwide" into this section. If the territory is to be a specific region or country, insert that information. As a general rule, restrict the territory to regions where the licensee has previously sold goods with success. If in doubt, simply limit the agreement to North America (the United States and Canada).

SAMPLE

Territory. The rights granted to Licensee are limited to _____
_____ (the "Territory").

Term

By including a Term provision in your agreement, you can limit how long the merchandise license lasts. As a general rule, the licensee wants permission for as long as possible in order to properly develop and exploit the work. You, as the licensor, are likely to prefer a shorter period. That way, if you're not happy with the licensor's performance or you want out for some other reason, you'll have less time to wait before the agreement comes to a natural ending point—for example, one year instead of two or three years.

The date that an agreement commences is usually referred to as the effective date. If the agreement has a fixed date of termination, say in ten years, you would start counting the ten years at the effective date.

The model agreement prohibits a term that is longer than U.S. copyright or design patent protection would last. This makes sense, because once these legal rights expire, the licensee should not have to pay to use the licensed work while the rest of the world can use it for free.

Even if no time limit is expressed, U.S. copyright law allows you, under some circumstances, to terminate the merchandise license after

35 years. This is true even if the agreement contains a statement that the license is "forever" or "in perpetuity." Several options are offered for the term.

SAMPLE

Term. The "Effective Date" of this Agreement is defined as the date when the Agreement commences and is established by the latest signature date.

[*Select one*]

☐ **Specified term with renewal rights.** This Agreement shall commence upon the Effective Date and shall extend for a period of years (the "Initial Term"). Following the Initial Term, Licensee may renew this Agreement under the same terms and conditions for consecutive periods (the "Renewal Terms"), provided that Licensee provides written notice of its intention to renew this Agreement within thirty (30) days before the expiration of the current term. In no event shall the Term extend beyond the period of United States copyright protection for the Work and design patent protection, if applicable.

☐ **Fixed term.** This Agreement shall commence upon the Effective Date and shall continue for unless sooner terminated pursuant to a provision of this Agreement.

☐ **Specified term with renewal rights.** This Agreement shall commence upon the Effective Date and shall extend for a period of _____ years (the "Initial Term"). Following the Initial Term, Licensee may renew this agreement under the same terms and conditions for _____ consecutive periods (the "Renewal Terms"), provided that Licensee provides written notice of its intention to renew this agreement within thirty (30) days before the expiration of the current term. In no event shall the Term extend beyond the period of United States copyright protection for the Work.

☐ **Term for as long as Licensee sells Licensed Products.** This Agreement shall commence upon the Effective Date as specified in Exhibit A and shall continue for as long as Licensee continues to offer the Licensed Products in commercially reasonable quantities or unless sooner terminated pursuant to a provision of this Agreement. In no event shall the Term extend beyond the period of U.S. copyright protection for the Work.

> ☐ **Term with renewal based upon sales.** This Agreement shall commence upon the Effective Date and shall extend for a period of _____ years (the "Initial Term") and may be renewed by Licensee under the same terms and conditions for consecutive _____-year periods (the "Renewal Terms"), provided that:
>
> (a) Licensee provides written notice of its intention to renew this Agreement within thirty days before the expiration of the current term, and
>
> (b) Licensee has met the sales requirements as established in Exhibit A.

Payments, Net Sales, and Fees

Under your license agreement, you will be paid a royalty, that is, a continuing payment based upon a percentage of the income from the licensed product. In other words, if the merchandise sells well, you'll receive more money. In some cases, a licensee must make payments in advance of royalties (known as "advances") or must pay fixed or "guaranteed minimum annual royalty" payments (see below) regardless of sales. In other words, money and time may be spent even if the licensed product is not successful. Below are definitions of some royalty terms you might need to use.

Gross sales refers to the total amount billed to customers. Net sales are usually defined as the licensee's gross sales minus certain deductions. In other words, the licensee calculates the total amount billed to customers and deducts certain items before paying the royalty. It is generally acceptable to deduct from gross sales any amounts paid for taxes, credits, returns, and discounts made at the time of sale. It is also common to deduct shipping (the cost of getting the products to the buyer).

An advance against royalties is an up-front payment to you, usually made at the time the license agreement is signed. An advance is almost always credited or "recouped" against future royalties, unless the agreement provides otherwise. It's as if the licensee is saying, "I expect you will earn at least $1,000 in royalties, so I am going to advance you that sum at the time I sign the agreement." When you start earning royalties, the licensee keeps the first $1,000 to repay the advance. If the licensor doesn't earn the $1,000 in royalties, the licensee takes a loss. You don't have to return the advance unless you breach the agreement.

A percentage of net sales (the licensed product royalty) is the most common form of licensing payment. Net sales royalty payments are computed by multiplying the royalty rate against net sales. For example, a royalty rate of 5% multiplied by net sales of $1,000 equals a net sales royalty of $50.

A per unit royalty is tied to the number of units sold or manufactured, not to the total money earned by sales. For example, under a per unit royalty you might receive 50 cents for each licensed product sold or manufactured. The licensee cannot choose both per unit and net sales royalties. If the licensee intends to license your work for a free distribution, for example, giving out hundreds of the products at a promotion, include the "manufactured" option. If the licensee will be offering your work for sale (not for free), include the "sold" option. Generally, net sales royalties are preferred over per unit royalties because revenue may come from sources such as sublicensing, in which case the total net sales will be easier to track.

A guaranteed minimum annual royalty payment (GMAR) is when the licensee promises that you'll receive a specific payment every year, regardless of how well the merchandise sells during each year. The licensee pays the GMAR at the beginning of the year. At the end of that year, if the earned royalties exceed the GMAR, you're paid the difference. If the GMAR exceeds the earned royalties, the licensee takes a loss. To avoid taking the loss, a licensee may insist that the agreement contain a clause stating that this difference will be carried forward and deducted against the next year's royalties. Also don't be surprised if the licensee wants to limit the initial term of the agreement. Otherwise, the licensee risks being locked into paying GMARs when the merchandise is not selling at all.

On rare occasions, a licensee may pay you a one-time license fee at the time of signing the agreement. This fee differs from an advance, because it is not deducted from royalties. The licensee may arrange to make the payment when the licensed product is first distributed. That way, if the licensed product is not produced, the licensee does not have to pay.

If the license agreement permits sublicensing, keep the provision for sublicensing revenue in the agreement.

SAMPLE

Payments. All royalties ("Royalties") provided for under this Agreement shall accrue when the respective Licensed Products are sold, shipped, distributed, billed, or paid for, whichever occurs first.

Net Sales. Net Sales are defined as Licensee's gross sales (that is, the gross invoice amount billed customers) less quantity discounts or rebates and returns actually credited. A quantity discount or rebate is a discount made at the time of shipment. No deductions shall be made for cash or other discounts, commissions, manufacturing costs, or uncollectible accounts, or for fees or expenses of any kind that the Licensee may incur in connection with the Royalty payments.

Fees.

[*Select one or more*]

☐ **Advance Against Royalties.** As a nonrefundable advance against Royalties (the "Advance"), Licensee agrees to pay to Licensor upon execution of this Agreement the sum of $_____ .

☐ **Licensed Product Royalty.** Licensee agrees to pay a Royalty of _____% percent of all Net Sales revenue of the Licensed Products ("Licensed Product Royalty").

☐ **Per Unit Royalty.** Licensee agrees to pay a Royalty of $_____ for each unit of the Licensed Product that is: [*select one*]

   ☐ manufactured.

   ☐ sold.

☐ **Guaranteed Minimum Annual Royalty Payment.** In addition to any other advances or fees, Licensee shall pay an annual guaranteed royalty (the "GMAR") as follows: $_____ . The GMAR shall be paid to Licensor annually on _____ . The GMAR is an advance against royalties for the 12-month period commencing upon payment.

☐ Royalty payments based on Net Sales made during any year of this Agreement shall be credited against the GMAR due for the year in which such Net Sales were made. In the event that annual royalties exceed the GMAR, Licensee shall pay the difference to Licensor. Any annual royalty payments in excess of the GMAR shall not be carried forward from previous years or applied against the GMAR.

☐ **License Fee.** As a nonrefundable, nonrecoupable fee for executing this license, Licensee agrees to pay to Licensor upon execution of this Agreement the sum of $_____ .

☐ **Sublicensing Revenues.** In the event of any sublicense of the rights granted pursuant to this Agreement, Licensee shall pay to Licensor _____% of all sublicensing revenues.

[*Optional*]

Payments and Statements to Licensor. Within thirty (30) days after the end of each calendar quarter (the "Royalty Period"), an accurate statement of Net Sales of Licensed Products along with any royalty payments or sublicensing revenues due to Licensor shall be provided to Licensor, regardless of whether any Licensed Products were sold during the Royalty Period. All payments shall be paid in United States currency drawn on a United States bank. The acceptance by Licensor of any of the statements furnished or royalties paid shall not preclude Licensor questioning the correctness at any time of any payments or statements.

Audits

In case one day you suspect that the licensee has failed to properly pay royalties, you'll want the right to perform an audit to detect and quantify the shortfall. The Audit provision describes when you (or your representative) can access licensee records. If the audit uncovers an error of a certain magnitude—usually a sum between $500 and $2,000—the licensee will have to not only compensate you for the shortfall, but pay for the audit, as well. Insert an amount in the blank space. If the audited sum is lower than this amount, you are the one who will have to pay for the audit.

SAMPLE

> **Audit.** Licensee shall keep accurate books of accounts and records covering all transactions relating to the license granted in this Agreement, and Licensor or its duly authorized representatives shall have the right, upon five days' prior written notice and during normal business hours, to inspect and audit Licensee's records relating to the Work licensed under this Agreement. Licensor shall bear the cost of such inspection and audit, unless the results indicate an underpayment greater than $ _____ for any six-month (6-month) period. In that case, Licensee shall promptly reimburse Licensor for all costs of the audit along with the amount due with interest on such sums. Interest shall accrue from the date the payment was originally due, and the interest rate shall be 1.5% per month, or the maximum rate permitted by law, whichever is less. All books of account and records shall be made available in the United States and kept available for at least two years after the termination of this Agreement.

Late Payments

To encourage prompt payment, this provision enables you to obtain interest on late payments—that is, to recover the money you might have earned in interest if you had placed the payment into an interest-bearing account.

SAMPLE

> **Late Payment.** Time is of the essence with respect to all payments to be made by Licensee under this Agreement. If Licensee is late in any payment provided for in this Agreement, Licensee shall pay interest on the payment from the date due until paid at a rate of 1.5% per month, or the maximum rate permitted by law, whichever is less.

Warranties and Indemnity

Warranties are contractual promises that you and the licensor will make. If you break one of these promises, you will—under the indemnity provision—have to pay for any costs that result. (The same will be true for the licensor.) In this way, warranties and indemnity work together.

A merchandise license can also be written without including warranties or indemnity provisions. They are recommended, but not essential for the agreement.

Warranties

In some agreements, warranties are labeled as "covenants" or "represent-ations." Regardless of the title, they are essentially the same things— promises made between the parties. For example, you might promise that you own the rights in the crafts product and that the crafts work doesn't infringe third-party rights. (Third parties are people who are not part of the agreement.) In case you feel uncomfortable making this kind of assurance, the model agreement provides a more palatable warranty, stating that you have "no knowledge as to any third-party claims." In other words, you recognize the remote possibility that the crafts work may infringe someone's copyright, but you—after performing a reasonable investigation—don't have any knowledge that it does.

You should ask that the licensee provide a warranty that sales and marketing of the licensed product will conform to applicable laws. A sample provision is included in the model merchandise agreement.

If an agreement includes a warranty but not an indemnity provision, the parties can still sue for "breach of warranty." However, you would have to go to court to for a decision on whether the breaching party must pay the costs or attorney fees associated with the breach.

SAMPLE

> **Licensor Warranties.** Licensor warrants that it has the power and authority to enter into this Agreement and has no knowledge as to any third-party claims regarding the proprietary rights in the Work that would interfere with the rights granted under this Agreement.

> **Licensee Warranties.** Licensee warrants that it will use its best commercial efforts to market the Licensed Products and that their sale and marketing shall be in conformance with all applicable laws and regulations, including but not limited to all intellectual property laws.

Indemnity

Indemnity is recommended, but is not essential for the agreement. A licensor who provides indemnity is agreeing to pay for the licensee's damages in certain situations. For example, if you indemnify the licensee against infringement, you will have to pay damages (and legal fees) if the licensee is sued by a company claiming that your work is a copy of its work. In this way, indemnity acts like a powerful shield. The licensee can deflect a lawsuit and make you pay for the damages and legal fees. Indemnity provisions are also sometimes referred to as "hold harmless" provisions, because the language for an indemnity provision often states that the "Licensor shall hold the Licensee harmless from any losses," and so on.

If possible, you should avoid indemnity, as it means taking on a legal obligation to pay someone else's legal costs. If a licensee is insistent, however, you may have to agree to this provision. But hold firm on insisting that the amount not be larger than any amounts you have received under the agreement.

In some cases, you may insist on establishing an indemnity fund. With such a fund, if indemnity is triggered, the licensee stops paying you royalties and places these payments into the fund. This deprives you of ongoing royalty payments but prevents you from having to pay out any additional money for indemnity. You may also request that the licensee provide you with indemnification as well. Indemnification would protect you from any third-party claims arising from illegal licensee business practices or from any additions or modifications that the licensee makes to your design.

SAMPLE

Indemnification by Licensor

[*Select one if appropriate*]

☐ **Licensor indemnification without limitations.** Licensor shall indemnify Licensee and hold Licensee harmless from any damages and liabilities (including reasonable attorney fees and costs) arising from any breach of Licensor's warranties as defined in Licensor's Warranties, above.

☐ **Licensor indemnification limited to amounts paid.** Licensor shall indemnify Licensee and hold Licensee harmless from any damages and liabilities (including reasonable attorney fees and costs) arising from any breach of Licensor's warranties as defined in Licensor's Warranties, above. Licensor's maximum liability under this provision shall in no event exceed the total amount earned by Licensor under this Agreement.

☐ **Licensor indemnification with limitations.** Licensor shall indemnify Licensee and hold Licensee harmless from any damages and liabilities (including reasonable attorney fees and costs) arising from any breach of Licensor's warranties as defined in Licensor's Warranties, above, provided:

(a) such claim, if sustained, would prevent Licensee from marketing the Licensed Products or the Work

(b) such claim arises solely out of the Work as disclosed to the Licensee, and not out of any change in the Work made by Licensee or a vendor

(c) Licensee gives Licensor prompt written notice of any such claim

(d) such indemnity shall only be applicable in the event of a final decision by a court of competent jurisdiction from which no right to appeal exists, and

(e) the maximum amount due from Licensor to Licensee under this paragraph shall not exceed the amounts due to Licensor under the Payment section from the date that Licensor notifies Licensee of the existence of such a claim.

☐ **Licensee Warranties.** Licensee warrants that it will use its best commercial efforts to market the Licensed Products and that their sale and marketing shall be in conformance with all applicable laws and regulations, including but not limited to all intellectual property laws.

Indemnification by Licensee. Licensee shall indemnify Licensor and hold Licensor harmless from any damages and liabilities (including reasonable attorney fees and costs):

(a) arising from any breach of Licensee's warranties and representation as defined in the Licensee Warranties, above

(b) arising out of any alleged defects or failures to perform of the Licensed Products or any product liability claims or use of the Licensed Products, and

(c) arising out of advertising, distribution, or marketing of the Licensed Products.

Intellectual Property Rights

If you have not filed a copyright registration or a design patent covering your work and do not plan to, the licensee may register for protection under this provision. For information about copyright registration, consult the Copyright Office website at www.copyright.gov. It is common for the licensee to deduct the reasonable costs of registration from future royalties.

SAMPLE

Intellectual Property Registration. Licensor may, but is not obligated to, seek in its own name and at its own expense appropriate copyright registrations or design patent registrations for the Work, if applicable. Licensor makes no warranty with respect to the validity of any copyright or design patent that may be granted. Licensor grants to Licensee the right to apply for registration of the Work or Licensed Products provided that such registrations shall be applied for in the name of Licensor and licensed to Licensee during the Term and according to the conditions of this Agreement. Licensee shall have the right to deduct its reasonable out-of-pocket expenses for the preparation and filing of any such registrations from future royalties due to Licensor under this Agreement. Licensee shall obtain Licensor's prior written consent before incurring expenses for any foreign copyright or design patent applications.

> **Compliance With Intellectual Property Laws.** The license granted in this Agreement is conditioned on Licensee's compliance with the provisions of the intellectual property laws of the United States and any foreign country in the Territory. All copies of the Licensed Product as well as all promotional material shall bear appropriate proprietary notices.

Credits

The Credit provision allows you to advise the licensee of any credit you want to appear on the merchandise. For instance, if I wanted to be credited for a photograph I was licensing, I would insert the following desired credit line:

SAMPLE

> © 2010 Rich Stim

The licensee's failure to include the credit could provide a basis for termination. The Credit section also provides the licensee with the right to use the licensor's name and trademark in advertising for the merchandised product. If you are an established crafts artist, the licensee will have a strong motivation to use your name (and maybe your image) in advertising and promotional materials.

SAMPLE

> **Licensor Credits.** Licensee shall identify Licensor as the owner of rights to the Work and shall include the following notice on all copies of the Licensed Products: "_____ . All rights reserved." Licensee may, with Licensor's consent, use Licensor's name, image, or trademark in advertising or promotional materials associated with the sale of the Licensed Products.

Infringement by Third Parties

Imitation may be a form of flattery, but it's also a form of infringement. Unethical competitors often create imitations of successful licensed products. If you do not have the money to fight an infringer, this provision allows the licensee to sue or settle with infringers. It provides for funding of a lawsuit and for determining how to divide any money that is recovered from the infringer. The provision in our model agreement establishes a 50/50 division of any award money after payment of attorney fees.

SAMPLE

> **Infringement by Third Parties.** In the event that either party learns of imitations or infringements of the Work or Licensed Products, that party shall notify the other in writing of the infringements or imitations. Licensor shall have the right to commence lawsuits against third persons arising from infringement of the Work or Licensed Products. In the event that Licensor does not commence a lawsuit against an alleged infringer within sixty (60) days of notification by Licensee, Licensee may commence a lawsuit against the third party. Before filing suit, Licensee shall obtain the written consent of Licensor to do so, and such consent shall not be unreasonably withheld. Licensor will cooperate fully and in good faith with Licensee for the purpose of securing and preserving Licensee's rights to the Work. Any recovery (including, but not limited to, a judgment, settlement, or license agreement included as resolution of an infringement dispute) shall be divided equally between the parties after deduction and payment of reasonable attorney fees to the party bringing the lawsuit.

Exploitation

When it comes to licensing your work, exploitation is a good thing. You want to be sure that the licensee won't simply sit on your work, which would prevent you from earning the royalties you're anticipating. If your agreement is an exclusive one, inaction by the licensee would be doubly frustrating, since you would be unable to license the product to anyone else. The exploitation provision addresses these concerns by setting a date by which the licensee must release the licensed product. Sometimes the release date is set to coincide with a specific trade show or a seasonal catalog. If the licensee fails to meet this date, you can claim that there has been a "material breach," which is a basis for termination of the license agreement.

SAMPLE

> **Exploitation Date.** Licensee agrees to manufacture, distribute, and sell the Licensed Products in commercially reasonable quantities during the term of this Agreement and to commence such manufacture, distribution, and sale by _____ . This is a material provision of this Agreement.

Advertising Budget

This optional provision provides an assurance that the licensee will allocate a budget to advertising your work.

> ☐ **Advertising Budget.** Licensee agrees to spend at least _____% of estimated annual gross sales for promotional efforts and advertising of the Licensed Products.

Approval of Samples and Quality Control

This provision gives you the right to look at and approve samples and prototypes of the artwork before it goes into full production. The provision gives the licensee an incentive to reproduce your work properly—and it prevents nasty surprises. If you have the clout and bargaining power, you may expand this provision to give you a right to inspect the manufacturing facilities and to reject any subcontracting manufacturing if their standards are insufficient.

SAMPLE

> **Approval of Samples and Quality Control.** Licensee shall submit a reasonable number of preproduction designs, prototypes, and camera-ready artwork prior to production, as well as preproduction samples of the Licensed Product to Licensor, to assure that the product meets Licensor's quality standards. In the event that Licensor fails to object in writing within ten (10) business days after the date of receipt of any such materials, such materials shall be deemed to be acceptable. At least once during each calendar year, Licensee shall submit two (2) production samples of each Licensed Product for review. Licensee shall pay all costs for delivery of these approval materials. The quality standards applied by Licensor shall be no more rigorous than the quality standards applied by Licensor to similar products.

Licensor Copies and Right to Purchase

You will probably want some free copies of the licensed product, for yourself and your close friends and relatives. This provision allows you and the licensee to specify how many you'll receive. The number you agree upon will probably depend on the value of the product and the size of the market—obviously, the licensee doesn't want you to undercut his profits by playing Santa Claus. If you think your generosity will exceed the number of free copies, you can negotiate for the right to purchase more product at the wholesale cost.

SAMPLE

> **Licensor Copies and Right to Purchase.** Licensee shall provide Licensor with _____ copies of each Licensed Product. Licensor has the right to purchase from Licensee, at Licensee's manufacturing cost, at least _____ copies of any Licensed Product, and such payments shall be deducted from Royalties due to Licensor.

Confidentiality

Though it may seem obvious that your discussions are confidential, you'd be surprised at how easy it is for you—or the other party—to forget this and disclose confidential information provided by one party. When you're deep in a conversation with your friend, hairdresser, or mechanic, it may seem so natural to say, "This company I'm dealing with is planning to expand into the fabric business." You've now revealed potentially important facts about the condition of the other party's business. Confidential information includes any information that gives a business an advantage and is maintained in confidence.

The Confidentiality clause below reminds each party to preserve the other's confidential information—and allows each to sue for breach of contract if the other slips up.

SAMPLE

> **Confidentiality.** The parties acknowledge that each may have access to confidential information that relates to each other's business (the "Information"). The parties agree to protect the confidentiality of the Information and maintain it with the strictest confidence, and no party shall disclose such information to third parties without the prior written consent of the other.

Insurance

Those patterned mugs may look innocent now, sitting on the shelf. But you should never underestimate the capacity of consumers to use products in a way that injures them—and then blame someone else for it. If a consumer is injured using the licensed product and claims it's defective, you and the licensee can be sued under a legal theory called "product liability."

For these reasons, you want to make sure that the licensee, as the one who'll be selling the merchandise, acquires product liability insurance. The first benefit of such insurance is that the insurance company—not you or the licensee—will have to defend the claim. That's a significant benefit, because legal fees can add up quickly, even in a case that you ultimately win. In addition, by requiring that the licensee name you in the policy, you will be shielded from paying damages in the event that a customer wins a product injury claim. The minimum amount of coverage inserted for the policy should be $1,000,000.

Product liability insurance doesn't usually cover trademark, patent, or copyright lawsuits. The licensee needs a separate business policy for protection against infringement claims.

SAMPLE

Insurance. Licensee shall, throughout the Term, obtain and maintain, at its own expense, standard product liability insurance coverage, naming Licensor as an additional named insured. Such policy shall provide protection against any claims, demands, and causes of action arising out of any alleged defects or failure to perform of the Licensed Products or any use of the Licensed Products. The amount of coverage shall be a minimum of $_____ , with no deductible amount for each single occurrence for bodily injury or property damage. The policy shall provide for notice to the Licensor from the insurer by registered or certified mail in the event of any modification or termination of insurance. The provisions of this section shall survive termination for three years.

Termination

Even without a termination provision, either party can terminate a merchandise license agreement if the other party commits a "material breach." A material breach means a substantial abuse of the agreement— for example, if the licensee uses the crafts work for purposes not described in the agreement.

Most licensors will insist upon a written termination provision and will seek some or all of the rights listed in our model agreement, including the right to terminate as to a specific portion of the territory if it is not exploited.

SAMPLE

Licensor's Right to Terminate. Licensor shall have the right to terminate this Agreement for the following reasons:

[*Select one or more*]

☐ **Failure to make timely payment.** Licensee fails to pay Royalties when due or fails to accurately report Net Sales, as defined in the Payment section of this Agreement, and such failure is not cured within thirty (30) days after written notice from the Licensor.

☐ **Failure to introduce product.** Licensee fails to introduce the product to market by the date set in the Exploitation section of this Agreement or to offer the Licensed Products in commercially reasonable quantities during any subsequent year.

☐ **Assignment or sublicensing.** Licensee assigns or sublicenses in violation of this Agreement.

☐ **Failure to maintain insurance.** Licensee fails to maintain or obtain product liability insurance as required by the provisions of this Agreement.

☐ **Failure to submit samples.** Licensee fails to provide Licensor with preproduction samples for approval.

☐ **Termination as to unexploited portion of territory.** Licensor shall have the right to terminate the grant of license under this Agreement with respect to any country or region included in the Territory in which Licensee fails to offer the Licensed Products for sale or distribution or to secure a sublicense agreement for the marketing, distribution, and sale of the product within two (2) years of the Effective Date.

Effect of Termination and Sell-Off Period

If the licensee breaches the agreement for any of the reasons provided under "Licensor's Right to Terminate"—for example, the licensee stops paying you royalties—the licensee should not be permitted to continue profiting from your art by selling off inventory. If the agreement has expired or ended amicably, however, it's reasonable to permit the licensee to sell off the remaining inventory during a fixed time period, say six months. Naturally, the licensee must also pay royalties and provide an accounting for these products.

SAMPLE

Effect of Termination. Upon termination of this Agreement ("Termination"), all Royalty obligations as established in the Payments section shall immediately become due. After the Termination of this license, all rights granted to Licensee under this Agreement shall terminate and revert to Licensor, and Licensee will refrain from further manufacturing, copying, marketing, distribution, or use of any Licensed Product or other product that incorporates the Work. Within thirty (30) days after Termination, Licensee shall deliver to Licensor a statement indicating the number and description of the Licensed Products that it had on hand or is in the process of manufacturing as of the Termination date.

Sell-Off Period. Licensee may dispose of the Licensed Products covered by this Agreement for a period of ninety (90) days after Termination or expiration, except that Licensee shall have no such right in the event this agreement is terminated according to the Licensor's Right to Terminate, above. At the end of the post-Termination sale period, Licensee shall furnish a royalty payment and statement as required under the Payment section. Upon Termination, Licensee shall deliver to Licensor all original artwork and camera-ready reproductions used in the manufacture of the Licensed Products. Licensor shall bear the costs of shipping for the artwork and reproductions.

Dispute Resolution

To avoid the high costs associated with formal court trials, many contracts now commit the parties to trying alternative methods of resolving their disputes first. Your two main choices are arbitration and mediation.

With arbitration, the parties hire one or more arbitrators—experts at resolving disputes—to evaluate the dispute and make a determination. Even if neither party is entirely happy with the arbitrator's decision, they have to live with it—that's why it's often called "binding arbitration."

With mediation, a neutral evaluator helps the parties settle their dispute themselves. That is, the mediator offers advice so that the parties can reach a solution together, but doesn't interject his or her own solution. Mediation and arbitration are referred to as alternative dispute resolution or ADR.

The model agreement includes two alternative dispute resolution provisions. The second is only for arbitration. The first provides for mediation first, then for arbitration if mediation fails. (For a discussion of the pros and cons of arbitration, see Chapter 11.)

SAMPLE

Dispute Resolution

[*Optional, select one*]

☐ **Mediation and Arbitration.** The parties agree that every dispute or difference between them arising under this Agreement shall be settled first by a meeting of the parties attempting to confer and resolve the dispute in a good faith manner. If the parties cannot resolve their dispute after conferring, any Party may require the other Party to submit the matter to nonbinding mediation, utilizing the services of an impartial professional mediator approved by all parties. If the parties cannot come to an agreement following mediation, the parties agree to submit the matter to binding arbitration at a location mutually agreeable to the parties. The arbitration shall be conducted on a confidential basis pursuant to the Commercial Arbitration Rules of the American Arbitration Association. Any decision or award as a result of any such arbitration proceeding shall include an assessment of costs, expenses, and reasonable attorney's fees and shall include a written record of the proceedings and a written determination of the arbitrators. An arbitrator experienced in copyright and merchandising law shall conduct any such arbitration. An award of arbitration shall be final and binding on the parties and may be confirmed in a court of competent jurisdiction.

☐ **Arbitration.** If a dispute arises under or relating to this Agreement, the parties agree to submit such dispute to binding arbitration in the state of _____ or another location mutually agreeable to the parties. The arbitration shall be conducted on a confidential basis pursuant

---

to the Commercial Arbitration Rules of the American Arbitration Association. Any decision or award as a result of any such arbitration proceeding shall be in writing and shall provide an explanation for all conclusions of law and fact and shall include an assessment of costs, expenses, and reasonable attorney fees. An arbitrator experienced in copyright and merchandising law shall conduct any such arbitration. An award of arbitration may be confirmed in a court of competent jurisdiction.

No Special Damages

If either party breaches the agreement, state laws provide that the non-breaching party can recover the amount of the loss directly resulting from the breach. For example, if the licensee fails to accurately pay royalties, you can sue to recover the unpaid amount, along with attorney fees if the agreement provides for such fees. However, under some state laws, claims may be made for additional damages—for example, special or punitive damages that are awarded to punish the breaching party. These are sometimes double or triple the amount of damage that the nonbreaching party actually suffered. If you and the other party agree that you don't want to expose each other to this level of risk, you can insert a No Special Damages provision into your agreement. This provision prevents either party from claiming any damages other than those actually suffered directly from the breach.

SAMPLE

No Special Damages. Licensor shall not be liable to Licensee for any incidental, consequential, punitive, or special damages.

Miscellaneous Provisions

Many agreements contain provisions entitled "Miscellaneous" or "General." These provisions actually have little in common with one another except for the fact that they don't fit anywhere else in the agreement. They're contract orphans and for that reason are usually dumped at the end of the agreement. Lawyers often refer to these provisions as "boilerplate." Don't be misled by the fact that boilerplate is buried at the back of the agreement. You'll be turning straight to that page if you're in the middle of a dispute with the licensee and need to know the procedures for resolving the dispute and how a court will enforce the agreement.

Even though the Miscellaneous and General provisions are important, they are not mandatory. In other words, if you and the licensee agree to leave them out, you can do so without affecting the validity of the remaining agreement. Below is a summary of common boilerplate provisions.

Entire Agreement

The Entire Agreement provision (sometimes referred to as the "Integration" provision) establishes that the agreement is the final version and that any further modification must be in writing. It prevents parties from later claiming, "But you told me such-and-such."

SAMPLE

> **Entire Agreement.** This is the entire agreement between the parties. It replaces and supersedes any and all oral agreements between the parties, as well as any prior writings. Modifications and amendments to this Agreement, including any exhibit or appendix hereto, shall be enforceable only if they are in writing and are signed by authorized representatives of both parties.

Successors and Assigns

In the event the agreement is assigned, or another company succeeds one of the parties—for example, a company buys the licensee—this provision assures that the acquiring party is bound by the Agreement.

SAMPLE

> **Successors and Assignees.** This Agreement binds and benefits the heirs, successors, and assignees of the parties.

Notices

The Notices provision tells each party how to alert the other one if a dispute arises. If a party fails to follow these notice procedures, he or she won't get very far toward resolving the dispute until proper notification has been provided.

SAMPLE

> **Notices.** Any notice or communication required or permitted to be given under this Agreement shall be sufficiently given when received by certified mail, or sent by facsimile transmission or overnight courier.

Governing Law

Every state has its own laws regarding contract interpretation. Though you might assume that the laws of the state in which you're currently sitting will govern your license agreement, that's not necessarily so. Parties in disputes over past contracts have been known to look around for states with laws that work to their advantage and argue that the other state's law applies. You can avoid this shopping-around game by inserting a simple provision—sometimes called a "Choice of Law" provision—stating which state's law will govern any lawsuit. Does it matter which state is chosen? Some states have a reputation for being better for certain kinds of disputes, but, generally, the differences between states' laws are not great enough to make this a major negotiating issue.

SAMPLE

> **Governing Law.** This Agreement will be governed by the laws of the State of
>
> _____ .

Waiver

A Waiver provision permits the parties to forgo or give up claim to a portion of the agreement without establishing a precedent for themselves. In other words, you don't have to enforce every part of the agreement every time you possibly could in order to keep it alive. For example, if you accept late royalty payments for two months (thereby waiving the portion of the contract that requires timely royalty payments), the Waiver provision says that you haven't established a precedent allowing late royalty payments.

SAMPLE

> **Waiver.** The failure to exercise any right provided in this Agreement shall not be a waiver of prior or subsequent rights.

Severability

This provision (sometimes referred to as the "Invalidity" provision) permits a court to sever (or take out) a portion of the agreement that's no longer good while keeping the rest of the agreement intact. Otherwise, if one portion of the agreement becomes invalid, a court may rule that the whole agreement has been dragged down into invalidity along with it.

SAMPLE

> **Severability.** If a court finds any provision of this Agreement invalid or unenforceable, the remainder of this Agreement will be interpreted so as best to carry out the parties' intent.

Attachments

The Attachment provision guarantees that any attachments (documents sometimes referred to as "exhibits," which are attached to the agreement) will be included as part of the agreement.

SAMPLE

Attachments and Exhibits. The parties agree and acknowledge that all attachments, exhibits, and schedules referred to in this Agreement are incorporated in this Agreement by reference.

No Agency

The relationship between you and the licensee is defined by the agreement. But to an outsider, it may appear that you have a different relationship, such as a partnership or joint venture. It's possible that an unscrupulous licensee will try to capitalize on this appearance and make a third-party deal. If that deal goes bad, you could find the third party coming to you to put matters right. In order to avoid liability for such a situation, most agreements include a provision disclaiming any relationship other than licensee/licensor.

SAMPLE

No Agency. Nothing contained herein will be construed as creating any agency, partnership, joint venture, or other form of joint enterprise between the parties.

Attorney Fees

The Attorney Fees provision establishes that the winner of a legal dispute receives payment for legal fees. Without this optional provision, each party has to pay its own attorney fees.

SAMPLE

> **Attorney Fees and Expenses.** The prevailing party shall have the right to collect from the other party its reasonable costs and necessary disbursements and attorney fees incurred in enforcing this Agreement.

Jurisdiction and Venue

In the event of a dispute, the Jurisdiction and Venue provision establishes which state and county the lawsuit or arbitration must be filed and heard in. Of course, each party will prefer going to court in its home county. Therefore, this section is optional and a matter of negotiation. If the section creates too much contention, remove it. In disputes over contracts that contain no reference to jurisdiction, the location is usually determined by whoever files the lawsuit. If a jurisdiction clause is used, it should list the same state as named in the Governing Law section (discussed above).

SAMPLE

> **Jurisdiction.** The parties consent to the exclusive jurisdiction and venue of the federal and state courts located in _____ [county], _____ [state], in any action arising out of or relating to this Agreement. The parties waive any other venue to which either party might be entitled by domicile or otherwise.

In Some States, Jurisdiction Clauses Are Invalid. In the past, many courts believed that citizens should not be able to bargain for jurisdiction (sometimes referred to as forum shopping), and these courts would not enforce jurisdiction provisions. Today, only three states—Alabama, Idaho, and Montana—refuse to honor jurisdiction provisions in agreements.

Assignability

Although you might think of your agreement as being between you and the licensee alone, that's not always the way business works. It is possible that the licensee may, at some point, wish to transfer the rights under your agreement to another company. Normal contract law allows her to do this by "assigning" her rights to a third party—unless you insert a provision to stop or control this.

For example, let's imagine that the licensee has two agreements with you: one to license your earring design and the other to license your bracelet design. The licensee later decides it only wants to concentrate on earrings. It wants to assign its rights in the bracelet design to a company that specializes in bracelet merchandising. You may—or may not—be happy with the change. For example, if the new company has a bad reputation when it comes to paying royalties, you're likely to regard this as a disaster. For this reason, our model agreement provides three choices regarding assignability.

The first option requires that your written consent be given for an assignment. Under this option, you can review the deal and decide, for any reason, that you don't like the assignment and won't have it.

The second choice also requires your written consent, but you must not refuse it without having a valid business reason. A valid business reason usually means an actual and substantial business risk—for example, the new company has a negative financial rating.

The third provision permits a transfer without your consent, so long as the new party is a company purchasing the licensee's business. Some licensees insist on this provision because they want the freedom to sell the whole company (and its license agreements).

SAMPLE

Assignability

[*Select one*]

☐ **Assignment requires licensor consent.** Licensee may not assign or transfer its rights or obligations pursuant to this Agreement without the prior written consent of Licensor. Any assignment or transfer in violation of this section shall be void.

☐ **Licensor consent not unreasonably withheld.** Licensee may not assign or transfer its rights or obligations pursuant to this Agreement without the prior written consent of Licensor. Such consent shall not be unreasonably withheld. Any assignment or transfer in violation of this section shall be void.

☐ **Licensor consent not required for assignment to parent or acquiring company.** Licensee may not assign or transfer its rights or obligations pursuant to this Agreement without the prior written consent of Licensor. However, no consent is required for an assignment or transfer that occurs: (a) to an entity in which Licensee owns more than 50% of the assets, or (b) as part of a transfer of all or substantially all of the assets of Licensee to any party. Any assignment or transfer in violation of this section shall be void.

Signatures

Each party must sign the agreement. If individuals are signing on behalf of a company, then the people who sign must have the authority to do so. Use the rules expressed in Chapter 11 to determine how the agreement should be signed.

SAMPLE

Signatures. Each party represents and warrants that on this date they are duly authorized to bind their respective principals by their signatures below.

Each party has signed this Agreement through its authorized representative. The parties, having read this Agreement, indicate their consent to the terms and conditions by their signatures below.

By: _____

Date: _____

Licensor Name: _____

By: _____

Date: _____

Licensee Name/Title: _____

Exhibit A

Agreements often have attachments known as "exhibits," which are stapled to the agreement. In license agreements, the exhibit summarizes some of the essential business elements. For example, in the model agreement, Exhibit A includes a description of the work, the licensed product, and, if applicable, the sales minimum required to renew the agreement. One important advantage of using an exhibit is that if you are dealing with multiple licensees or if you are licensing more than one item to one licensee, you may be able to keep the body of the agreement the same and only change the exhibit.

SAMPLE

Exhibit A

The Property _____

Licensed Products _____ _____

Sales Requirements: $ _____ in Gross Sales per year.

Right of First Refusal

Although we do not include this section, some merchandise agreements include a provision known as a right of first refusal. Its purpose is to give the licensee the first shot at licensing any new works from you. For example, if you previously licensed a series of lighting fixture designs, the licensee will want the first opportunity to license your new designs. If another company makes a better offer than the licensee, this provision gives the licensee a period of time to match the offer.

SAMPLE

> **Right of First Refusal.** Licensor may identify and develop new works suitable to be used as Licensed Products ("New Works"). Licensee shall have the first right to license such New Works, and the parties shall negotiate in good faith to reach agreement as to the terms and conditions for such license. In the event that the parties fail to reach agreement and Licensor receives an offer from a third party for the New Works, Licensee shall have 30 days to notify Licensor whether Licensee desires to execute a license on similar terms and conditions. In the event that Licensee matches any third-party terms and conditions, Licensor shall enter into a License Agreement with Licensee and terminate negotiations with any third parties.

FORM ON CD-ROM
You can find the full text of the Merchandise License Agreement on the CD-ROM at the back of the book.

Licensing Worksheet

I've provided this Merchandise License Worksheet to help you keep track of the elements in your merchandise license agreement. The idea is that as you are negotiating with a licensee, you can keep track of the terms that you agree upon and later plug that into the merchandise license agreement.

FORM ON CD-ROM
The Merchandise License Worksheet is included on the CD-ROM at the back of this book.

Merchandise License Worksheet

Licensee

Name of Licensee Business _____

Licensee Address _____

Licensee Business Form

   ☐ sole proprietorship   ☐ general partnership   ☐ limited partnership

   ☐ corporation   ☐ limited liability company

State of incorporation _____

Name and position of person signing for Licensee _____

Property Definition

Design Patent No. _____

Design Patent Application Serial No. _____

Copyrightable Features _____

_____

Copyright Registration No(s). _____

Trade Secrets _____

_____

Trademarks _____

_____

Trademark Registration No(s). _____

Licensed Products Definition

Industry (Have you limited the license to a particular industry?) _____

Product (Have you limited the license to a particular product or products?) _____

_____

Territory

   ☐ Worldwide; or

   ☐ Countries _____

   ☐ States _____

Rights Granted (*check those rights granted to Licensee*)

☐ sell	☐ import	☐ advertise
☐ lease	☐ make or manufacture	☐ promote
☐ distribute	☐ right to improvements	☐ other rights _____
☐ use	☐ derivatives (copyright)	☐ other rights _____
☐ revise	☐ copy (copyright)	☐ other rights _____

Rights Reserved

☐ all rights reserved (except those granted in license)

☐ no rights reserved

☐ specific rights reserved

Have you signed any other licenses? ☐ Yes ☐ No   If so, do you need to reserve specific rights? _____

Term

Have you agreed upon:

☐ a fixed term (How long? _____)

☐ a term limited by design patent length

☐ unlimited term until one party terminates

☐ an initial term with renewals (see below)

☐ other _____

Renewals

If you have agreed upon an initial term with renewals:

How many renewal periods? _____

How long is each renewal period? _____

What triggers renewal?

☐ Licensee must notify of intent to renew

☐ Licensor must notify of intent to renew

☐ Agreement renews automatically unless Licensee indicates it does not want to renew.

Net Sales Deductions

What is the Licensee permitted to deduct when calculating net sales?

☐ quantity discounts ☐ debts & uncollectibles ☐ sales commissions

☐ fees ☐ promotion and marketing costs ☐ freight & shipping

☐ credits & returns ☐ other

Is there a cap on the total amount of the deductions? ☐ Yes ☐ No

If so, how much? _____

Royalty Rates

☐ Licensed Products _____%

☐ Combination Products _____%

☐ Accessory Products _____%

☐ Per-Use Royalty _____% or Usage Standard _____

☐ Other Products _____ _____%

☐ Other Products _____ _____%

Do you have any sliding royalty rates? ☐ Yes ☐ No

Advances and Lump Sum Payments

☐ Advance $_____ ☐ Date Due _____

☐ Lump Sum Payment(s) $_____ ☐ Date Due _____

Guaranteed Minimum Annual Royalty (GMAR)

☐ GMAR $_____ ☐ Date Due _____

☐ Does the GMAR carry forward credits?

☐ Does the GMAR carry forward deficiencies?

Audit Rights

No. of audits permitted per year _____

No. of days' notice _____

Taxes

n 1989, Paul Bechtelheimer and his wife Nelda sold their home in Kansas and bought a Pace Arrow motor home outfitted with heat, running water, air conditioning, a refrigerator, a stove, a microwave, a washer, a dryer, two television sets, a couch, a chair, and a bed. They hitched a trailer containing their inventory to the motor home and traveled the country, attending over 40 crafts shows a year. At the shows, they sold lamps, figurines, and woodcuts, all in a Southwestern motif. In 1990 the couple bought a mobile home in Florida, where they stayed for approximately 30 to 50 days a year.

When paying their income taxes, the Bechtelheimers deducted their travel expenses—the costs of traveling to and selling at crafts shows. The tax law provides that you can deduct travel expenses (including amounts expended for meals and lodging) while away from home in the pursuit of a trade or business (26 U.S.C. § 162). However, there's a catch. A taxpayer is not away from home if the home travels with him. After a dispute arose with the IRS, a federal judge ruled the Bechtelheimers were always "at home," even while on the road. Their motor home—not their mobile home in Florida—qualified as their "home" as the term is used in § 162(a)(2) of the tax code. One important factor was that the couple used the Florida mobile home as their studio to work on and store their crafts. Even when they were in Florida, they lived and slept in the motor home. The deduction was void, and the couple was required to pay the government back taxes. (*In re Bechtelheimer*, 239 B.R. 616 (M.D. Fla.1999).)

As the Bechtelheimer case demonstrates, an honest error in judgment can result in an unexpected tax burden. This chapter will provide information and resources to help you avoid such problems. Although tax laws are complex and sometimes unpredictable, by following the basic rules in this chapter, you can maximize your tax benefits with the minimum risk.

It's possible for you to handle all of your own tax issues and IRS forms—many crafts people manage all things taxable. Others hire tax professionals to take care of everything for them. And many more crafts workers are somewhere in between, relying on both professional and self help. Your approach depends on how complex your tax affairs are and whether you have the time, energy, and desire to do some or all of the work yourself.

In this chapter I focus on three things: paying your taxes, claiming deductions, and understanding the distinction between a hobby and a business—a distinction that can save you a great deal of money at tax time.

Even if you are paying a professional to handle your taxes, you should read this chapter and familiarize yourself with basic tax rules. After all, your expenditures—and therefore potential deductions—will be occurring throughout the year. And the ultimate legal responsibility for your taxes lies with you, not your accountant. The more you know, the less chance there is that errors will slip by you—and the more you can save.

References are provided throughout this chapter to IRS publications and other related reading. You can obtain IRS publications by calling the IRS at 800-TAX-FORM, visiting your local IRS office, or downloading the publications at www.irs.gov.

Other helpful tax sites are 1040.com (www.1040.com), offering state and federal links, and H&R Block (www.hrblock.com).

CAUTION

This chapter is focused primarily on tax issues for self-employed individuals, that is, sole proprietorships. Many of the rules in this chapter will also apply if you operate your crafts business with someone other than your spouse—that is, if your business is a partnership or some other business form. For example, it offers some tax advice for owners of partnerships, corporations, limited liability companies, and corporations. However, for specific tax advice for these business forms and regarding tax audits, consult a tax professional or review *Tax Savvy for Small Business* (Nolo) or *Stand Up to the IRS* (Nolo), both by Frederick W. Daily.

Hobby vs. Business—What's the Difference?

If you treat your crafts activities as a business, you can deduct your losses from all your income including your salary, your spouse's income, or interest and investment income. That's a big benefit. You can also carry over deductions from year to year.

If you treat your crafts activities as a hobby, you can deduct your expenses from your hobby income only. So if you lose $5,000 on your crafts hobby, you can't deduct it from your other income. This is the "hobby loss rule." And a hobbyist can't carry over deductions to use them in future years when income starts rolling in; they're lost forever.

How the IRS Judges Your Business

So, if you want to claim the maximum tax benefits, you need to meet the IRS standards for a business (also known as the hobby loss rule). The key to meeting this standard is to demonstrate that your primary motive is to earn a profit and that you continuously and regularly engage in your business over a substantial period.

Here are the IRS rules:

- If you earned a profit from your business in any three of the last five years, the IRS presumes it is a business and is unlikely to question you about it.
- If you didn't earn a profit in any three of the last five years, you will have to show that you behave as if you want to earn a profit (explained below).

> **TIP**
>
> **When do you have a profit?** You have a profit when the taxable income from an activity is more than the deductions for it—that is, you are not claiming a loss. There is no set amount or percentage of profit you need to earn to satisfy the IRS.

Proving a Profit Motive

If you're audited and you can't show a profit, the IRS will still consider your enterprise a business if you can prove you are guided by a profit motive. The IRS measures your profit motive by looking at five "business behavior" factors. Studies show that taxpayers who satisfy the first three factors—you act like you're in business, you demonstrate expertise, and you show time and effort expended—are routinely classified as businesses even if they don't expect to profit for years.

Act like you're in business. Keeping good books and other records goes a long way to show that you carry on activities in a businesslike manner. For example, husband and wife sculptors were able to claim business losses by providing records of exhibits at museums and galleries and testimonials to their skill and sales potential from art experts. (*Rood v. U.S.*, 184 F.Supp. 791 (D. Minn. 1960).)

Acquire expertise within your industry. It helps to show that you're industry-savvy. For example, an inventor developed a miles-per-gallon indicator but gave up on it after learning that General Motors was developing something similar. The tax court found a profit motive in the inventor's decision to drop the project; it showed he was savvy enough to realize he couldn't compete against GM. (*Maximoff v. Commissioner*, T.C. Memo 1987-155.)

Work regularly. The IRS is looking for proof that you work regularly and continuously, not sporadically, on your crafts business. What's "regularly and continuously"? One court accepted 20 to 30 hours per week (*Maximoff v. Commissioner*, T.C. Memo 1987-155); another accepted 25 hours per week for three years, then five to ten hours per week for two years (*Luow v. Commissioner*, T.C. Memo 1971-326). When a taxpayer couldn't establish the time spent, a court called it a hobby (*Everson v. Commissioner*, 2001 TNT 115-8).

Establish a record. Having a record of success in other businesses in the past—whether or not they are related to your current business—creates the likelihood that your activities are a business.

Earn some profits. Even if you can't satisfy the three-out-of-five-years profit test, earning a profit one year after years of losses helps show you are in a business.

Something else to keep in mind—the IRS is skeptical of taxpayers who claim large business losses from their crafts businesses, but who have substantial income from other sources.

If you need more assistance wrestling with the hobby loss rule, check out the small business owners section of the IRS website at www.irs.gov/businesses/small/index.html.

Paying Taxes

Preparing and paying taxes for your crafts business is more complicated than it is when you work as someone else's employee. You'll have plenty of new tax forms to complete, new rules to follow, and strategic decisions to make. The good news is that you can easily tackle your new paperwork using a Web-based or software tax preparation program, once you know your obligations.

The basic formula for paying tax on a crafts business is the same as paying tax on a salary or other sources of income. You pay tax on your net income—the money you earn less your deductions. As the owner of a crafts business, however, you have some additional tax obligations.

For example, you have to pay self-employment taxes, which fund your Social Security and Medicare contributions. It gets more complicated if you have employees because you'll have to pay part of their Social Security and Medicare payments, pay federal unemployment tax, and withhold (and periodically send to the government) income tax from your employees. And you'll probably have to pay your income taxes in four installments throughout the year, rather than all at once on April 15.

Will You Get Audited?

These days, most people who disobey tax rules have a good chance of escaping the IRS's clutches—generally only between 1% and 1.2% of taxpayers are audited each year. Most of these audits are triggered by a computer analysis known as the discriminate function system (or DIF), which looks for red flags in a tax return. Several factors arouse suspicion:

- the individual filing has substantial assets
- the deduction is very high, perhaps tens of thousands of dollars, and
- the business is one that could be considered a leisure activity.

When suspicious factors light up, the odds of being selected by the DIF system increase. However, be aware that every once in a while, the IRS breaks from this pattern and selects an otherwise unlikely candidate for audit. As tax expert and Nolo author Steve Fishman puts it, "It all depends if you want to play what they call 'the audit lottery.' You can do that and you may win. You may not. It's up to you."

How Businesses Are Taxed

How you pay taxes on your business profits will depend on how you have structured your crafts business. If you're like the hundreds of thousands of other crafts business operators, you're likely operating as a single-owner sole proprietorship. If you're operating with someone else, you're most likely a partnership. If you're concerned with personal liability, you may have formed a limited liability company (LLC) or corporation.

For tax purposes, however, there are only two categories of business taxpayers: those who pay tax on business income on their individual tax returns (called pass-through entities, because income and expenses pass through the business to the owner) and those that must pay their own taxes.

Most likely, you are a pass-through entity. Sole proprietorships, partnerships, LLCs, and S corporations (corporations that elect to be taxed like a partnership) are all pass-through entities. A pass-through entity does not pay its own taxes. Instead, its profits or losses pass through to the owners, who must report those amounts on their personal tax returns.

Here are the basic rules:

Sole proprietors. Sole proprietors report business income and expenses on IRS Schedule C, *Profit or Loss From Business*, which they have to file along with their personal tax returns (IRS Form 1040).

Partners. Partners report their share of partnership income and expenses on IRS Schedule E, *Supplemental Income and Loss*, which they must file along with their 1040s. In addition, the partnership itself must file an informational return (IRS Form 1065, *U.S. Return of Partnership Income*) and provide each partner with an IRS Schedule K-1, *Partner's Share of Income, Credits, Deductions, etc.*, which lists each partner's share of income and expenses.

S corporations. Shareholders in S corporations report income and expenses on their personal tax returns (IRS Schedule C, *Profit or Loss From Business*, and IRS Form 1040). In addition, the S corporation must file IRS Form 1120S, *U.S. Income Tax Return for an S Corporation*. This return gives the IRS information, but you don't use it to figure tax owed.

LLCs. LLC members report their income and expenses just like sole proprietors if they have one-member LLCs. In a multimember LLC, members report their income and expenses just like partners. A multimember LLC also has to file IRS Form 1065, *U.S. Return of Partnership Income,* and issue an IRS Schedule K-1 to each member. (LLCs may, however, choose to be taxed as C corporations by filing IRS Form 8832, *Entity Classification Election*.)

C corporations. Shareholders in C corporations differ from their business brethren because the C corporation is the only business form that is not a pass-through entity. A C corporation must file its own tax return and pay its own taxes on corporate income. (It does so by filing IRS Form 1120, *U.S. Corporation Income Tax Return*.) Corporate shareholders have to pay personal income tax (on the 1040) only on any business income paid out to them as compensation or dividends. This is where the potential tax-saving benefits of incorporating come from: Because shareholders can decide how much corporate income to distribute and how much to retain in the corporation, they can allocate most of the money to the taxpayer with the lowest rates—usually, the corporation.

How Businesses Report Income			
Type of Business	Owner Pays Tax on Personal Tax Return	Business Pays Tax Itself	Business Must File Its Own Tax Return
Sole proprietor	✓		
Partnership	✓		✓
One-member LLC	✓		
Multimember LLC	✓		✓
S corporation	✓		✓
C corporation		✓	✓

Taxes Your Crafts Business Will Have to Pay

There are three basic types of taxes a typical self-employed business-person might have to pay: income taxes, self-employment taxes, and employment taxes. In addition, if you sell goods or services on which your state imposes a sales tax, you will have to collect this money and periodically hand it over to your state taxing authority.

Income taxes. You will have to pay income taxes on the net profit your crafts business earns. The federal government imposes an income tax, as do the governments of most states. Some local governments also get into the act by taxing businesses within their jurisdictions; a few use an income tax, while others use some other method (an inventory, payroll, or business equipment tax, for example). (Here's good news for those who live in Alaska, Florida, Nevada, South Dakota, Texas, Washington, and Wyoming—these states don't impose income taxes.)

Self-employment taxes. You are responsible for paying your own Social Security and Medicare taxes. Unlike employees, whose employers are legally required to chip in for half of these amounts, you will have to pay the entire bill—currently, a 12.4% Social Security tax and a 2.9% Medicare tax on all of your taxable income from self-employment. However, you are entitled to deduct half of these taxes from your gross income for purposes of calculating your income tax, so the total effective self-employment tax rate is about 12%. To report and pay self-employment taxes, you must file IRS Form SE, *Self-Employment Tax*, along with your annual tax return.

Employment taxes. In the event you have employees, you will have to pay half of their Social Security and Medicare taxes, as well as unemployment tax and perhaps temporary disability tax (to your state taxing authority). You'll also have to withhold taxes from your employees' paychecks and deposit them with the IRS. To report and pay unemployment tax, you file IRS Form 940, *Employer's Annual Federal Unemployment Tax (FUTA) Tax Return*. To report all withholdings and pay your share of Social Security and Medicare, you must file IRS Form 941, *Employer's Quarterly Federal Tax Return*. The rules for employment taxes can get pretty tricky, and many employers are required to make quarterly filings with the IRS. For more information, check out IRS Publication 15 (Circular E), *Employer's Tax Guide* (you can get it at www.irs.gov).

Sales tax. Almost every state has a sales tax. You're undoubtedly used to paying sales tax as a consumer, but now that you're in business, you'll be on the other end of the transaction: You'll be responsible for collecting sales tax from your customers and paying that money to the state. State sales tax rules vary considerably: Some states tax only sales of goods, while others also tax services; in every state, certain sales are exempt from tax (that is, you don't have to collect or pay tax on the sale), but every state's list of exempt transactions is different, and states have different rules about when and how you must submit the tax you collect to the state taxing authority. To find the rules in your state, your best bet is to go straight to your state tax agency for help (you can find a list of links at www.irs.gov). You can also get a lot of good basic information, as well as details about every state's sales tax scheme, at www.toolkit.cch.com. There's additional sales tax information in Chapter 1.

Paying Estimated Taxes

Your crafts business clients and customers don't withhold taxes from what they pay you. This is a financial advantage for you; you not only receive the full amount you are owed, but also have greater freedom to plan your finances. The IRS is not so enthusiastic, however; it wants to get your tax dollars right away, rather than waiting for you to pay the whole tab on April 15.

That's why self-employed people have to pay estimated taxes—taxes on their estimated annual incomes, paid in four installments over the course of each year. These payments must include both estimated income tax and estimated self-employment taxes.

Estimated Tax Payment Schedule	
Income received	**Estimated tax due**
January 1 through March 31	April 15
April 1 through May 31	June 15
June 1 through August 31	September 15
September 1 through December 31	January 15 of the following year

You don't have to pay estimated taxes until you earn some income. For example, if your business doesn't bring in any income by March 31, you don't have to make an estimated tax payment on April 15.

Not everyone has to pay estimated taxes. You don't if:

- you expect to owe less than $1,000 in federal tax for the year
- you paid no taxes last year, if you were a U.S. citizen and your tax return covered the full 12-month period, or
- your crafts business is a C corporation and you receive dividends or distributions of profits from your corporation on which you will owe less than $500 in tax for the year. (You don't have to pay estimated taxes on salary you receive from your corporation; instead, you report that income and pay tax on it annually, on your personal tax return.)

But even if you don't have to pay estimated taxes, you might want to do it anyway. Paying estimated taxes spreads your tax bill over the entire year, so you won't have to come up with all of the money at once. On the other hand, as long as you really have enough socked away to cover your bill, paying it all at once will give you the benefit of that money—and its interest-earning power—for a longer period of time.

No tax last year = no estimated tax this year. No matter how much money you earn or how much you expect to owe in federal income and self-employment tax, you have no obligation to pay estimated taxes if you had no tax liability in the previous year. This is true regardless of the discrepancy between this year's and last year's earnings. However, you must have filed a tax return for the previous year in order to take advantage of this rule.

There are three ways to figure out how much estimated tax to pay. The easiest method is to simply pay exactly what you owed in federal tax the previous year (or a bit more, if you earned more than $150,000). However, if you don't expect to owe as much this year, you may want to look into the second and third methods listed below; although they are more complicated, they could result in a lower tax bill.

Pay what you paid last year. To use this method, simply divide your total federal tax payments for the previous year by four, then pay that amount when estimated taxes are due. (If you earn more than $150,000 annually—$75,000 for married people filing separately—you'll have to pay 110% of your previous year's tax bill.) As long as you pay this amount, you won't owe the IRS any penalties, even if your current year's income is higher and you end up owing more tax at the end of the year.

Make payments based on your estimated income. If you expect to earn less this year than you did last year, you might save money by making tax payments based on this year's estimated taxable income. The catch, of course, is that it can be very tough to estimate income and expenses ahead of time. The IRS knows this, and won't charge you any penalties as long as your estimated payments cover at least 90% of the current year's tax bill (of course, you will have to pay the additional tax). To use this method, estimate your total taxable income for the year, calculate the tax you will owe (don't forget self-employment taxes), and pay one quarter of that amount when each estimated payment falls due.

Make payments based on your estimated quarterly income. Under this method, you calculate your taxable income (including prorated deductions) at the end of each payment period, then pay that amount on the due date. This is probably the toughest method to use, but may be worthwhile if your income fluctuates a lot throughout the year (for example, if your business is intensely seasonal). It allows you to pay little or no estimated tax during your "dry" periods, and save your tax bills for more profitable days.

Preparing Your Taxes

Before you sit down to fill in your tax forms, I advise following a two- (okay, sometimes three-) step process. First, do as much research as you need to understand the decisions you'll have to make. For example, as I'll explain, you often have a choice of either depreciating a major purchase or deducting its entire cost in the year you buy it. Only you can decide which makes more sense for your business, and you'll probably need to learn more about each option to make the right choice.

> RESOURCE
> **The best place to start is the IRS website, www.irs.gov.** You can find a lot of useful articles and links on its home page for small businesses and the self-employed, and its free publications are loaded with information. You can download your tax forms here, too.

Once you are ready to actually prepare your returns, you have a number of options, ranging from filling in the forms yourself to hiring a certified public accountant to do your taxes. Often, the best choice falls in the middle of this range: using a Web-based or software program to complete your tax forms. These programs are cost-effective, can save you a lot of time and stress, and will help you not only complete the forms properly, but also figure out when you need more information to make the right decision.

Unreported Income Is a No-No

Although many taxpayers fear an audit of their claimed deductions, the IRS is actually much more interested in income than expenses. Unreported income is often the first thing auditors look for, and they will be very suspicious if you have significant deposits beyond the income you claimed on your return, even if those deposits are to your personal account. If you have significant nontaxable income, make sure to keep the records you'll need to prove where it came from.

And don't expect the IRS to take your word for it, especially if you claim that the money belongs to someone else and just happened to find its way into your bank account. Judging from cases decided by the U.S. Tax Court, this is a fairly popular argument that is extremely likely to fail, unless you can show written proof of your claim and it looks like something other than a tax evasion ploy.

Keeping Records for the IRS

If you face an audit, the IRS is not going to take your word for anything. You'll have to come up with receipts, cancelled checks, bank statements, and other records to support both the amount of income you claimed and any business deductions you took. You really can throw it all in a shoebox if you want, but most business owners find it easier to use a set of file folders or an accordion file (you can buy one that's already labeled with common business expense categories at an office supply store).

Here's a brief rundown on what you need to keep as proof of income and expenses:

To document income, you'll need copies of your bank statements, copies of checks you've deposited, copies of any 1099s you received, and, if you have nontaxable income, copies of documents showing the source of that income (for example, from an inheritance). Remember, the IRS is less interested in the business income you reported than in the income it thinks you failed to report. This means your job is not really to prove the amount of income your business earned, but to prove that any income you didn't report came from a nontaxable source.

To document most business expenses, you must keep records showing what you bought, who you bought it from, how much you paid, and the date of the purchase. In most cases, you can prove this with your receipt and a cancelled check or credit card statement (which proves that the receipt is really yours).

To document vehicle expenses, you must keep records of the dates of all business trips, your destination, the business purpose of your trip (for example, to meet with a client or scout a retail location), and your mileage.

To document meals and entertainment, you must keep records of what you paid for, who you bought it from, how much you paid, the date of purchase, who you were with, and the business purpose of your meeting. The first four facts are often included on a receipt; the remaining two you can record in a date book or calendar.

To document your use of property, you must keep records of how much time you spent using it for business and using it for other purposes. This rule applies to "listed property," items that the IRS believes people often use for personal purposes, including computers and cameras. (You can find "listed property" in IRS Publication 946, *How to Depreciate Property*.) You might also want to keep track of the time you spend in your home office, to prove that you used it regularly. You can keep these records in a log or journal.

Don't expect the IRS to allow your tax deductions if you don't keep records to back them up. If you have no records at all, your deductions will be disallowed in an audit, and you might face penalties as well. If you can prove that you had some business-related expenses of a type that makes sense for your line of work, the IRS may still allow a deduction, but it will be much smaller than what you claimed. Under the *Cohan* rule (named for a tax suit against entertainer George Cohan), if you can show some proof that you incurred deductible expenses, the IRS can estimate those expenses and allow a deduction for that amount. But, as you might expect, the IRS's estimates will be low. And this rule doesn't apply to expenses for travel, vehicles, gifts, and meals and entertainment. The IRS requires more detailed records for these types of deductions.

How Long Should You Keep Records?

In most situations, the IRS has up to three years to audit you after you file a tax return (or after the date when your tax return was due, if you filed early). However, if the IRS claims that you have unreported income exceeding 25% of the income you did report, it has six years to audit you. And if you didn't file a return or the IRS claims that your return was fraudulent, there is no audit deadline; you're always fair game.

Based on these rules, some experts advise that you simply give up and keep all of your tax records forever. There's certainly no harm in keeping all of your actual tax returns forever; they don't take up much space and can help you track the financial life of your business over time. The supporting documents are another story. Unless you filed a fraudulent return (and this is something only you can decide), you can generally get rid of supporting documents six years after you file your tax returns.

Tax Deductions

You probably already know one of the cardinal rules of business: You have to spend money to make money. The good news is that the government is prepared to give you some of that money back by allowing you to deduct most of what you spend on your crafts business.

When you consider what a great deal the government is offering, you'll realize how important it is to understand tax deductions. By letting you deduct your expenses, the government is essentially offering to pick up part of the tab for your venture. After you factor in federal income taxes, state income taxes, and self-employment taxes, every dollar you spend on deductible business expenses could save you more than 40 cents on your tax bill. The offer is on the table; it's up to you to take advantage of it by claiming every tax deduction to which you're entitled.

What's a Tax Deduction Worth?

A deduction is the cost or value of something that you can subtract from your gross income (all the money you earn) to determine your taxable income (the amount on which you have to pay tax). It's not a dollar-for-dollar proposition: You don't save the entire amount you paid for deductible goods and services. But because you don't have to pay tax on this amount, a deduction can save you almost half of what you spend.

The exact amount you'll save by taking a deduction depends on your tax bracket—the tax rate that applies to your income. The higher your bracket, the more every deduction is worth. Here's an example to show you how it works:

> **EXAMPLE:** Simon spends $2,000 on a computer for his crafts business. He's in the 25% federal income tax bracket. By deducting the cost of the computer, he doesn't have to pay tax on $2,000 of his income. That saves him 25% of $2,000, or $500. But that's not all. The state where Simon does business imposes a 6% income tax, so Simon saves an additional $120 there. And Simon doesn't have to pay self-employment taxes—the amount self-employed people have to chip in to fund their Social Security and Medicare—on this money, either. The self-employment tax rate works out to about 12%, for an additional $240 savings. Simon ends up saving $860, almost half of what he paid for his computer.

Tax Deduction Basics

How much you can deduct and when you can take the deduction depend on the type of expense. There are four basic categories of deductions, and the rules for each are a bit different.

Start-up expenses. Money that you spend before your business is up and running—such as the cost of researching what kind of business to start or advertising your grand opening—are start-up expenses. When it comes to dealing with these expenses, you can either treat them as part of your basis in the business, or deduct them over time. You may deduct up to $5,000 of them right away; you must deduct the remainder over the first 180 months you are in business.

Operating expenses. Once you are in business, your day-to-day costs are operating expenses. These might include money you spend on office rent, employee salaries, travel, professional services, office supplies, advertising, interest on business loans or purchases, and so on. As long as you aren't paying for something that you will use for more than a year (such as a vehicle or computer—see below), you can deduct these expenses in the year when you spend the money. The IRS has created special rules for operating expenses that it believes are often overstated or abused: travel, vehicle, and entertainment expenses. (These are covered in more detail below.)

Capital expenses. If you buy things for your business that have a useful life of more than one year—like a car, studio furniture, or machinery—then you have purchased a long-term asset. You usually have the choice of either depreciating these assets (deducting a portion of the cost for each year of the item's useful life, as determined by the IRS) or deducting them all at once. (See "Deducting Long-Term Assets," below, for more information.)

Inventory. Special rules apply to inventory, the crafts products you make or buy to sell to customers. You must wait until you sell inventory to deduct the cost of making or buying it. This is why so many businesses are desperate to get rid of their inventory at the end of the year: They want to take a larger deduction, and they want to minimize their burden when it comes time to count inventory for tax purposes.

Seven Often-Overlooked Deductions

Many crafts business owners miss out on valuable business deductions simply because they don't know which expenses they can deduct. Dan Hoffman, CPA and director of the San Francisco-based accounting firm Lautze & Lautze (www.lautze.com), says that business owners often forget to deduct:

Bad debts. If someone owes your business money and it's starting to look like you're never going to get paid back, you might be able to deduct the amount of the bad debt.

Casualty losses. If your crafts business property is damaged or destroyed by fire, vandalism, flood, or some other sudden, unexpected, or unusual event, you can claim the amount of the loss as a deduction—but only to the extent that the loss isn't covered by insurance.

Dues, subscriptions, and fees. Dues or fees you pay to professional organizations—such as a trade association or membership group—are deductible business expenses. So are charges for subscriptions to professional, technical, or trade journals in your field.

Education expenses. If you buy books, take a crafts course, or attend a convention to keep up with the latest trends in your field, you can deduct your costs. As long as the expenditure improves your crafts-related skills, it's deductible.

Phone bills. If you have a separate business line in your studio office, you should deduct not only the costs associated with that phone, but also the cost of occasional business calls you make from your cell phone or personal phone line.

Retirement plans. You can deduct the money you contribute to most types of retirement plans that you set up for yourself or your employees. And if you qualify, you can deduct some of the start-up and administrative costs of a pension plan you establish for your employees. (See IRS Form 8881, *Credit for Small Employer Pension Plan Startup Costs*, for more information.)

Federal and state tax credits. Tax credits may be available to businesses that help further particular civic goals—for example, by hiring employees through a welfare-to-work program, doing business in designated "empowerment" or "renewal" zones (communities that are struggling economically), or using solar energy. You can find information on federal credits in IRS Publication 334, *Tax Guide for Small Business*; for information on state credits, contact your state taxing authority.

Postponing Start-Up Costs

If you've already incurred start-up costs, you'll have to follow the rules laid out above. And, if you won't spend more than $5,000 on start-up expenses, you can simply deduct them all at once. However, if you're looking at more than $5,000 in future start-up costs, it's worth taking a couple of steps to avoid having to spread out part of your deduction over the next 15 years. The key is to start your crafts business before you lay out significant amounts of money; that way, your expenses are usually immediately deductible. If you will offer services, your business starts when you first make your services available to the public, whether or not you actually have any customers. If you'll be making products, you're in business once you start the process, even if you have not yet solicited any sales or completed any crafts products. Here are two ways to convert what would be start-up costs into immediately deductible business expenses:

Postpone major purchases until you're up and running. Once you hang out your shingle, you can buy that fancy computer system and office furniture, or shell out thousands of dollars for advertising.

Postpone paying for purchases. If you absolutely have to pay for some expensive items or services before you open your doors, buy them on credit (or ask to be billed later). As long as you're a cash-basis taxpayer, you haven't actually incurred an expense until the money leaves your wallet. And as long as you pay the bill after you start up, you'll probably have an immediately deductible expense.

Deducting Home Office Expenses

It's possible you run your crafts business from your home. If you do, you may be able to deduct expenses relating to your home workspace. Although commonly referred to as the "home office" deduction, this deduction actually applies to any home space you use for your crafts business, including a studio, workshop, or office.

Whether or not you qualify for a home office deduction, you can always deduct the direct costs of running your crafts business—for example, if you buy a computer to use in your business, pay for high-speed Internet access to do your work, or use your personal phone for business calls, you may deduct those costs whether or not you claim the home office deduction. But using the home office deduction allows you to claim a portion of the costs of your home—rent, utility bills, cleaning services, homeowner fees, and so on—as a business expense.

To qualify for the home office deduction, you must first satisfy the IRS's threshold test:

You use your home workspace exclusively for business, not for personal or other purposes. You don't have to devote an entire room to your business to qualify; you can use a portion of a room as a home office, as long as you use it exclusively for business. If you mix business with pleasure—for example, you use your workspace to correspond with clients and handle business bookkeeping, but also to play online poker and pay household bills—then you won't qualify for the home office deduction.

You must also use your home office regularly and exclusively. The IRS has never clearly explained exactly what it considers regular use. One court found 12 hours a week sufficiently regular, but no one really knows how low you can go. If you use your home office exclusively and regularly for business, you will qualify for the home office deduction if you meet one of these five additional tests:

- **Your home office is your principal place of business.** If you do all or almost all of your crafts work in your home office, you meet this test. If you work in more than one location, however, you'll have to show that you do your most important business activities at home or that you do your administrative or management tasks at home. For example, if you do your primary crafts work at weekend crafts fairs, you will qualify for the home office deduction if you do your planning, scheduling, billing, and so forth at home.

- **You meet customers at home on a regular basis.** For example, if you create custom work for clients in your home, you may take the home office deduction.

- **You use a separate freestanding structure on your property exclusively for business.** Some examples might be a detached garage, cottage, or workshop.
- **You store inventory or product samples at home.** However, you cannot have an outside office or other workplace outside your home. You don't have to use your storage space exclusively for business to qualify—regular use is enough.

Your Home Office Might Be a Vehicle

You don't have to live and work in a house to take the home office deduction: Apartments, condominiums, or even motor homes, houseboats, and other vehicles that double as your home and workspace can qualify, but you must meet the tests set out above. The combined facts that you own a vehicle that you use as a residence and you run a business are not enough, in themselves, to prove your entitlement to the deduction.

Don't expect the IRS to believe that you use most of a small home exclusively for your business, especially if you don't live alone. IRS auditors have homes, too, and they understand that it's very difficult to devote your only bedroom or all of your shared living space exclusively to your business.

For example, one taxpayer claimed that he used the "great room"—a combination living and dining room—of his rented house exclusively for his real estate business. The tax court didn't buy it, primarily because his home had only one bedroom and a kitchenette in addition to that great room, and his girlfriend lived with him. Although the court didn't doubt that he did some work at home, it refused to accept his argument that he and his girlfriend did all of their living, dining, and entertaining in the bedroom (or that the sofa and dining room table were used exclusively for work). (*Szasz v. Commissioner of Internal Revenue*, TC Summary Opinion 2004-169.)

On the other hand, if you can prove that you really do use a lot of your living space for work, you might have a good claim. For example, a professional concert violinist successfully claimed the home office deduction for her entire living room, even though she shared a one-bedroom apartment with her husband and young daughter. The court noted that her living room contained no typical furnishings, only shelves for sheet music, recording equipment, a small table, and a chair for her practice sessions (and her daughter was not allowed to play there). (*Popov v. Commissioner of Internal Revenue*, 246 F.3d 1190 (9th Cir. 2001).)

What You Can Deduct

Using the home office deduction, you can deduct a portion of your household expenses, including:

- rent
- mortgage interest and property taxes (the advantage of taking a portion of these costs as a business deduction rather than a personal deduction—as you are entitled to do on IRS Schedule A, *Itemized Deductions*—is that it reduces your business income and so your self-employment taxes)
- condominium or homeowners' association fees
- depreciation on a home you own
- utilities
- insurance
- maintenance and cleaning
- security costs, and
- casualty losses.

The exact amount you can deduct depends on how much of your home you use for work. There are two ways to measure this:

Using the room method, you divide the number of rooms you use for business by the total number of rooms in your home (not including bathrooms, closets, and other storage areas). For example, if you use the spare bedroom of your four-room home for business, you can deduct 25% of your household expenses.

Under the square footage method, you divide the square footage of the area you use for work by the total square footage of your home (you don't have to include stairways, hallways, landings, entries, attics, or garages in your calculations). For example, if you use a 10' × 20' room as an office in your 1,000-square-foot home, your home office deduction percentage is 20%.

In addition to deducting a portion of overall household expenses, you may deduct 100% of any expense that is solely for your home office. For example, if you pay someone to paint the entire interior of your home (including your work area), you may deduct only the home office portion of the cost. But if you hire a painter just to paint your home office, you can deduct the entire amount.

Five Home Office Deduction Tips

Plenty of taxpayers don't take a home office deduction because they believe it is likely to trigger an audit. The IRS says such beliefs are misguided, but it never hurts to cover your bases. Follow these five tips to maximize your benefits—and minimize your chances of losing an audit.

Devote a separate room exclusively to your crafts business. While you can take a home office deduction even if you use only a portion of a room for work, it's much easier to designate an entire room: The math is easier, you won't have to worry about physically separating your work from your personal space, and you'll have an easier time satisfying the IRS that you use your office exclusively for work.

Do the math to figure out which method yields the highest deduction. Of course it's easier just to count rooms, but take the time to measure your square footage as well. Depending on your home's layout, it may give you a bigger deduction.

Create visual aids. Take a picture of your home office and draw up a simple diagram of your home layout showing the space you use for business. This can help you prove, if it's ever necessary, that you claimed the correct percentage.

Keep a record of home office activities and save receipts. If customers visit, ask them to sign a log book. Note the time you spend on business in your date book or calendar. Save bills and receipts for home-office related expenses (rent, utility payments, or house-cleaning fees, etc.) along with your other business records.

Use your home office as your business address. It will be easier to prove that your home is your principal place of business if you designate it as such. Have business mail delivered there and put your address on business correspondence, cards, and your letterhead.

Inventory Is Not a Business Expense

As someone who makes (and buys) goods, you are entitled to deduct the cost of those goods actually sold on your tax return. This is what you spent for the goods or their actual market value if they've declined in value since you bought them. However, this deduction is separate from the business expense deduction. Instead, you deduct the cost of goods you've sold from your business receipts to determine your gross profit from the business. Your business expenses are then deducted from your gross profit to determine your net profit, which is taxed. Crafts businesses must determine the value of their inventories at the beginning and the end of each tax year using an IRS-approved accounting method. Conducting inventories can be burdensome.

> **RESOURCE**
>
> **For more information on inventories,** see the Cost of Goods Sold section in Chapter 7 of IRS Publication 334, *Tax Guide for Small Businesses*; and IRS Publication 538, *Accounting Periods and Methods*; as well as Publication 970, *Application to Use LIFO Inventory Method.* You can obtain these and all other IRS publications by calling the IRS at 800-TAX-FORM, visiting your local IRS office, or downloading the publications from the IRS (www.irs.gov).

Deducting Long-Term Assets

Long-term assets are things that have a useful life of more than one year, as determined by the IRS. Examples include computers, equipment, machinery, and furniture. There are two ways to deduct long-term assets. You can:

- deduct them immediately under Section 179 of the Internal Revenue Code if they meet the requirements, or
- depreciate them (deduct a portion of the value each year of the item's useful life).

Special Rules for Computers, Cell Phones, and Other Potential Toys

The IRS has created special rules for things that can easily be used for personal purposes, including computers, vehicles, cell phones, stereo equipment, and cameras. For these types of property (called "listed" property), you are required to keep a log proving that you use the item for business, even if you use it only for business and never for fun. The only exception is computers: If you use your computer exclusively for business, you don't have to keep a log. The moral of the story, for many small business owners, is that it makes more sense to buy a separate computer solely for business use than to go through the hassle of making a note every time you (or a family member) log on.

Section 179

Using Section 179 allows you to deduct long-term assets in the year when you buy them. You can't deduct more than you earn for the year, but you may carry over a Section 179 deduction to a future year, when your business is doing better. If you're fortunate enough to have skyrocketing profits, you can deduct up to a current limit of $250,000 (for tax year 2009). (And in 2009, businesses that exceed the $250,000 deduction limit can take a bonus depreciation of 50% on the amount that exceeds the limit.)

Section 179 is only for tangible personal property—in other words, you can't use it to deduct the cost of land or buildings, or intellectual property, such as patents and copyrights. To take the deduction, you must use the item more than half of the time for business in the year in which you buy it. This means that if you buy an item for personal use (such as a computer or desk) and then start using it in your business more than one year later, you can't use Section 179. It also means that if you use an item at least half of the time for personal (nonbusiness) purposes, you can't take the deduction. If you use the item more than half of the time for business, you may deduct only a percentage of what you paid—for example, if you paid $2,000 for a computer that you use 75% of the time for business, you can deduct $1,500.

Depreciation

Depreciation spreads your deduction out over the useful life of a long-term asset—three to seven years for most business equipment and electronics. Rather than deducting the entire cost at once, you take the deduction in installments, according to one of several formulas accepted by the IRS. Depreciation is pretty complicated; the IRS guide to the subject (Publication 946, *How to Depreciate Property*) is more than 100 pages long. There are exceptions, limits, and traps for unwary deduction claimers. If you're planning to use depreciation, get some accounting assistance.

Does Depreciation Ever Make Sense?

Unless you buy more than the limit worth of business property in a single year ($250,000 in tax year 2009), you'll probably be able to deduct long-term assets right away under Section 179. So why would anyone ever depreciate these assets instead?

Generally, they wouldn't (unless they use the item less than half of the time for business, in which case they cannot use Section 179). In a couple of situations, however, spreading out your deductions makes sense:

You need to show a profit. If you're pushing up against the IRS's hobby loss rule (discussed earlier in this chapter), you may need to show a profit in order to prove that you're really running a business. Depreciation gives you a smaller deduction, which might mean the difference between a profit and a loss.

You expect to earn more in the future. If you expect to be in a higher tax bracket later, you might want to depreciate. Because the value of a tax deduction depends on your tax rate, a deduction will save you more in taxes if your earnings are higher.

Deducting Vehicle Expenses

Chances are that you do some driving for your crafts business—to pick up supplies, visit clients, go to the post office, and more. If you do, you have the choice of two different ways to calculate your vehicle deduction: the standard mileage rate or the actual expense method.

If you use the standard mileage rate, you can claim a set deduction (55 cents per mile for 2009; you can always find the current rate at www.irs.gov) for every mile you drive for business. You can claim a few additional expenses—including parking fees and tolls—on top of the mileage rate. You can't deduct the cost of repairs, maintenance, gas, insurance, or other costs of operating your car, because these costs are figured into the standard rate. You can use the standard rate only for a car that you own. If you don't use the standard rate in the first year when you drive your car for business, you won't be able to use it for that car, ever.

To use the actual expense method, you can deduct all of your car-related costs—including interest payments, insurance, license fees, oil and gas, repairs and so on—for business use of your car. You can also depreciate the car, which means you take a set deduction each year to reflect the car's declining value over time. If you also use the car for personal reasons, you can deduct only a portion of your expenses. Using the actual expense method is much more time-consuming than using the standard mileage rate, but it might be worth the extra work if you have an expensive car and so can take a fairly hefty depreciation deduction.

Whichever method you use, you'll have to keep careful records. Because the IRS believes that taxpayers often overstate how much they use their cars for business, it has some special rules for vehicle deductions. You'll have to keep track of your business and personal mileage; the easiest way to do this is to keep a log in your car and record the odometer reading at the beginning and end of every business-related drive. If you use the actual expense method, you'll also need to keep records of all of your vehicle expenses.

Deducting Travel Expenses

If you travel overnight for your crafts business, you can deduct your airfare, accommodations, and more. And the IRS doesn't require you to travel steerage; you can deduct your costs even if you stay at four-star hotels and enjoy the comforts of the first-class cabin.

However, the IRS also knows that most of us aren't going to travel to a distant city and spend our every waking moment working—we also want to see the sights. So it has created a set of rules delineating exactly which costs you can deduct and how much of your trip has to be business related in order to take a deduction. These rules depend on where you travel and how long you stay.

If you travel within the United States, your transportation costs (air and cab fare, for example) are deductible as long as you spend at least half of your trip on business. On days when you're doing business, you can also deduct your "destination" expenses, such as hotel costs, 50% of your meal expenses (see below for more on this 50% rule), local transportation (including car rental), telephone bills, and so on. On days when you're just having fun, you can't deduct these costs. And you can't deduct the cost of a spouse or other companion who comes along for the ride unless that person is your employee and has a genuine business reason for tagging along.

State Your Business

It isn't enough to keep records of what you paid for airfare, car rental, meals, and so on; you must also have some proof that you actually did business on your trip, in case you're audited. Take notes in your date book or calendar indicating whom you met with, sales calls, and other business activities. Keep copies of the business cards of people you spoke to, contracts you entered into, or other written records of the work you did.

If you travel outside the United States, the rules depend on the length of your trip. If you're gone for fewer than seven days, you can deduct your transportation costs and your destination expenses for days you spend working. If your trip lasts more than seven days and you spend more than 75% of your time on business, the same rules apply. However, if you spend between 50% and 75% of your time on business, you may deduct only the business percentage of your transportation costs (you can still deduct destination costs for the days you spend working). And if you spend less than 50% of your time working, none of your costs are deductible.

Although these rules may already seem complicated, there are many more that are too detailed to explain here. The IRS has really gone to town in imposing requirements for travel deductions because this is an area where there has been a lot of abuse. As a result, there are special rules for cruises, conventions, side trips, and more. For all the details, read IRS Publication 463, *Travel, Entertainment, Gift, and Car Expenses.*

Deducting Meals and Entertainment

If you entertain customers, advisers, suppliers, or other business-related associates, you may be able to deduct 50% of your costs. However, because lots of people have cheated on this deduction, there are many rules about what you can deduct and how you can prove that you really had a business purpose.

To claim a deduction, you must be with someone who can benefit your business in some way; you can't deduct the cost of entertaining family friends, for example, unless they also do business with you. In addition, you must actually discuss business before, during, or after the event. If you plan to claim that you discussed business during the event, you won't be able to deduct much more than meals, because the IRS believes that most types of entertainment—going to the theater, a ball game, or a cocktail lounge, for example—are not conducive to serious business discussions.

The IRS won't accept certain expenses as entertainment costs, including the cost of renting or buying an entertainment facility (such as a fishing lodge or tennis court), club dues, membership fees, or the cost of nonbusiness guests. This is another area where the rules can get pretty complicated. For more information, see IRS Publication 463, *Travel, Entertainment, Gift, and Car Expenses.*

Lawyers, Contracts, and Lawsuits

n September 1999, artist Crispina ffrench (www.crispina.com)
was surprised to discover a catalog company selling copies of her
"Hood and Pocket Sweater." Every element of Crispina's sweater
had been duplicated, including the nine mismatched wool panels,
exposed stitching, exposed half-inch hems, six-sided kangaroo pouch,
and hood with external hem. Adding to the annoyance, the catalog
copy trumpeted the fact that the sweaters were "one-of-a-kind" and
"imported," as if the foreign origins added to the sweater's cachet.
Crispina had achieved considerable attention, including a mention in
the *New York Times*, for her hand-made sweaters—produced in her
Massachusetts studio using a special process she created to preserve and
enhance recycled fabrics.

Crispina and I knew that it would be an uphill battle to protect her
clothing designs under principles of copyright or trade dress, so we
agreed to take a reasonable, nonthreatening approach. My letter to the
company ended with the hope that the company could "quickly and
fairly resolve this matter without litigation."

Within two weeks, the president of the catalog company had
written back and thanked me for bringing the matter to the company's
attention. He explained that the company had no intention of infringing
Crispina's design, and that they had discontinued selling the product.
The matter ended quietly. Crispina provided me with memorable
compensation—one of her sweaters!

Most legal altercations don't end this quickly and peacefully. But
Crispina's case demonstrates that when you're involved in a legal
squabble, you need not assume the worst and start out swinging a big
stick. Sometimes disputes can be resolved peacefully and reasonably and
sometimes, yes, sometimes, people do the right thing. If I had written
a typical attorney letter threatening litigation or demanding financial
damages, it's possible that the fight would have dragged on much longer
than was necessary (and my wife might not have ended up with that
fabulous sweater).

In this case, Crispina might have achieved the same result on her
own. Unfortunately, that's not true in most infringement battles—a
misbehaving company will usually take notice only if a cease and

desist demand arrives with a legal letterhead. When you do need legal help—whether to draft a contract or stop an infringer—you may find it frightening to be thrown into the world of legal fees and legalese. This chapter is designed to remove that fear.

Hiring Lawyers for Routine Business

If you're like most small business owners, the only time you'll need a lawyer is to take care of some paperwork. For example, you may:

- be forming a business entity such as a corporation, LLC, or partnership
- need a contract prepared
- need to review and negotiate a lease
- want to register a trademark, copyright, or patent, or
- need to file special tax or business documentation.

> **RESOURCE**
> **You can also choose to handle many of the above matters yourself.** See Nolo's website (www.nolo.com) for helpful books and software.

Lawyers who prepare and review legal documents are referred to as "business" or "transactional" lawyers (versus "litigators," who primarily resolve disputes). Sometimes a general business lawyer can handle all your transactional work. However, sometimes you'll need a specialist for certain documentation—for example, negotiating a lease may require the help of a real estate lawyer, while filing a trademark registration might best be done with the help of a trademark lawyer.

Try to find a lawyer who seems interested in your crafts business and either already knows a lot about your field or seems genuinely eager to learn more about it. Avoid the lawyer who's aloof and doesn't want to get involved in learning the nitty-gritty details of what you do. Some lawyers are hypercautious nitpickers who get unnecessarily bogged down in legal minutiae while a valuable business opportunity slips away. You want a lawyer who blends sound legal advice with a practical approach—someone who figures out a way to do something, not one who offers reasons why it can't be done.

Working with a business attorney is fairly straightforward—you gather and maintain documents and make decisions based upon your attorney's advice. Below are some tips for saving money with your business attorney:

- **Group together your legal affairs.** You'll save money if you consult with your business lawyer on several matters at one time. For example, in a one-hour conference, you may be able to review the annual updating of your corporate record book, renew your Web hosting agreement, and check over a noncompetition agreement you've drafted for new employees to sign.

- **Use flat fees.** When hiring a business attorney, you may be able to obtain a fixed fee for certain transactional work. Flat fees give your business some predictability; you're not waiting for a billing surprise at the end of the month.

- **Help out.** You or your employees can do a lot of work yourselves. Help gather documents needed for a transaction. Write the first couple of drafts of a contract, then give your lawyer the relatively inexpensive task of reviewing and polishing the document.

- **Avoid spending too much time on contract negotiations.** Lawyer's fees can quickly get out of control if negotiations for contracts drag on too long. Contracts sometimes go through many drafts. As long as you and your attorney are conscientious, you can get away with fewer drafts. Make sure you and the attorney are in agreement as to the goals of the contract negotiation. Tell your lawyer your priorities. Once you have achieved most or all of your goals, be flexible about remaining issues so that you can save time.

- **Use other professionals.** Often, nonlawyer professionals perform some business tasks better and at lower cost than lawyers do. For example, look to management consultants for strategic business planning, real estate brokers or appraisers for valuation of properties, accountants for preparation of financial proposals, insurance agents for advice on insurance protection, and CPAs for the preparation of tax returns.

Hiring Lawyers for Legal Disputes

When you hire an attorney because you're in the midst of a dispute, you're often looking for a different type of legal animal. You're seeking someone who can defend your turf against others who threaten your livelihood. But don't assume you need the biggest ape in the jungle. Sometimes, a shrewd negotiator or a logical, methodical attorney can be the ideal choice to end a dispute amicably. Below are a few tips for dealing with legal disputes and legal fees:

- **Avoid lawsuits that go on forever.** Beware of litigation! It often costs $10,000 or more, and the main ones who profit are the lawyers. If you're in a dispute, before screaming "I'll see you in court!" ask your attorney for a realistic assessment of your odds for success and the potential costs. The assessment and underlying reasoning should be in plain English. If a lawyer can't explain your situation clearly to you, he won't be able to explain it clearly to a judge or jury. Also, ask your attorney about alternative dispute resolution methods such as arbitration and mediation. Finally, keep in mind that some lawyers are greedy, and the longer the dispute drags out, the more the attorney will earn.

- **Be skeptical about large windfalls.** Being legally right about something doesn't necessarily mean being entitled to financial damages. One of the first questions that judges and arbitrators usually ask is whether the complaining party has actually suffered any injury. For example, has an infringing copy of your work deprived you of revenue? Can you prove it? Has a similar trademark reduced your sales? Again, what's the proof? What are the real damages? If you are involved in a contract dispute, be aware that you will rarely obtain a financial windfall. The best that you can usually hope for is for payment of what you would have received if the contract had been performed according to plan.

- **Encourage settlement.** A settlement is a contract signed by both parties, usually executed at the time one party pays the other. A negotiated settlement saves money (litigation costs) and time (you avoid waiting three years for the case to end). Better still, it results in a guaranteed payment (unlike a court judgment that must be collected and enforced). These advantages create an incentive for you to accept less money in a settlement than you would demand in a court case. When deciding whether to accept a settlement, you and your lawyer should consider your likelihood of winning in court and estimate any resulting award of damages if you were to lose.

- **Consider small claims court.** Small claims court judges resolve disputes involving relatively modest amounts of money. (You can sue for between $2,000 and $25,000, depending on your state.) The people or businesses involved normally present their cases to a judge or court commissioner without the help of lawyers. Small claims court rules are designed not to overwhelm the participants with legal or procedural formalities. The judge makes a decision (a judgment) reasonably promptly, often the same day as the hearing. Although procedural rules dealing with when and where to file and serve papers are established by each state's laws and differ in detail, the basic approach to properly preparing and presenting a small claims case is remarkably similar everywhere. For more information, read *Everybody's Guide to Small Claims Court*, by Ralph Warner (Nolo).

Finding the Right Lawyer

The novelist Robert Smith-Surtees said there are three sorts of lawyers: able, unable, and lamentable. In this section, I'll provide some suggestions for avoiding the latter two.

At least 24 states have organizations that provide legal services and information to the arts community at a reduced rate. To find such an organization near you, check the national directory on the website of the Volunteer Lawyers for the Arts (VLA), the granddaddy of the organizations (www.vlany.org). Click "Resources" on the home page, and then click "National Directory."

These organizations provide low-income artists with free or low-cost legal advice. Contact the organization nearest you to see if you qualify. If you don't meet the financial requirements for free legal help, groups like the California Lawyers for the Arts and VLA can save you money through lawyer referral services. Each organization maintains a directory of local attorneys who handle arts-related legal issues. Many offer reduced rates for an initial visit. For example, the CLA will arrange a half-hour consultation with an attorney for $35—a savings of about $70 off a private attorney's normal fee. This initial consultation may be enough to tell you whether or not you should pursue a dispute.

Legal organizations can also save you money on legal fees by offering workshops on topics such as "Copyright Infringement," "Trademark 101," or "Starting and Operating a Nonprofit Corporation." Finally, the mediation and arbitration services provided by these organizations can save you money, as explained below.

If you live in an area that does not have a VLA-style group, your best bet for finding the right lawyer is to get recommendations from other crafts artists or organizations. Talk to crafts artists who have actually used a particular lawyer's services. Find out what the person liked about the lawyer, and why. Ask how the legal problem turned out—was the lawyer successful? Ask about the lawyer's legal abilities, communication skills, and billing practices. If you have a problem related to copyrights, trade secrets, patents, or trademarks, you can ask the American Intellectual Property Law Association (AIPLA); (www.aipla.org) to refer you to an experienced lawyer. A few other sources you can turn to for possible candidates include the director of your state or local chamber of commerce or a law librarian who can identify lawyers in your state who have written books or articles on arts or business law.

RESOURCE

Nolo's Lawyer Directory. Nolo, the publisher of this book, has a lawyer directory that can help you find a lawyer in your area. Check it out at www.nolo.com.

Fees and Fee Agreements

You may have heard the joke about the new client who asked the lawyer, "How much do you charge?"

"I charge $200 to answer three questions," replied the lawyer.

"Isn't that a bit steep?"

"Yes," said the lawyer. "What's your third question?"

As the joke indicates, it's important to get a clear understanding about how fees will be computed when you hire a lawyer. And as you bring new tasks to the lawyer, ask specifically about the charges for each. Many lawyers initiate fee discussions, but others forget or are shy about doing so. Bring up the subject yourself. Insist that the ground rules be clearly established. In California, all fee agreements between lawyers and clients must be in writing if the expected fee is $1,000 or more, or is contingent on the outcome of a lawsuit. In any state, it's a good idea to put your fee agreement in writing.

There are four basic ways that lawyers charge.

By the hour. In most parts of the United States, you can get competent services for your small business for $150 to $300 an hour. The cheapest hourly rate isn't necessarily the best deal. A novice who charges only $80 an hour may take three hours to review a contract. A more experienced lawyer who charges $200 an hour may do the same job in half an hour and make better suggestions. Take into account the lawyer's knowledge and reputation and the personal rapport the two of you have—or don't have.

Flat fees. Sometimes a business lawyer quotes a flat fee for a specific job. For example, the lawyer may offer to draw up a distribution agreement for $300, or review and edit your online terms and conditions for $500. You pay the same amount regardless of how much time the lawyer spends.

Contingent fee. A contingent fee is a percentage (commonly 33%) of the amount the lawyer obtains for you in a negotiated settlement or through a trial. If the lawyer recovers nothing for you, there's no fee. However, the lawyer does generally expect reimbursement for out-of-pocket expenses, such as filing fees, long-distance phone calls, and transcripts of testimony. Contingent fees are common in personal injury lawsuits but relatively unusual in small business cases.

Annual fee. You may be able to hire a lawyer for a flat annual fee to handle all of your routine legal business. Obviously, the key to making this arrangement work is to have a written agreement clearly defining what's routine and what's extraordinary.

What Is a Retainer?

A retainer is an advance payment to an attorney. The attorney places the retainer in a bank account (in some states, this must be an interest-bearing account) and deducts money from the account at the end of each month to pay your bill. When the money is depleted, the attorney may ask for a new retainer. If the retainer is not used up at the end of the services, the attorney must return what's left. The amount of the retainer usually depends on the project. For example, retainers for litigation tend to run between $2,000 and $5,000. Some attorneys use the term "retainer" to refer to a monthly fee that the attorney keeps regardless of whether any legal services are performed. In other words, you are paying a monthly fee just to keep the attorney available to you. I recommend against this type of arrangement.

To save yourself money and grief when dealing with an attorney, follow these tips:

- **Keep it short.** If you are paying your attorney on an hourly basis, keep your conversations short—the meter is always running. Avoid making several calls a day. Instead, consolidate your questions and ask them all in one conversation.
- **Get a fee agreement.** Make sure that your fee agreement gives you the right to an itemized statement along with the bill, detailing the work done and time spent. Some state statutes and bar associations require a written fee agreement—for example, California requires that attorneys provide a written agreement when the fee will exceed $1,000.

- **Review billings carefully.** Your lawyer's bill should be clear. Do not accept summary billings such as the single phrase "litigation work" used to explain a block of time for which you are billed a great deal of money.
- **Watch out for hidden expenses.** Find out what expenses you must cover. Watch out if your attorney wants to bill for services such as word processing or administrative services. This means you will be paying the secretary's salary. Also beware of fax and copying charges. Some firms charge clients per page for incoming and outgoing faxes—and the per-page cost can be artificially high.

Educate yourself. Legal websites such as Nolo (www.nolo.com), Justia (www.justia.com), and FindLaw (www.findlaw.com) will help you keep up with specific legal developments that your lawyer may have missed. Send pertinent articles to your lawyer—this can dramatically reduce legal research time—and encourage your lawyer to do the same for you.

Show that you're an important client. The single most important thing you can do to tell your lawyer how much you value the relationship is to pay your bills on time. Also, let your lawyer know about plans for expansion and your company's possible future legal needs. And if your business wins an award or otherwise is recognized as being a leader in its field, let your lawyer know about it—everyone feels good when an enterprise they're associated with prospers. Also, let your lawyer know when you recommend her to business colleagues.

Evaluating Your Attorney's Services

How do you know if your lawyer is doing a good job? Generally, you can measure a professional's performance (whether it is a doctor, lawyer, or dentist) by observing whether the professional:

- provides you with accurate and understandable advice
- permits you to make an informed decision as to how to proceed, and
- works with you to efficiently resolve conflicts and solve problems.

If your attorney is not fulfilling all three of these requirements then there is a problem in the attorney-client relationship. For example, there is generally a problem if:

- your attorney is not returning phone calls within 48 hours
- the bills you're receiving are disproportionate to what the attorney predicted and there is no adequate explanation, or
- you are unable to understand why your attorney is doing certain things or your attorney speaks down to you.

As a general rule, if you leave the lawyer's office confused or unclear as to your course of action, then there is a problem. After all, the primary purpose of an attorney is to counsel you as to your legal options. If you don't understand these options, then the attorney has failed. This doesn't mean that the lawyer will always present a black and white explanation. There are many gray areas in the law. For example, the law regarding business names is often murky. A good attorney will explain this murkiness and evaluate your chances of success if a dispute arises over the use of your intended name.

Firing Your Attorney

You can always fire your lawyer. (You're still obligated to pay outstanding bills, though.) But bear in mind that switching attorneys is a nuisance, and you may lose time and money.

How do you fire an attorney? Notify the attorney by letter that you are terminating services and that you request the return of your files. The attorney will probably retain a copy of your files and return the originals to you. Despite your obligation to pay any outstanding bills, the attorney is not allowed to withhold your files until you pay.

If your attorney is representing you to a third party, for example, to a manufacturer, you should also notify the third party that you are no longer working with the attorney and that future correspondence should be sent to you (at least until you retain a new attorney). The easiest way to switch attorneys is to find a new attorney and have that attorney terminate the old relationship. That is, before terminating one attorney, you would have another attorney prepare to take over any outstanding legal work.

Using Contract Provisions to Avoid Legal Costs and Hassles

Below is a discussion of four contract provisions usually found at the end of standard business agreements. These provisions can level the playing field between you and a more well-heeled adversary. Ultimately, they can limit how much you spend on lawyers, court costs, and damages if you're on the losing end of a dispute. Unfortunately, because these provisions equalize the relationship, one party sometimes rejects them during contract negotiations.

> **TIP**
> **You don't need a contract to use arbitration or mediation.**
> However, if the contract doesn't require one of these alternatives, both parties must agree to the procedure beforehand. If you get into a dispute and only one party wants to use the procedure, that party will be out of luck.

Agreeing to Mediation

Many disputes are resolved privately through mediation, an informal procedure in which the parties submit their dispute to an impartial mediator who assists them in reaching a settlement. The settlement decision is not binding, and the parties can disregard the result. That's the key to mediation—nobody is bound by the outcome. Below is sample language you can add to a contract to require mediation of any dispute.

SAMPLE

> **Mediation.** The Parties agree that every dispute or difference between them arising under this Agreement shall be settled first by a meeting of the Parties attempting to confer and resolve the dispute in a good faith manner. If the Parties cannot resolve their dispute after conferring, any Party may require the other Parties to submit the matter to nonbinding mediation, utilizing the services of an impartial professional mediator approved by all Parties.

Agreeing to Arbitration

With arbitration, the parties hire one or more arbitrators—experts at resolving disputes—to evaluate the dispute and to make a determination. Arbitration is often used if the parties fail to reach a settlement during mediation of their dispute. It has both good and not-so-good aspects. Here's an overview of the pros and cons:

Arbitration Pros: Arbitration is usually less expensive and more efficient than litigation. Moreover, the parties can select an arbitrator who has knowledge in the crafts or small business field.

Arbitration Cons: The parties usually have no right to discovery—that is, the process used during litigation in which the parties must reveal documents and disclose information about their cases. (However, you can include a requirement for discovery in the arbitration provision or agree to it later.) Unlike a court ruling, a binding arbitration ruling is not appealable and can only be set aside by a judge if the arbitrator was biased or the arbitration ruling violated public policy. Arbitrators must be paid, and these fees can run to $10,000 or more. Most participants in arbitration hire attorneys, so you will not avoid paying attorney fees. In short, some arbitrations—though it is not common—become as expensive (or more expensive) than a lawsuit. (After all, you don't have to pay for the services of a judge in court litigation.)

Many associations offer private arbitration. The best-known of these is the American Arbitration Association (AAA; www.adr.org). However, if you're in a dispute that needs mediating or arbitrating, first try an arts organization such as the CLA or VLA. For examples of provisions that will guarantee that the arbitration is handled by this type of organization, check the CLA website at www.calawyersforthearts.org/aams.html.

Below is sample contract language requiring the parties to arbitrate any dispute.

SAMPLE

> **Arbitration.** If a dispute arises under or relating to this Agreement, the Parties agree to submit such dispute to binding arbitration in the state of _____
> _____ of or another location mutually agreeable to the Parties. The arbitration shall be conducted on a confidential basis pursuant to the Commercial Arbitration Rules of the American Arbitration Association. Any decision or award as a result of any such arbitration proceeding shall be in writing and shall provide an explanation for all conclusions of law and fact and shall include the assessment of costs, expenses, and reasonable attorney fees. An arbitrator experienced in copyright and merchandising shall conduct any such arbitration. An award of arbitration may be confirmed in a court of competent jurisdiction.

Deciding Who Pays Attorney Fees

Many agreements have an "attorney fees and costs" clause. This clause usually provides that if you and the other party end up in a legal battle over the contract, the loser will have to pay the winning (or "prevailing") party's attorney fees plus the costs of preparing the case, including service of process, depositions, court filings, and expert witness fees. The clause will apply to disputes that have gone to arbitration, too, since one or both of you may hire lawyers to help you prepare for your case. (Normally, the clause will not apply to lawyers you might hire to help you prepare for mediations.)

An attorney fees clause has the laudable effect of making both of you think twice before initiating arbitration or bringing a lawsuit that you aren't quite sure you can win, since the consequences of losing can be quite expensive.

Below is contract language you can use to require the winner of a dispute to pay attorney fees and costs.

SAMPLE

> **Attorney Fees and Expenses.** The prevailing party shall have the right to collect from the other party its reasonable costs and necessary disbursements and attorney fees incurred in enforcing this Agreement.

Deciding on Jurisdiction

In the event of a dispute, this provision establishes in which state (and county) the lawsuit or arbitration must be filed. One way to limit your expenses is to guarantee that jurisdiction is in your home county, if possible. That way, you avoid the expense of traveling to a distant location to fight your legal battle. As you can imagine, this section is sometimes a matter of heated discussion. If there is no reference to jurisdiction, the location is usually determined by whoever files a lawsuit. If a jurisdiction clause is used, it should list the same state as the contract provision that describes which state's law governs the agreement (known as the "Governing Law" provision).

Below is contract language you can use to decide in advance where any litigation will take place.

SAMPLE

> **Jurisdiction.** The parties consent to the exclusive jurisdiction and venue of the federal and state courts located in [county], [state], in any action arising out of or relating to this Agreement. The parties waive any other venue to which either party might be entitled by domicile or otherwise.

How to Use the CD-ROM

The CD-ROM included with this book can be used with Windows computers. It installs files that use software programs that need to be on your computer already. It is not a stand-alone software program.

In accordance with U.S. copyright laws, the CD-ROM and its files are for your personal use only.

Please read this appendix and the Readme.htm file included on the CD-ROM for instructions on using the CD-ROM. For a list of files and their file names, see the end of this appendix.

Note to Macintosh users: This CD-ROM and its files should also work on Macintosh computers. Please note, however, that Nolo cannot provide technical support for non-Windows users.

Note to eBook users: You can access the CD-ROM files mentioned here from the bookmarked section of the eBook, located on the left-hand side.

How to View the README File

To view the "Readme.htm" file, insert the CD-ROM into your computer's CD-ROM drive and follow these instructions:

Windows XP and Vista
1. On your PC's desktop, double-click the **My Computer** icon.
2. Double-click the icon for the CD-ROM drive into which the CD-ROM was inserted.
3. Double-click the file "Readme.htm."

Macintosh
1. On your Mac desktop, double-click the icon for the CD-ROM that you inserted.
2. Double-click the file "Readme.htm."

Installing the Files Onto Your Computer

To work with the files on the CD-ROM, you first need to install them onto your hard disk. Here's how:

Windows XP and Vista

Follow the CD-ROM's instructions that appear on the screen.
  If nothing happens when you insert the CD-ROM, then:
  1. Double-click the **My Computer** icon.
  2. Double-click the icon for the CD-ROM drive into which the CD-ROM was inserted.
  3. Double-click the file "Setup.exe."

Macintosh

If the **Craft Guide CD** window is not open, double-click the **Craft Guide CD** icon. Then:
  1. Select the **Crafts Forms** folder icon.
  2. Drag and drop the folder icon onto your computer.

Where Are the Files Installed?

Windows

By default, all the files are installed to the **CraftsGuide** folder in the **Program Files** folder of your computer. A folder called **CraftsGuide** is added to the **Programs** folder of the **Start** menu.

Macintosh

All the files are located in the **CraftsGuide** folder.

Using the Word Processing Files to Create Documents

The CD-ROM includes word processing files that you can open, complete, print, and save with your word processing program. All word processing files come in rich text format and have the extension ".rtf." For example, the file for the Nondisclosure Agreement discussed in Chapter 4 is on the file "Nondisclosure.rtf." RTF files can be read by most recent word processing programs including MS *Word*, Windows *WordPad*, and recent versions of *WordPerfect*.

The following are general instructions. Because each word processor uses different commands to open, format, save, and print documents, refer to your word processor's help file for specific instructions.

Do not call Nolo's technical support if you have questions on how to use your word processor or your computer.

Opening a File

You can open word processing files in any of the three following ways:

1. Windows users can open a file by selecting its "shortcut."
   - Click the Windows **Start** button.
   - Open the **Programs** folder.
   - Open the **Crafts Forms** folder.
   - Click the shortcut to the file you want to work with.
2. Both Windows and Macintosh users can open a file by double-clicking it.
   - Use **My Computer** or **Windows Explorer** (Windows XP or Vista) or the **Finder** (Macintosh) to go to the **Crafts Forms** folder.
   - Double-click the file you want to open.
3. Windows and Macintosh users can open a file from within their word processor.
   - Open your word processor.
   - Go to the **File** menu and choose the **Open** command. This opens a dialog box.
   - Select the location and name of the file. (You will navigate to the version of the **Crafts Forms** folder that you've installed on your computer.)

Editing Your Document

Here are tips for working on your document.

Refer to the book's instructions and sample agreements for help.

Underlines indicate where to enter information, frequently including bracketed instructions. Delete the underlines and instructions before finishing your document.

Signature lines should appear on a page with at least some text from the document itself.

Editing Files That Have Optional or Alternative Text

Some files have check boxes that appear before text. Check boxes indicate:

- Optional text that you can choose to include or exclude.
- Alternative text that you select to include, excluding the other alternatives.

When you are using the CD-ROM, we recommend doing the following:

Optional text

Delete optional text you do not want to include and keep that which you do. In either case, delete the check box and the italicized instructions. If you choose to delete an optional numbered clause, renumber the subsequent clauses after deleting it.

Alternative text

Delete the alternatives that you do not want to include first. Then delete the remaining check boxes, as well as the italicized instructions that you need to select one of the alternatives provided.

Printing Out the Document

Use your word processor's or text editor's **Print** command to print out your document.

Saving Your Document

Use the "Save As" command to save and rename your document. You will be unable to use the "Save" command because the files are "read-only." If you save the file without renaming it, the underlines that indicate where you need to enter your information will be lost, and you will be unable to create a new document with this file without recopying the original file from the CD-ROM.

Files on the CD-ROM

Form Title	Source Chapter	RTF File Name
Invoice	1	Invoice.rtf
Consignment Agreement	1	Consignment.rtf
Commission Agreement	1	Commission.rtf
Collection Letter #1	1	Collection1.rtf
Collection Letter #2	1	Collection2.rtf
Collection Letter #3	1	Collection3. rtf
Work-Made-for-Hire Agreement	4	WorkHire.rtf
Nondisclosure Agreement	4	Nondisclosure.rtf
Sales Representative Agreement	4	SalesRep.rtf
Partnership Agreement	5	Partnership.rtf
Basic Copyright Assignment	6	Assignment.rtf
Artwork Assignment Agreement	6	ArtAssign.rtf
Unlimited Personal Release Agreement	6	Unlimited.rtf
Limited Personal Release Agreement	6	Limited.rtf
Merchandise License Agreement	9	MerchLicense.rtf
Merchandise License Worksheet	9	MerchWksht.rtf

Index

NOLO® *Keep Up to Date*

 Go to **Nolo.com/newsletters/index.html** to sign up for free newsletters and discounts on Nolo products.

- **Nolo Briefs.** Our monthly email newsletter with great deals and free information.

- **Nolo's Special Offer.** A monthly newsletter with the biggest Nolo discounts around.

- **BizBriefs.** Tips and discounts on Nolo products for business owners and managers.

- **Landlord's Quarterly.** Deals and free tips just for landlords and property managers, too.

 Don't forget to check for updates at **Nolo.com.** Under "Products," find this book and click "Legal Updates."

Let Us Hear From You

 Comments on this book? We want to hear 'em. Email us at feedback@nolo.com.

CRBIZ1

NOLO® *Online Legal Forms*

Nolo offers a large library of legal solutions and forms, created by Nolo's in-house legal staff. These reliable documents can be prepared in minutes.

Create a Document

- **Incorporation.** Incorporate your business in any state.
- **LLC Formations.** Gain asset protection and pass-through tax status in any state.
- **Wills.** Nolo has helped people make over 2 million wills. Is it time to make or revise yours?
- **Living Trust (avoid probate).** Plan now to save your family the cost, delays, and hassle of probate.
- **Trademark.** Protect the name of your business or product.
- **Provisional Patent.** Preserve your rights under patent law and claim "patent pending" status.

Download a Legal Form

Nolo.com has hundreds of top quality legal forms available for download—bills of sale, promissory notes, nondisclosure agreements, LLC operating agreements, corporate minutes, commercial lease and sublease, motor vehicle bill of sale, consignment agreements and many, many more.

Review Your Documents

Many lawyers in Nolo's consumer-friendly lawyer directory will review Nolo documents for a very reasonable fee. Check their detailed profiles at **www.nolo.com/lawyers/index.html**.

Nolo's Bestselling Books

Legal Guide for Starting and Running a Small Business
$39.99

Business Loans from Family & Friends
$29.99

The Small Business Start-Up Kit
$29.99

Marketing Without Advertising
$20.00

Every Nolo title is available in print and for download at Nolo.com.